JUMP Math 5.2
Book 5 Part 2 of 2

Contents

jump math
MULTIPLYING POTENTIAL.

Contents

PART 1
Patterns & Algebra

Number Sense

Measurement

Probability & Data Management

Geometry

PART 2
Patterns & Algebra

Number Sense

Measurement

Probability & Data Management

Geometry

Children will need to answer the questions marked with a [book icon] in a notebook. Grid paper and notebooks should always be on hand for answering extra questions or when additional room for calculation is needed. Grid paper is also available in the BLM section of the Teacher's Guide.

The [octagon icon] means "Stop! Assess understanding and explain new concepts before proceeding."

Brandon makes a garden path using 2 triangular stones for every 1 square stone.
He writes an **equation** that shows how to calculate the number of triangles from the number of squares.

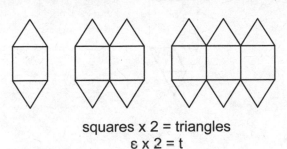

squares x 2 = triangles
$\varepsilon \times 2 = t$

Squares (s)	2 × s = t	Triangles (t)
1	2 × [1] = 2	2
2	2 × [2] = 4	4
3	2 × [3] = 6	6

----

1. Each chart represents a different design for a path. Complete the charts.

a)

Squares (s)	3 × s = t	Triangles (t)
1	3 × [1] = 3	3
2	3 × [2] = 6	6
3	3 × [3] = 9	9

b)

Squares (s)	4 × s = t	Triangles (t)
1	4 × [1] =	4
2	4 × [2] =	8
3	4 × [3] =	12

2. Write a rule that tells you how to calculate the number of triangles from the number of squares.
Then write a formula using **s** for the number of squares and **t** for the number of triangles.

a)

Squares	Triangles
1	4
2	8
3	12

Multiply by 4.

4 × s = t

b)

Squares	Triangles
1	5
2	10
3	15

multiply by 5

5×S=t

c)

Squares	Triangles
1	2
2	4
3	6

multiply by 2

2×S=t

d)

Square	Triangles
1	6
2	12
3	18

multiply by 6

6×S=t

3. Wendy makes brooches using squares (s) and triangles (t). Complete the chart. Write a formula
(such as 4 × **s** = **t**) for each design.

a)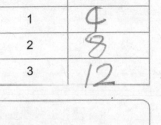

Squares	Triangles
1	4
2	8
3	12

b)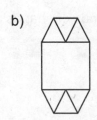

Squares	Triangles
1	6
2	12
3	18

c)

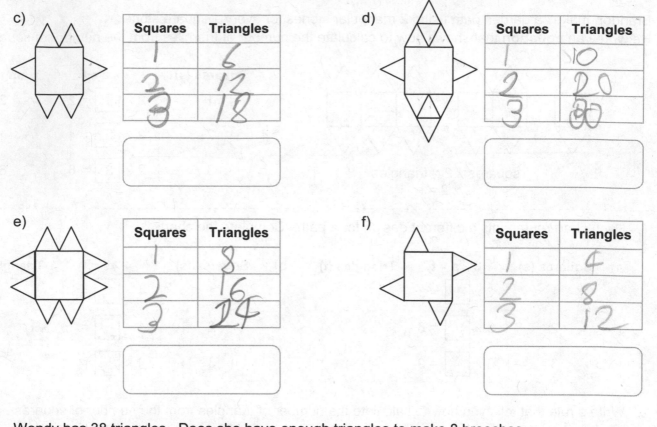

Squares	Triangles
1	6
2	12
3	18

d)

Squares	Triangles
1	10
2	20
3	30

e)

Squares	Triangles
1	8
2	16
3	24

f)

Squares	Triangles
1	4
2	8
3	12

4. Wendy has 38 triangles. Does she have enough triangles to make 8 brooches using the design shown? How can you tell without making a chart?

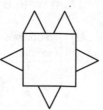

5. Create a design using squares (s) and triangles (t) to go with each formula.

   a) $3 \times s = t$

   b) $5 \times s = t$

6. Create a design with two kinds of shapes and then write a formula for your design.

In an auditorium, the number of chairs in each row is always 2 greater than the row number.
Sadia writes an equation that shows how to calculate the number of chairs from the row number.

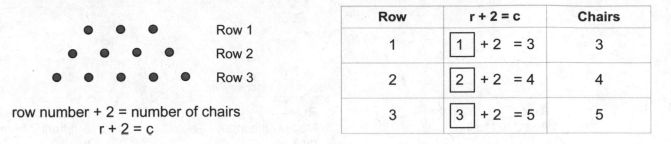

Row	r + 2 = c	Chairs
1	1 + 2 = 3	3
2	2 + 2 = 4	4
3	3 + 2 = 5	5

row number + 2 = number of chairs
r + 2 = c

---

1. Each chart represents a different arrangement of chairs. Complete the charts.

a)

Row	r + 2 = c	Chairs
1	1 + 2 = 3	3
2	☐ + 2 =	
3	☐ + 2 =	

b)

Row	r + 5 = c	Chairs
1	☐ + 5 =	
2	☐ + 5 =	
3	☐ + 5 =	

2. Say what number you must add to the row number to get the number of chairs.
   Write a formula using **r** for the row number and **c** for the number of chairs.

a)

Row	Chairs
1	4
2	5
3	6

Add 3.

r + 3 = c

b)

Row	Chairs
1	6
2	7
3	8

c)

Row	Chairs
1	5
2	6
3	7

d)

Row	Chairs
7	10
8	11
9	12

3. Complete the charts. Then write a formula for each arrangement of chairs.

a)

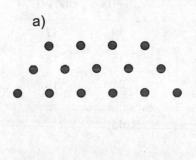

Row	Chairs

b)

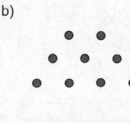

Row	Chairs

4. Apply the given rule to the numbers in the input column. Write your answer in the output column.

a)

INPUT	OUTPUT
1	
2	
3	

Rule:
Add 2 to the input.

b)

INPUT	OUTPUT
5	
6	
7	

Rule:
Multiply the input by 3.

c)

INPUT	OUTPUT
5	
4	
7	

Rule:
Subtract 2 from the input.

d)

INPUT	OUTPUT
32	
8	
40	

Rule:
Add 3 to the input.

e)

INPUT	OUTPUT
8	
9	
10	

Rule:
Add 10 to the input.

f)

INPUT	OUTPUT
4	
5	
6	

Rule:
Multiply the input by 4.

5. For each chart, give a rule, which tells you how to make the output numbers from the input numbers.

a)

INPUT	OUTPUT
2	5
3	6
4	7

Rule:

Add 3.

b)

INPUT	OUTPUT
3	7
5	9
7	11

Rule:

c)

INPUT	OUTPUT
1	5
2	10
3	15

Rule:

d)

INPUT	OUTPUT
3	9
2	6
1	3

Rule:

e)

INPUT	OUTPUT
2	8
4	16
6	24

Rule:

f)

INPUT	OUTPUT
19	17
15	13
21	19

Rule:

Complete the T-table for each pattern.
Then write a rule that tells you how to calculate the output numbers from the input numbers.

1.

Number of Vertical Lines	Number of Horizontal Lines	Rule:

2.

Number of Squares	Number of Triangles	Rule:

3.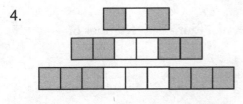

Number of Triangles	Number of Circles	Rule:

4.

Number of Light Squares	Number of Dark Squares	Rule:

5.

Number of Light Squares	Number of Dark Squares	Rule:

6. Make a T-table and write a rule for the following patterns in your notebook.

Figure 1   ◁   Figure 2   ◁ ◁   Figure 3   ◁ ◁ ◁

7. How many triangles are needed for 8 squares in the pattern in Question 6? How do you know?

PA5-27: Direct Variation

Fill in the chart and find a rule for the number of blocks in each figure, as shown in part a).

1. a)

Figure 1   Figure 2   Figure 3

Rule: ___2 × Figure Number___

Figure Number	Number of Blocks
1	
2	
3	

b)

Figure 1   Figure 2   Figure 3

Rule: _____

Figure Number	Number of Blocks

c)

Figure 1   Figure 2   Figure 3

Rule: _____

Figure Number	Number of Blocks

d)

Figure 1   Figure 2   Figure 3

Rule: _____

Figure Number	Number of Blocks

> In each example above, you can find the **total number of blocks** by *multiplying*
> the **Figure Number** by the **number of blocks in the first figure**.
> In such cases, <u>the number of blocks</u> is said to vary **directly** with the <u>Figure Number</u>.

2. Circle the sequences where the number of blocks varies <u>directly</u> with the Figure Number.

a)

Figure Number	Number of Blocks
1	4
2	8
3	12

b)

Figure Number	Number of Blocks
1	5
2	11
3	17

c)

Figure Number	Number of Blocks
1	5
2	10
3	15

d)

Figure Number	Number of Blocks
1	7
2	14
3	23

jump math
MULTIPLYING POTENTIAL.

Patterns & Algebra 2

1. In each pattern below, the number of *shaded* blocks increases <u>directly</u> with the Figure Number.
   The *total* number of blocks, however, <u>does not</u> increase directly.

   i) Write a rule for the number of *shaded* blocks in each sequence.
   ii) Write a rule for the *total number* of blocks in each sequence.

a)

Figure 1   Figure 2   Figure 3

Rule for the number of shaded blocks:

2 × Figure Number

Rule for the total number of blocks:

2 × Figure Number + 1

b)

Figure 1   Figure 2   Figure 3

Rule for the number of shaded blocks:

_____

Rule for the total number of blocks:

_____

c)

Figure 1   Figure 2   Figure 3

Rule for the number of shaded blocks:

_____

Rule for the total number of blocks:

_____

d)

Figure 1   Figure 2   Figure 3

Rule for the number of shaded blocks:

_____

Rule for the total number of blocks:

_____

e) Rule for the number of shaded blocks:

_____

Rule for the total number of blocks:

_____

Figure 1   Figure 2   Figure 3

2. Draw or build a sequence of figures that might go with the following tables.
   Shade the part of each figure that varies directly with the Figure Number.

a)

Figure Number	Number of Blocks
1	3
2	5
3	7

b)

Figure Number	Number of Blocks
1	4
2	6
3	8

c)

Figure Number	Number of Blocks
1	6
2	10
3	14

1. Fill in the chart using the rule.

a) Rule: <u>Multiply by 3 and add 2</u>

INPUT	OUTPUT
1	
2	
3	

Gap: _____

b) Rule: <u>Multiply by 3 and add 1</u>

INPUT	OUTPUT
1	
2	
3	

Gap: _____

c) Rule: <u>Multiply by 4 and add 2</u>

INPUT	OUTPUT
1	
2	
3	

Gap: _____

d) Rule: <u>Multiply by 2 and add 5</u>

INPUT	OUTPUT
1	
2	
3	

Gap: _____

e) Compare the **gap** in each pattern above to the rule for the pattern. What do you notice?

_____

_____

2. For each pattern below, make a T-table as shown.

Fill in the total number of blocks (shaded and unshaded) and the gap.

Can you predict what the gap will be for each pattern before you fill in the chart?

Figure Number	Number of Blocks
1	
2	
3	

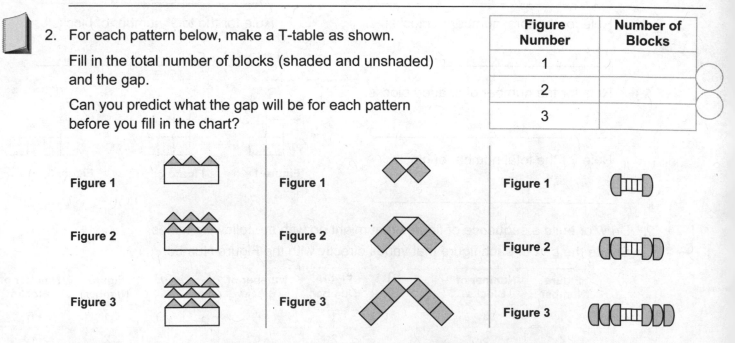

Figure 1

Figure 2

Figure 3

Figure 1

Figure 2

Figure 3

Figure 1

Figure 2

Figure 3

Can you write a rule for each pattern that tells how to find the number of blocks from the figure number?

Patterns & Algebra 2

In the T-table, the output is calculated from the input by **two** operations.

To find the rule …

INPUT	OUTPUT
1	5
2	8
3	11

<u>Step 1</u>: Find the step (or gap) between the numbers in the OUTPUT column.

<u>Step 2</u>: Multiply the input numbers by the gap.

<u>Step 3</u>: What must you add to each number in the second column to get the output?

INPUT	INPUT × GAP	OUTPUT
1		5
2		8
3		11

3
3

INPUT	INPUT × GAP	OUTPUT
1	3	5
2	6	8
3	9	11

3
3

INPUT	INPUT × GAP	OUTPUT
1	3	5
2	6	8
3	9	11

3
3

Add 2.

Step 4: Write a rule for the T-table.

<u>Multiply the INPUT by 3 and add 2</u>

----

1. Follow the steps shown above to find the rule that tells you how to calculate the OUTPUT from the INPUT.

a)

INPUT	INPUT × GAP	OUTPUT
1		5
2		9
3		13

Add _____

Rule: Multiply by _____ and add _____.

b)

INPUT	INPUT × GAP	OUTPUT
1		3
2		5
3		7

Add _____

Rule: Multiply by _____ and add _____.

c)

INPUT	INPUT × GAP	OUTPUT
1		7
2		10
3		13

Add _____

Rule: Multiply by _____ and add _____.

d)

INPUT	INPUT × GAP	OUTPUT
1		6
2		8
3		10

Add _____

Rule: Multiply by _____ and add _____.

2. Write a rule that tells you how to calculate the OUTPUT from the INPUT.

a)

INPUT	INPUT× GAP	OUTPUT
1		9
2		14
3		19

Multiply by _____ and Add _____

b)

INPUT	INPUT × GAP	OUTPUT
1		12
2		18
3		24

Multiply by _____ and Add _____

c)

INPUT	INPUT × GAP	OUTPUT
1		6
2		10
3		14

Multiply by _____ and Add _____

d)

INPUT	INPUT × GAP	OUTPUT
1		6
2		11
3		16

Multiply by _____ and Add _____

3. Write the rule that tells you how to calculate the OUTPUT from the INPUT (in this case you will have to subtract rather than add).

a)

INPUT	INPUT × GAP	OUTPUT
1		4
2		9
3		14

Multiply by _____ and Subtract _____

b)

INPUT	INPUT × GAP	OUTPUT
1		1
2		4
3		7

Multiply by _____ and Subtract _____

c)

INPUT	INPUT × GAP	OUTPUT
1		2
2		6
3		10

Multiply by _____ and Subtract _____

d)

INPUT	INPUT × GAP	OUTPUT
1		5
2		11
3		17

Multiply by _____ and Subtract _____

 jump math
MULTIPLYING POTENTIAL.

Patterns & Algebra 2

4. Write the rule that tells you how to make the OUTPUT from the INPUT.
   (Each rule involves <u>two</u> operations: either multiplication and addition or multiplication and subtraction.)

a)

Input	Output
1	4
2	7
3	10

Rule:

b)

Input	Output
1	6
2	11
3	16

Rule:

c)

Input	Output
1	7
2	10
3	13

Rule:

d)

Input	Output
1	9
2	13
3	17

Rule:

e)

Input	Output
1	1
2	4
3	7

Rule:

f)

Input	Output
1	22
2	32
3	42

Rule:

5. Write a rule that tells you how to make the OUTPUT from the INPUT. (Each rule may involve either one or two operations. For some charts you may have to guess and check.)

a)

Input	Output
1	2
2	7
3	12
4	17

Rule:

b)

Input	Output
1	3
2	9
3	15
4	21

Rule:

c)

Input	Output
1	5
2	6
3	7
4	8

Rule:

d)

Input	Output
1	5
2	7
3	9
4	11

Rule:

e)

Input	Output
3	9
5	15
1	3
7	21

Rule:

f)

Input	Output
3	7
7	15
2	5
1	3

Rule:

 jump math
MULTIPLYING POTENTIAL

Patterns & Algebra 2

6. Draw Figure 4 and fill in the T-table.

a)

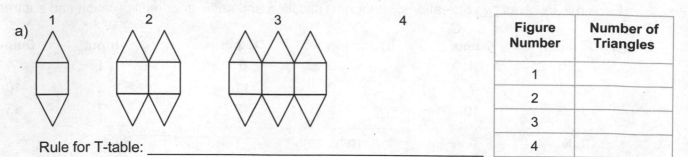

Figure Number	Number of Triangles
1	
2	
3	
4	

Rule for T-table: _____

Use your rule to predict how many triangles will be needed for Figure 9: _____

b)

Figure Number	Perimeter
1	
2	
3	
4	

Rule for T-table: _____

Use your rule to predict the perimeter of Figure 11: _____

c)

Figure Number	Number of Squares
1	
2	
3	
4	

Rule for T-table: _____

Use your rule to predict the number of squares Figure 8 will have: _____

d)

Figure Number	Line Segments
1	
2	
3	
4	

Rule for T-table: _____

Use your rule to predict how many line segments Figure 23 will have: _____

PA5-31: Patterns Created Using One Operation

1. Write the correct symbol (+ or ×) in the circle to show what operation was used.

   a) 6 ◯ 2 = 8   b) 3 ◯ 1 = 3   c) 4 ◯ 3 = 7   d) 2 ◯ 5 = 10

   e) 8 ◯ 1 = 9   f) 4 ◯ 5 = 9   g) 2 ◯ 3 = 6   h) 3 ◯ 4 = 12

   i) 4 ◯ 2 = 8   j) 5 ◯ 1 = 6   k) 6 ◯ 3 = 9   l) 4 ◯ 1 = 4

2. Write the correct symbol (+, −, or ×) in the circle to show what operation was used.

   a) 8 ◯ 4 = 32   b) 3 ◯ 2 = 6   c) 3 ◯ 3 = 9   d) 5 ◯ 1 = 4

   e) 2 ◯ 4 = 8   f) 4 ◯ 4 = 8   g) 7 ◯ 3 = 4   h) 9 ◯ 3 = 12

   i) 9 ◯ 3 = 6   j) 5 ◯ 1 = 6   k) 5 ◯ 1 = 5   l) 8 ◯ 14 = 22

3. Continue the following sequences by **multiplying** each term by the given number.

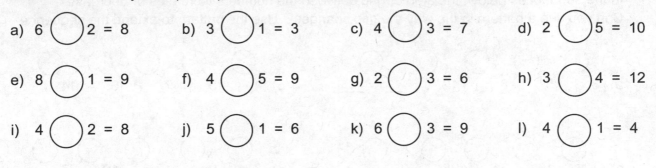

   a) 2 $\overset{×3}{}$ 6, ____ , ____ , ____   b) 1 $\overset{×3}{}$ 3, ____ , ____ , ____

   c) 3 $\overset{×2}{}$ 6, ____ , ____ , ____   d) 1 $\overset{×6}{}$ 6, ____ , ____ , ____

4. Each term in the sequence below was made by **multiplying** the previous term by a fixed number. Find the number and continue the sequence.

   a) 2 $\overset{×}{}$ 4 , 8 , _____ , ____   b) 3 $\overset{×}{}$ 9 , 27 , _____ , ____

   c) 1 $\overset{×}{}$ 5 , 25 , _____ , ____   d) 2 $\overset{×}{}$ 10 , 50 , _____ , ____

5. Each sequence was made using one operation: **multiplication**, **addition**, or **subtraction**. Continue the sequence.

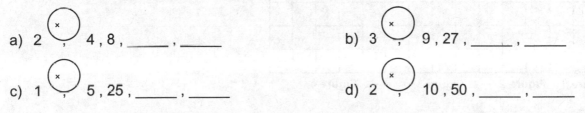

   a) 1 , 2 , 4 , _____ , ____   b) 5 , 8 , 11 , _____ , ____   c) 18 , 14 , 10 , _____ , ____

   d) 3 , 6 , 12 , _____ , ____   e) 14 , 18 , 22 , _____ , ____   f) 1 , 3 , 9 , _____ , ____

6. Write a rule for each sequence in Question 5.
   (The rule for the first sequence is: Start at 1, multiply by 2.)

1. In the sequences below, the step or gap between the numbers increases or decreases.
    Can you see a pattern in the way the gap changes? Use the pattern to extend the sequence.

a) 3 , 5 , 8 , 12 , ____ , ____

b) 4 , 5 , 7 , 10 , 14 , ____ , ____

c) 13 , 16 , 21 , 28 , ____ , ____

d) 7 , 9 , 13 , 19 , 27 , ____ , ____

e) 28 , 22 , 17 , 13 , ____ , ____

f) 52 , 42 , 34 , 28 , ____ , ____

g) 62 , 53 , 46 , 41 , ____ , ____

h) 310 , 280 , 255 , 235 , 220 , ____ , ____

2. Complete the T-table for Figure 3 and Figure 4. Then use the pattern in the gap to predict the number
    of squares needed for Figures 5 and 6.

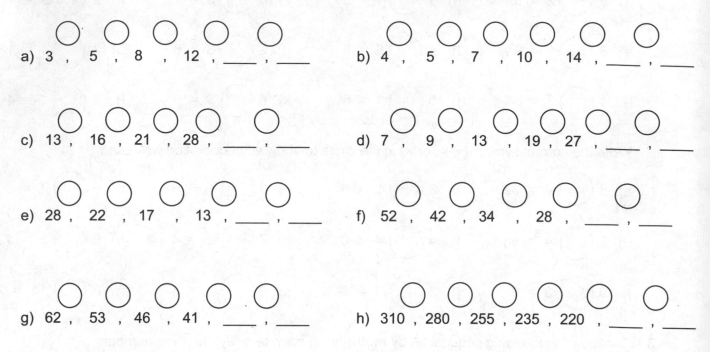

Figure	Number of Squares
1	2
2	5
3	
4	
5	
6	

Write the number of squares added each time here

3. Make a T-table to predict how many triangles will be needed for Figure 6.

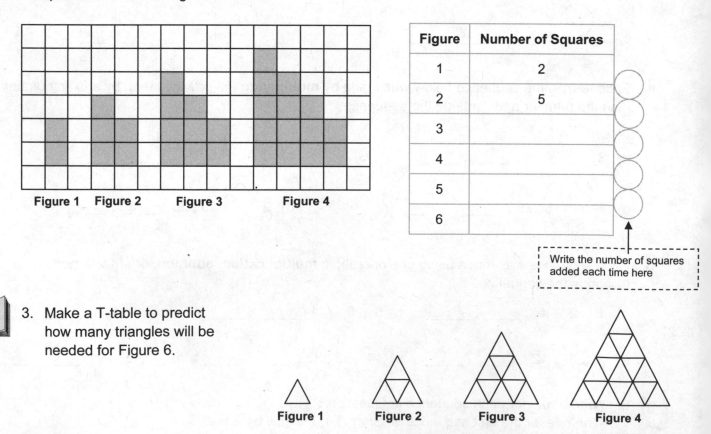

Figure 1   Figure 2   Figure 3   Figure 4

PA5-32: Patterns with Increasing & Decreasing Steps
(continued)

4. In each sequence below, the gap changes in a regular way. Write a rule for each pattern.

a) 2 , 5 , 10 , 17 , 26
    (+3) (+5) (+7) (+9)

    Rule: Start at 2. Add 3, 5, 7 ... (The gap increases by 2.)

b) 7 , 11 , 9 , 13 , 11
    (+4) (-2) (+4) (-2)

    Rule : Start at 7. Add 4, then subtract 2. Repeat.

c) 1 , 2 , 4 , 7 , 11

    Rule: _____

d) 6 , 8 , 5 , 7 , 4

    Rule: _____

e) 24 , 23 , 20 , 15 , 8

    Rule: _____

f) 17 , 20 , 25 , 32 , 41

    Rule: _____

5. Write a rule for each pattern. Then give the value of the 5th term.

    a) 0 , 3 , 8 , 15   b) 1 , 3 , 9 , 27

6. Write a rule for the number of shaded squares or triangles in each figure.
    Use your rule to predict the number of shaded parts in the 5th figure.
    HINT: To count the number of triangles in the last figure in b), try skip counting by 3s.

a)

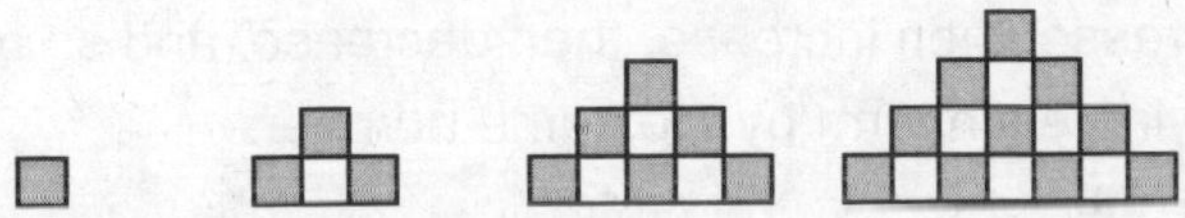

Figure 1   Figure 2   Figure 3   Figure 4

b)

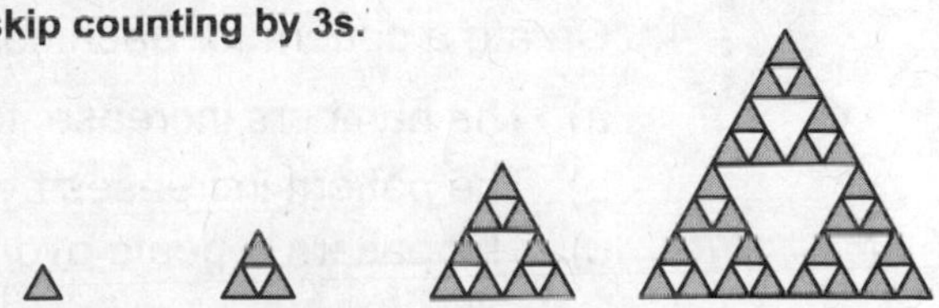

Figure 1   Figure 2   Figure 3   Figure 4

1. Extend each pattern for the next 3 terms. Then write a rule for the pattern.

   a) 357 , 362 , 367 , 372 , 377 , _____ , _____ , _____

      Rule: _____

   b) 6 , 10 , 7 , 11 , 8 , 12 , _____ , _____ , _____

      Rule: _____

   c) 42 , 40 , 37 , 33 , _____ , _____ , _____

      Rule: _____

2. Use the letters of the alphabet to continue the following patterns.

   A B C D E F G H I J K L M N O P Q R S T U V W X Y Z

   a) A , C , E , G , ____ , ____   b) A , D , G , J , ____ , ____

   c) Z , X , V , T , ____ , ____   d) Z , U , P , K , ____ , ____

   e) A , C , F , J , O , ____   f) Z , Y , W , T , ____ , ____

3. Continue the patterns.

   a) M N , M M N N , M M M ____ , _____   b) 2 T , 22 T , 222 T , _____ , _____

   c) R r R, R r r r R, R r r r r r R, _____   d) 030, 060, 090, 030, _____ , _____ , _____

   e) AA, AB, AC, AD, ____ , ____   f) AA3, AB6, AC9, AD12, _____

   g)

			1			
		2	3	2		
	3	4	5	4	3	
4	5	6	7	6	5	4

   h)

			5			
		5	10	5		
	5	10	15	10	5	
5	10	15	20	15	10	5

4. Create a pattern for each condition.

   a) The numbers increase, then decrease, then increase, then decrease, and so on.
   b) The pattern increases by multiplying each term by the same number.
   c) The pattern repeats every four terms.

5. Create your own pattern using the letters of the alphabet. Write a rule for your pattern.

PA5-34: Patterns with Larger Numbers

1. Use addition or multiplication to complete the following charts.

a)
Days	Hours
1	24
2	
3	
4	
5	

b)
Years	Days
1	365
2	
3	

c)
Tonnes	Kilograms
1	1000
2	
3	
4	

2. a) A hummingbird takes 250 breaths per minute.

   How many breaths would a hummingbird take in 3 minutes?

   b) About how many breaths do you take in a minute?

   c) About how many breaths would you take in 3 minutes?

   d) How many more breaths would a hummingbird take in 3 minutes than you would take?

3. Can you find the answer quickly by grouping the terms in a clever way?

   a) $52 - 52 + 52 - 52 + 52 - 52 + 52$

   b) $375 + 375 + 375 - 75 - 75 - 75$

4.

   In a leap year, February has 29 days.

   There is a leap year every 4 years.

   The year 2008 is a leap year.

   Is the year 2032 a leap year?

5. Use multiplication or a calculator to find the first few products. Look for a pattern. Use the pattern you've discovered to fill in the rest of the numbers.

   a) 37 x 3 = _____

   37 x 6 = _____

   37 x 9 = _____

   _____ = _____

   _____ = _____

   b) 1 x 1 = _____

   11 x 11 = _____

   111 x 111 = _____

   _____ = _____

   _____ = _____

BONUS

6. Using a calculator, can you discover any patterns like the ones in Question 5?

jump math
MULTIPLYING POTENTIAL.

Patterns & Algebra 2

PA5-35: Introduction to Algebra

1. Some apples are inside a box and some are outside. The total number of apples is shown. Draw the missing apples in the box provided.

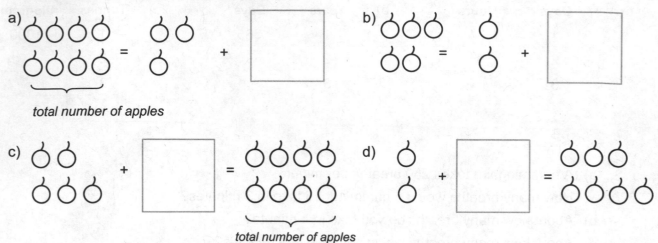

total number of apples

total number of apples

2. Draw the missing apples in the box given. Then write an equation (with numbers) to represent the picture.

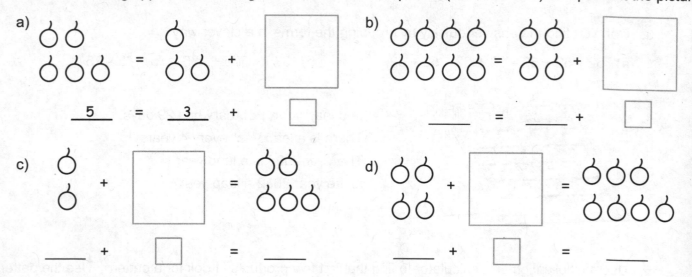

3. Write an equation for each situation. (Use a box to stand for the unknown quantity.)

   a) There are 9 apples altogether.
      5 are outside of a box.
      How many are inside?

      9 = 5 + ☐

   b) There are 7 apples altogether.
      3 are outside of a box.
      How many are inside?

   c) There are 8 pears altogether.
      3 are inside a bag.
      How many are outside?

   d) 10 students are in a library.
      2 are inside the computer room.
      How many are outside?

   e) 7 children are in a gym.
      2 are in the pool.
      How many are out of the pool?

   f) Rena has 13 stamps.
      5 are Canadian.
      How many are from other countries?

   g) 15 children are in a camp.
      9 are girls.
      How many are boys?

   h) 9 dogs are in a pet store.
      5 are puppies.
      How many are adults?

jump math
MULTIPLYING POTENTIAL.

Patterns & Algebra 2

PA5-36: Algebra

1. Tim took some apples from a box. Show how many apples were in the box originally.

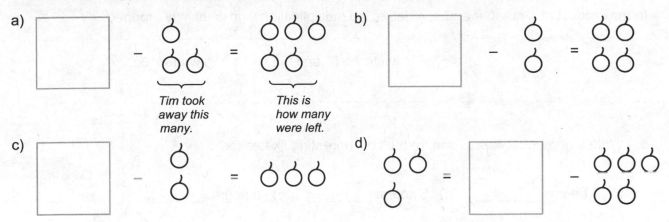

2. Show how many apples were in the box originally. Then write an equation to represent the picture.

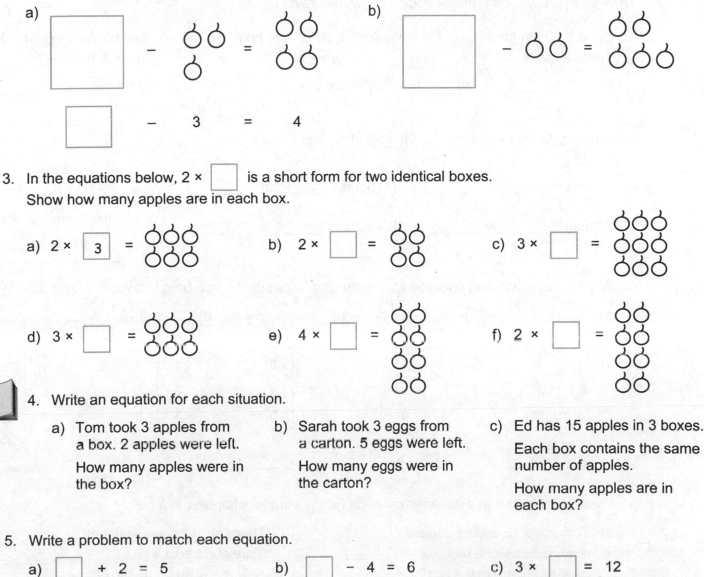

3. In the equations below, 2 × ☐ is a short form for two identical boxes.
   Show how many apples are in each box.

4. Write an equation for each situation.

   a) Tom took 3 apples from a box. 2 apples were left.

   How many apples were in the box?

   b) Sarah took 3 eggs from a carton. 5 eggs were left.

   How many eggs were in the carton?

   c) Ed has 15 apples in 3 boxes. Each box contains the same number of apples.

   How many apples are in each box?

5. Write a problem to match each equation.

   a) ☐ + 2 = 5

   b) ☐ − 4 = 6

   c) 3 × ☐ = 12

PA5-37: Variables

A **variable** is a letter or symbol (such as **x**, **n**, or **h**) that represents a number.

In the product of a number and a variable, the multiplication sign is usually dropped.

> $3 \times T$ is written $3T$ and $5 \times z$ is written $5z$.

---

1. Write a numerical expression for the cost of renting skates for...

   a) 2 hours: __3 × 2__   b) 5 hours: _____   c) 6 hours: _____

   Rent a pair of skates
   $3 for each hour

2. Write an expression for the distance a car would travel at ...

   a) Speed: 60 km per hour   b) Speed: 80 km per hour   c) Speed: 70 km per hour
      Time: 2 hours   Time: 3 hours   Time: h hours

      Distance: _____ km   Distance: _____ km   Distance: _____ km

3. Write an algebraic expression for the cost of renting skis for ...

   a) h hours: _____ or _____   b) t hours: _____ or _____

   c) x hours: _____ or _____   d) n hours: _____ or _____

   Rent a pair of skis
   $ 5 per hour

4. Write an equation that tells you the relationship between the numbers in column A and column B.

   a)   b)   c)   d)   e)

A	B		A	B		A	B		A	B		A	B
---	---		---	---		---	---		---	---		---	---
1	4		1	2		1	3		1	3		1	5
2	5		2	4		2	4		2	6		2	10
3	6		3	6		3	5		3	9		3	15

   __$A + 3 = B$__   __$2 \times A = B$__   _____   _____   _____

5. Use the variable x to write an expression for the number of apples in a box.

   a) There are 10 apples altogether.   b) There are 12 apples altogether.
      4 are outside of a box.   7 are outside of a box.
      How many are in the box?   How many are in the box?

PA5-38: Equations

1. Find the number that makes each equation true (by guessing and checking) and write it in the box.

a) ☐ + 3 = 9

b) ☐ + 2 = 5

c) ☐ + 4 = 10

d) 8 − ☐ = 6

e) 18 − ☐ = 14

f) 10 − ☐ = 7

g) 2 × ☐ = 8

h) 5 × ☐ = 20

i) 3 × ☐ = 12

j) ☐ ÷ 3 = 2

k) ☐ ÷ 5 = 3

l) ☐ ÷ 2 = 5

BONUS

m) 7 + 3 = 6 + ☐

n) 10 − 3 = ☐ + 2

o) ☐ + ☐ + 3 = 7

p) 9 = 1 + 2 + ☐

q) 7 + 8 = ☐ + 2

r) ☐ + 12 = 20 − 7

s) 5 × ☐ = 9 + 11

t) ☐ ÷ 2 = 7 − 4

u) 2 × 3 = ☐ ÷ 5

2. Find a set of numbers that makes each equation true. (Some questions have more than one answer.)
   NOTE: In a given question, congruent shapes represent the <u>same</u> number.

a) ☐ + ☐ + ◯ = 10

b) ☐ + ☐ + ◯ = 8

c) ◇ + ◇ + ◯ + ◯ = 8

d) ☐ + △ + ◯ = 9

3. Find two answers for the equation.

☐ + ☐ + ◯ = 7   ☐ + ☐ + ◯ = 7

4. Find a single number that makes both equations true.   ☐ + ☐ = 4   ☐ × ☐ = 4

5. Find three different numbers that make both equations true.

☐ + △ + ◯ = 6   and   ☐ × △ × ◯ = 6

Patterns & Algebra 2

6. Find a combination of numbers that make the equation true. (You cannot use the number 1.)

a) ☐ × △ = 6

b) ☐ × △ = 8

c) ☐ × ◯ = 10

d) ☐ × 3 = 3 × ☐

e) ☐ × ☐ × ◯ = 12

f) ☐ × ☐ × ◯ = 18

g) 3 × 10 = 2 × ☐ × △

7. Complete the patterns.

a) 10 + [1] = ◯

10 + [2] = ◯

10 + [3] = ◯

10 + ☐ = ◯

b) 10 − [1] = ◯

10 − [2] = ◯

10 − ☐ = ◯

10 − ☐ = ◯

c) 10 × [1] = ◯

10 × [2] = ◯

10 × ☐ = ◯

10 × ☐ = ◯

8. For each pattern in Question 7, say how the number in the circle changes as the number in the box increases by one.

9. When the number in each box below <u>doubles</u>, what happens to the product? (Use the pattern to fill in the numbers in the last question.)

5 × ☐ = 10   5 × ☐ = 20   5 × ☐ = 40   5 × ☐ = ____

10. Knowing that 6 is double 3, and that 7 × 3 = 21, how can you find 7 × 6 = 42 without multiplying 7 × 6?

11.

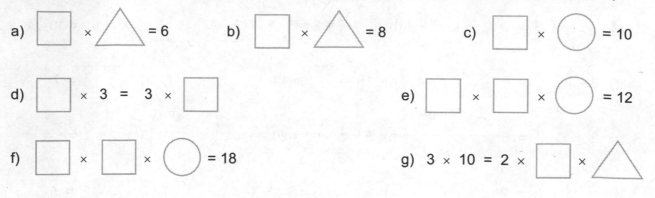

Fran threw 3 darts and scored 10 points.

The dart in the centre ring is worth more than the others.

Each dart in the outer ring is worth more than two points.

How much is each dart worth?

HINT: How can an equation like the one in 2 a) help you solve the problem?

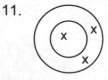
 jump math
MULTIPLYING POTENTIAL

Patterns & Algebra 2

1. The picture shows how many chairs can be placed at each arrangement of tables.

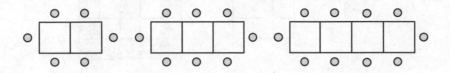

   a) Make a T-table and state a rule that tells the relationship between the number of tables and the number of chairs.

   b) How many chairs can be placed at 15 tables?

2. Julia makes an ornament using triangles and squares. She has 16 squares.

   How many triangles will she need to make ornaments with all 16 squares?

3. Raymond is 400 km from home Wednesday morning.

   He cycles 65 km toward home each day.

   How far away from home is he by Saturday evening?

4. Explain why the underlined term is or is not the next step in the pattern.

   a) 127, 124, 121, <u>118</u>
   b) 27, 31, 35, <u>40</u>
   c) 7, 5, 8, 6, <u>9</u>

5. A recipe calls for 3 cups of flour for every 4 cups of water.

   How many cups of water will be needed for 18 cups of flour?

6. Find the mystery numbers.

   a) I am a 2 digit number. I am a multiple of 4 and 6. My tens digit is 2.

   b) I am between 20 and 40. I am a multiple of 3. My ones digit is 6.

7. Every 6th person who arrives at a book sale receives a free calendar.
   Every 8th person receives a free book.

   Which of the first 50 people receive a book and a calendar?

8. Describe how each picture was made from the one before.

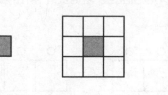

9. What strategy would you use to find the 63rd shape in the pattern below?

    What is the shape?

10. Paul shovelled 26 sidewalks in 4 days.

    Each day, he shovelled 3 more sidewalks than the day before.

    How many sidewalks did he shovel each day?
    Guess and check!

11. A camp offers 2 ways to rent a sailboat.

    You can pay $8.50 for the first hour and $4.50 for every hour after that.

    Or, you can pay $6.00 for every hour.

    If you wanted to rent the sailboat for 5 hours, which way would you choose to pay?

12. The picture shows how the temperature inside a cloud changes at different heights.

    a) Does the temperature increase or decrease at greater heights?

    b) What distance does the arrow represent in real life?

    c) Measure the length of the arrow.

    d) What is the scale of the picture?

        _____ cm = _____ m

13. Marlene says she will need 27 blocks to make Figure 7.

    Is she right? Explain.

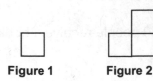

Figure 1   Figure 2   Figure 3

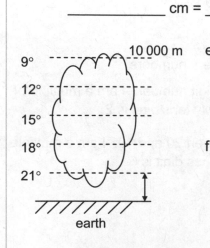

earth

e) Do temperatures change by the same amount each time?

f) If the pattern continued, what would the temperature be at:
    i)   12 000 m?
    ii) 14 000 m?

Patterns & Algebra 2

Fractions name equal parts of a whole.

The pie is cut into 4 equal parts.

3 parts out of 4 are shaded.

$\frac{3}{4}$ of a pie is shaded.

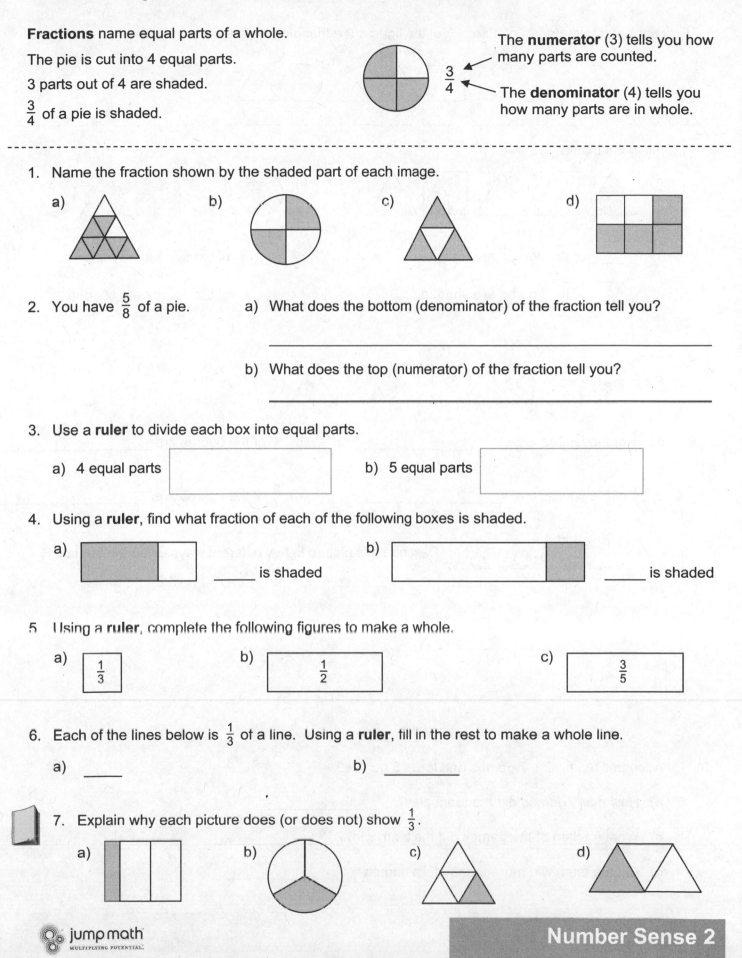

The **numerator** (3) tells you how many parts are counted.

$\frac{3}{4}$

The **denominator** (4) tells you how many parts are in whole.

1. Name the fraction shown by the shaded part of each image.

   a)   b)   c)   d)

2. You have $\frac{5}{8}$ of a pie.   a) What does the bottom (denominator) of the fraction tell you?

   _____

   b) What does the top (numerator) of the fraction tell you?

   _____

3. Use a **ruler** to divide each box into equal parts.

   a) 4 equal parts   b) 5 equal parts

4. Using a **ruler**, find what fraction of each of the following boxes is shaded.

   a)   _____ is shaded   b)   _____ is shaded

5. Using a **ruler**, complete the following figures to make a whole.

   a) $\frac{1}{3}$ b) $\frac{1}{2}$ c) $\frac{3}{5}$

6. Each of the lines below is $\frac{1}{3}$ of a line. Using a **ruler**, fill in the rest to make a whole line.

   a) _____   b) _____

7. Explain why each picture does (or does not) show $\frac{1}{3}$.

   a)   b)   c)   d)

jump math
MULTIPLYING POTENTIAL.

Number Sense 2

NS5-62: Equal Parts of a Set

Fractions can name parts of a set: $\frac{3}{5}$ of the figures are triangles, $\frac{1}{5}$ are squares and $\frac{1}{5}$ are circles.

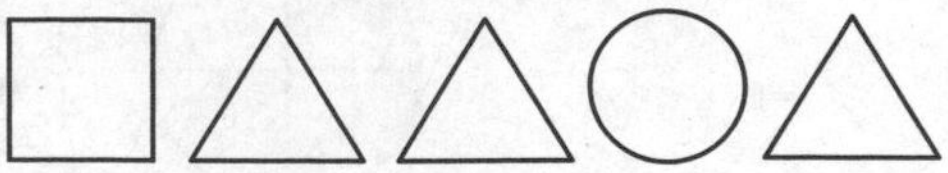

1. Fill in the blanks.

a) 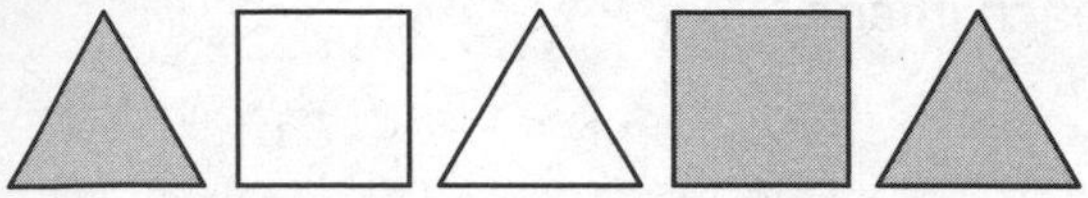

______ of the figures are triangles.

______ of the figures are shaded.

b) 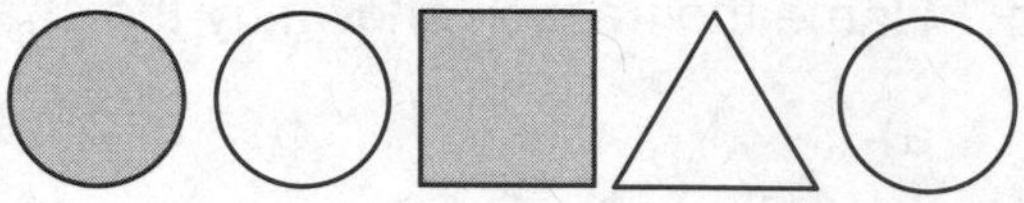

______ of the figures are squares.

______ of the figures are shaded.

2. Fill in the blanks. 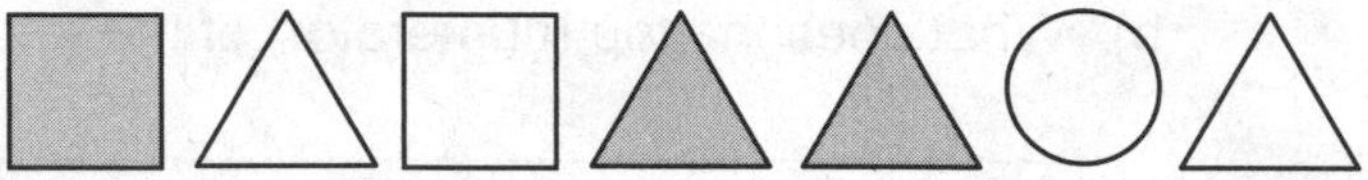

a) $\frac{4}{7}$ of the figures are ____________________

b) $\frac{2}{7}$ of the figures are ____________________

c) $\frac{1}{7}$ of the figures are ____________________

d) $\frac{3}{7}$ of the figures are ____________________

3. 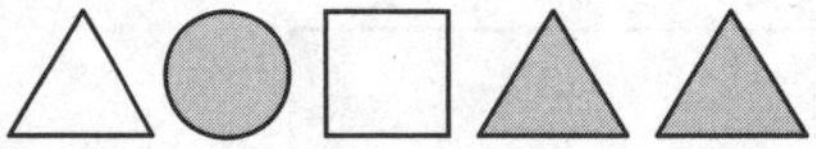 Describe this picture in two different ways using the fraction $\frac{3}{5}$.

4. A football team wins 7 games and loses 5 games.

a) How many games did the team play? ______________

b) What fraction of the games did the team win? ______________

c) Did the team win more than half its games? ______________

5.

	Number of boys	Number of girls
The Smith Family	2	3
The Sinha Family	1	2

a) What fraction of the children in each family are boys?

Smiths _____   Sinhas _____

b) What fraction of all the children are boys? _____

6. What fraction of the letters in the word "Canada" are ...

a) vowels? _____

b) consonants? _____

7. Express 7 months as a fraction of one year: _____

8. Write a fraction for each statement.

a) [ ] of the figures have 4 vertices

b) [ ] of the figures have more than 4 sides

c) [ ] of the figures have exactly one right angle

d) [ ] of the figures have exactly 2 pairs of parallel sides

9. Write two fraction statements for the figures in Question 8 above.

10. Draw a picture to solve the puzzle.

a) There are 7 circles and squares.

$\frac{2}{7}$ of the figures are squares.

$\frac{5}{7}$ of the figures are shaded.

Three circles are shaded.

b) There are 8 triangles and squares.

$\frac{6}{8}$ of the figures are shaded.

$\frac{2}{8}$ of the figures are triangles.

One triangle is shaded.

1.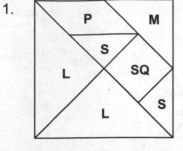

    In a tangram …

    - 2 small triangles (**S**) cover a medium triangle (**M**)
    - 2 small triangles (**S**) cover a square (**SQ**)
    - 2 small triangles (**S**) cover a parallelogram (**P**)
    - 4 small triangles (**S**) cover a large triangle (**L**)

    What fraction of each shape is covered by a <u>single</u> small triangle?

    a)   b)   c)

    d)   e)   f)

2. What fraction of each shape is shaded? Explain how you know.

    a)   b)   c)   d)

3. What fraction of the trapezoid is covered by a <u>single</u> small triangle?

    Show your work.

4. If ▧ = red and ▦ = blue, approximately what fraction of each flag is shaded red? Explain.

    a)   b)   c)   d)

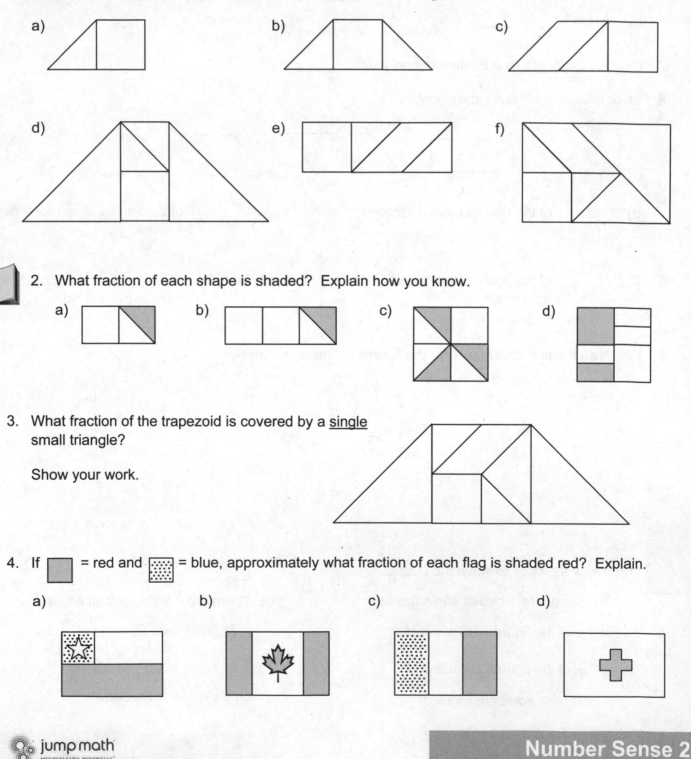

1.

    What fraction has a greater numerator, $\frac{2}{6}$ or $\frac{5}{6}$? _____

    Which fraction is greater? _____

    Explain your thinking. _____

    _____

2. Circle the greater fraction in each pair.

    a) $\frac{6}{16}$ or $\frac{9}{16}$ b) $\frac{5}{8}$ or $\frac{3}{8}$ c) $\frac{24}{25}$ or $\frac{22}{25}$ d) $\frac{37}{53}$ or $\frac{27}{53}$

3. Two fractions have the same <u>denominators</u> (bottoms) but different <u>numerators</u> (tops).
    How can you tell which fraction is greater?

    _____

4. Circle the greater fraction in each pair.

    a) $\frac{1}{8}$ or $\frac{1}{9}$ b) $\frac{12}{12}$ or $\frac{12}{13}$ c) $\frac{6}{225}$ or $\frac{5}{125}$

5. Fraction A and Fraction B have the same <u>numerators</u> but different <u>denominators</u>. How can you tell
    which fraction is greater?

    _____

6. Write the fractions in order from least to greatest.

    a) $\frac{2}{3}$, $\frac{1}{3}$, $\frac{3}{3}$ b) $\frac{9}{10}$, $\frac{2}{10}$, $\frac{1}{10}$, $\frac{5}{10}$

    c) $\frac{1}{7}$, $\frac{1}{3}$, $\frac{1}{13}$ d) $\frac{2}{11}$, $\frac{2}{5}$, $\frac{2}{7}$, $\frac{2}{16}$

7. Circle the greater fraction in each pair.

    a) $\frac{2}{3}$ or $\frac{2}{9}$ b) $\frac{7}{17}$ or $\frac{11}{17}$ c) $\frac{6}{288}$ or $\frac{6}{18}$

8. Which fraction is greater, $\frac{1}{2}$ or $\frac{45}{100}$? Explain your thinking.

9. Is it possible for $\frac{2}{3}$ of a pie to be bigger than $\frac{3}{4}$ of another pie? Show your thinking with a picture.

NS5-65: Mixed Fractions

Mattias and his friends ate the amount of pie shown.

They ate three and three quarter pies altogether (or $3\frac{3}{4}$ pies).

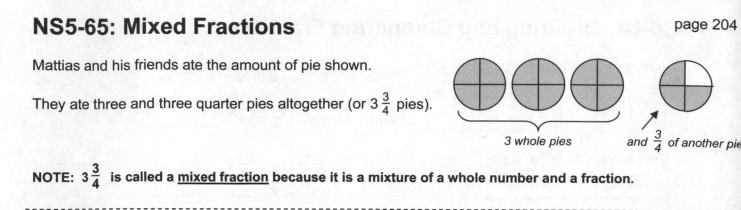

3 whole pies

and $\frac{3}{4}$ of another pie

NOTE: $3\frac{3}{4}$ is called a __mixed fraction__ because it is a mixture of a whole number and a fraction.

----

1. Write how many __whole__ pies are shaded.

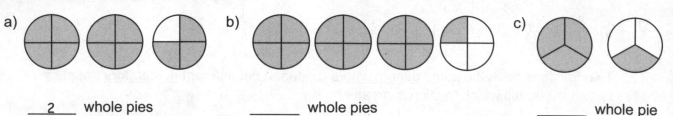

   a) ___2___ whole pies

   b) _____ whole pies

   c) _____ whole pie

2. Write the fractions as __mixed fractions__.

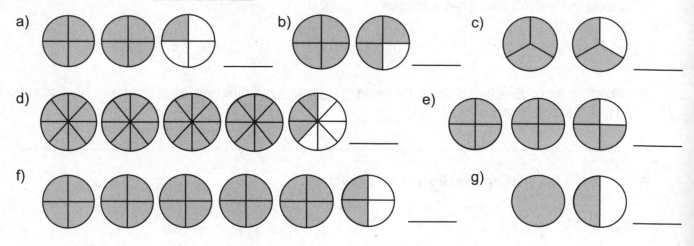

3. Shade the amount of pie given in bold.
   NOTE: There may be more pies than you need.

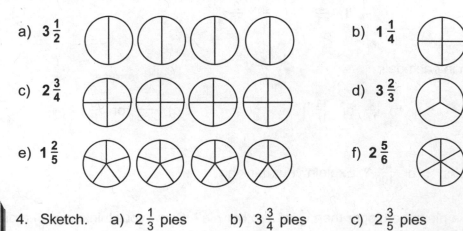

   a) $3\frac{1}{2}$

   b) $1\frac{1}{4}$

   c) $2\frac{3}{4}$

   d) $3\frac{2}{3}$

   e) $1\frac{2}{5}$

   f) $2\frac{5}{6}$

4. Sketch.   a) $2\frac{1}{3}$ pies   b) $3\frac{3}{4}$ pies   c) $2\frac{3}{5}$ pies   d) $3\frac{1}{2}$ pies

jump math
MULTIPLYING POTENTIAL

Number Sense 2

NS5-66: Improper Fractions

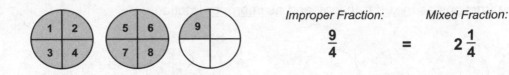

Improper Fraction: Mixed Fraction:

$$\frac{9}{4} \quad = \quad 2\frac{1}{4}$$

Huan-Yue and her friends ate **9** quarter-sized pieces of pizza. Altogether they ate $\frac{9}{4}$ pizzas.

NOTE: When the numerator of a fraction is larger than the denominator, the fraction represents *more than* a whole. Such fractions are called <u>improper fractions</u>.

---

1. Write these fractions as <u>improper</u> fractions.

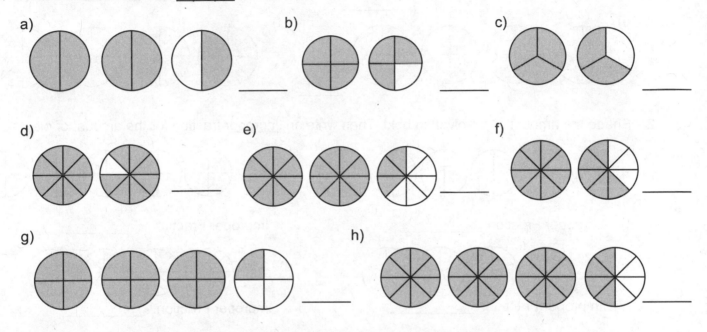

a)

b)

c)

d)

e)

f)

g)

h)

2. Shade one piece at a time until you have shaded the amount of pie given.

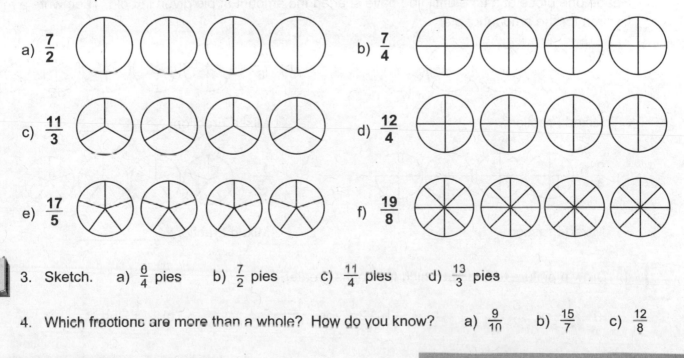

a) $\frac{7}{2}$

b) $\frac{7}{4}$

c) $\frac{11}{3}$

d) $\frac{12}{4}$

e) $\frac{17}{5}$

f) $\frac{19}{8}$

3. Sketch.   a) $\frac{8}{4}$ pies   b) $\frac{7}{2}$ pies   c) $\frac{11}{4}$ pies   d) $\frac{13}{3}$ pies

4. Which fractions are more than a whole? How do you know?   a) $\frac{9}{10}$ b) $\frac{15}{7}$ c) $\frac{12}{8}$

NS5-67: Mixed and Improper Fractions

1. Write these fractions as <u>mixed</u> fractions and as <u>improper</u> fractions.

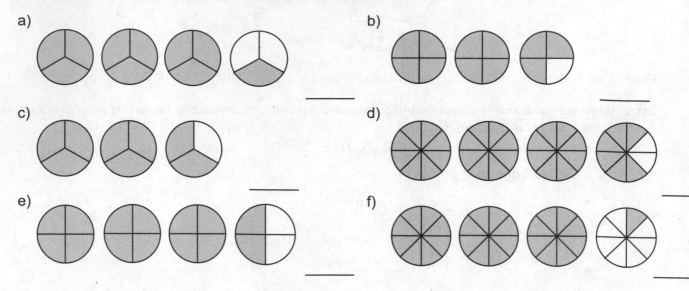

a) _____

b) _____

c) _____

d) _____

e) _____

f) _____

2. Shade the amount of pie given in bold. Then write an <u>improper</u> fraction for the amount of pie.

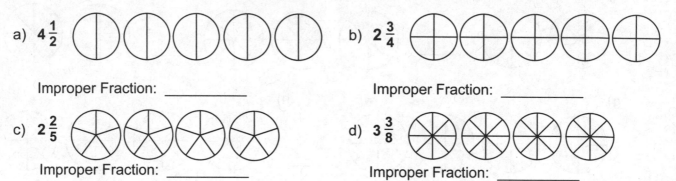

a) $4\frac{1}{2}$

Improper Fraction: _____

b) $2\frac{3}{4}$

Improper Fraction: _____

c) $2\frac{2}{5}$

Improper Fraction: _____

d) $3\frac{3}{8}$

Improper Fraction: _____

3. Shade one piece at a time until you have shaded the amount of pie given in bold. Then write a <u>mixed</u> fraction for the amount of pie.

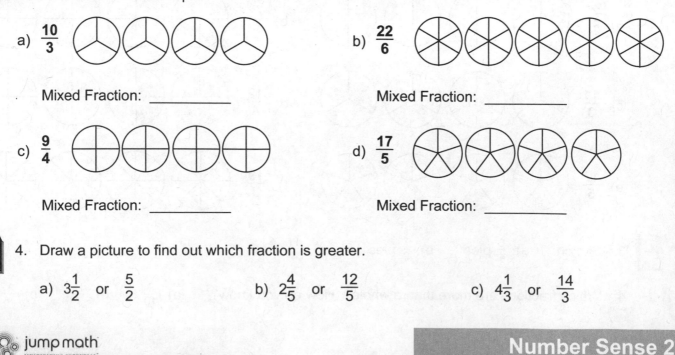

a) $\frac{10}{3}$

Mixed Fraction: _____

b) $\frac{22}{6}$

Mixed Fraction: _____

c) $\frac{9}{4}$

Mixed Fraction: _____

d) $\frac{17}{5}$

Mixed Fraction: _____

4. Draw a picture to find out which fraction is greater.

a) $3\frac{1}{2}$ or $\frac{5}{2}$ b) $2\frac{4}{5}$ or $\frac{12}{5}$ c) $4\frac{1}{3}$ or $\frac{14}{3}$

NS5-68: Mixed Fractions (Advanced)

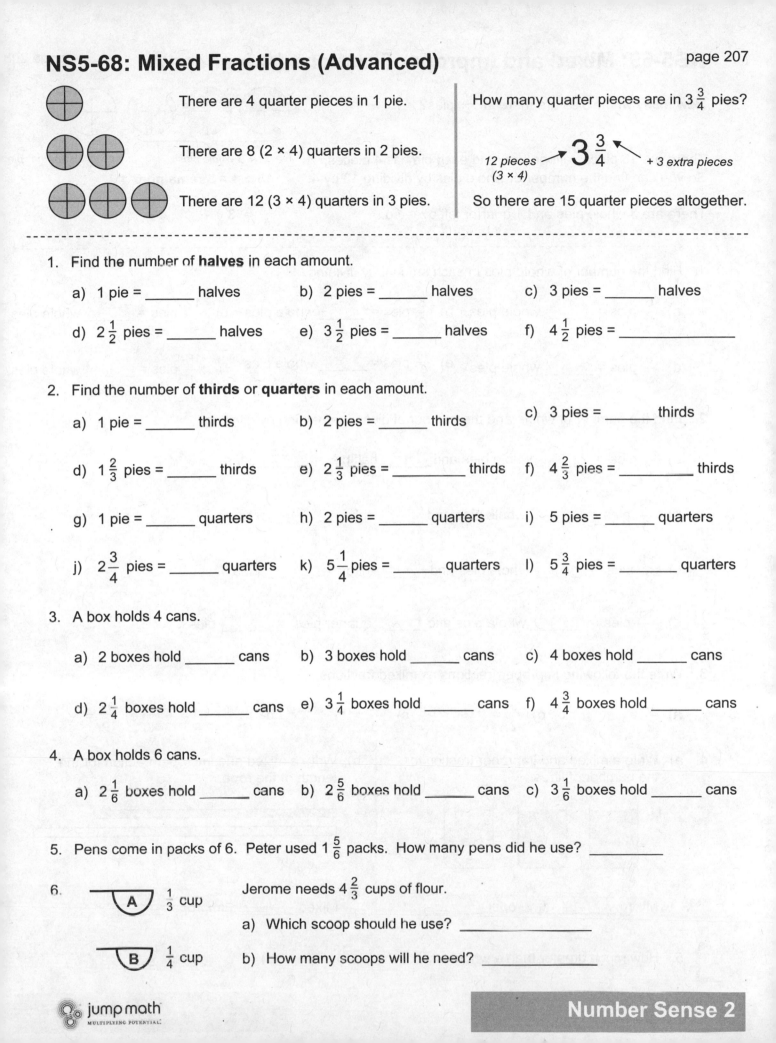

There are 4 quarter pieces in 1 pie.

There are 8 (2 × 4) quarters in 2 pies.

There are 12 (3 × 4) quarters in 3 pies.

How many quarter pieces are in $3\frac{3}{4}$ pies?

12 pieces (3 × 4) → $3\frac{3}{4}$ ← + 3 extra pieces

So there are 15 quarter pieces altogether.

---

1. Find the number of **halves** in each amount.

   a) 1 pie = _____ halves

   b) 2 pies = _____ halves

   c) 3 pies = _____ halves

   d) $2\frac{1}{2}$ pies = _____ halves

   e) $3\frac{1}{2}$ pies = _____ halves

   f) $4\frac{1}{2}$ pies = _____

2. Find the number of **thirds** or **quarters** in each amount.

   a) 1 pie = _____ thirds

   b) 2 pies = _____ thirds

   c) 3 pies = _____ thirds

   d) $1\frac{2}{3}$ pies = _____ thirds

   e) $2\frac{1}{3}$ pies = _____ thirds

   f) $4\frac{2}{3}$ pies = _____ thirds

   g) 1 pie = _____ quarters

   h) 2 pies = _____ quarters

   i) 5 pies = _____ quarters

   j) $2\frac{3}{4}$ pies = _____ quarters

   k) $5\frac{1}{4}$ pies = _____ quarters

   l) $5\frac{3}{4}$ pies = _____ quarters

3. A box holds 4 cans.

   a) 2 boxes hold _____ cans

   b) 3 boxes hold _____ cans

   c) 4 boxes hold _____ cans

   d) $2\frac{1}{4}$ boxes hold _____ cans

   e) $3\frac{1}{4}$ boxes hold _____ cans

   f) $4\frac{3}{4}$ boxes hold _____ cans

4. A box holds 6 cans.

   a) $2\frac{1}{6}$ boxes hold _____ cans

   b) $2\frac{5}{6}$ boxes hold _____ cans

   c) $3\frac{1}{6}$ boxes hold _____ cans

5. Pens come in packs of 6. Peter used $1\frac{5}{6}$ packs. How many pens did he use? _____

6.
   A $\frac{1}{3}$ cup

   B $\frac{1}{4}$ cup

   Jerome needs $4\frac{2}{3}$ cups of flour.

   a) Which scoop should he use? _____

   b) How many scoops will he need? _____

Number Sense 2

NS5-69: Mixed and Improper Fractions (Advanced)

How many whole pies are there in $\frac{13}{4}$ pies?

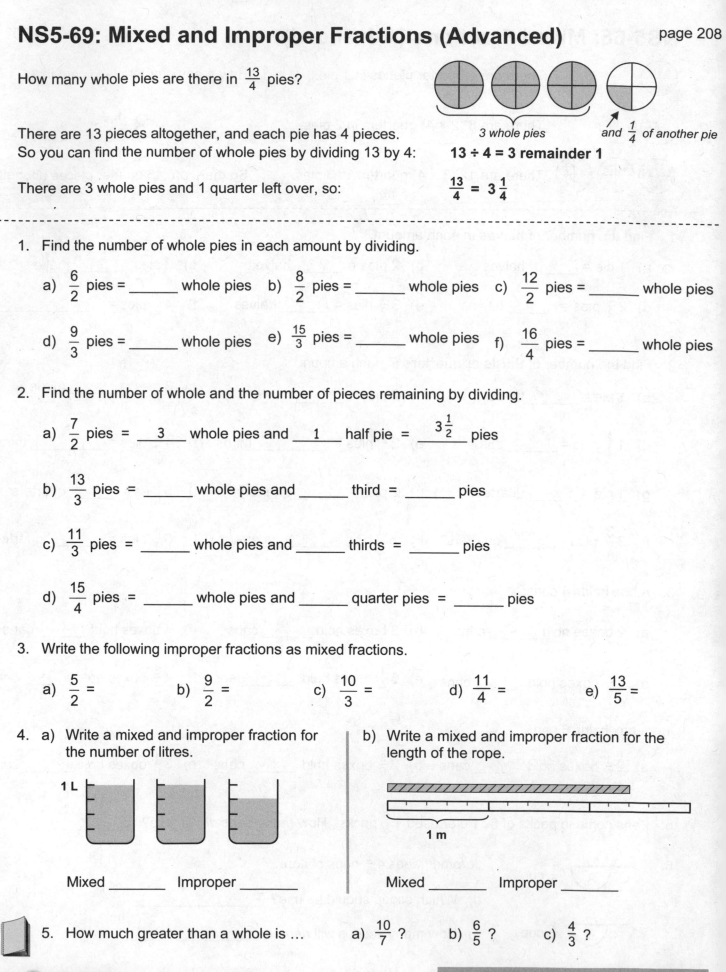

3 whole pies   and $\frac{1}{4}$ of another pie

There are 13 pieces altogether, and each pie has 4 pieces.
So you can find the number of whole pies by dividing 13 by 4:   **13 ÷ 4 = 3 remainder 1**

There are 3 whole pies and 1 quarter left over, so: $\frac{13}{4} = 3\frac{1}{4}$

- -

1. Find the number of whole pies in each amount by dividing.

   a) $\frac{6}{2}$ pies = _____ whole pies   b) $\frac{8}{2}$ pies = _____ whole pies   c) $\frac{12}{2}$ pies = _____ whole pies

   d) $\frac{9}{3}$ pies = _____ whole pies   e) $\frac{15}{3}$ pies = _____ whole pies   f) $\frac{16}{4}$ pies = _____ whole pies

2. Find the number of whole and the number of pieces remaining by dividing.

   a) $\frac{7}{2}$ pies = ___3___ whole pies and ___1___ half pie = $3\frac{1}{2}$ pies

   b) $\frac{13}{3}$ pies = _____ whole pies and _____ third = _____ pies

   c) $\frac{11}{3}$ pies = _____ whole pies and _____ thirds = _____ pies

   d) $\frac{15}{4}$ pies = _____ whole pies and _____ quarter pies = _____ pies

3. Write the following improper fractions as mixed fractions.

   a) $\frac{5}{2}$ =   b) $\frac{9}{2}$ =   c) $\frac{10}{3}$ =   d) $\frac{11}{4}$ =   e) $\frac{13}{5}$ =

4. a) Write a mixed and improper fraction for the number of litres.

   b) Write a mixed and improper fraction for the length of the rope.

   1 L

   Mixed _____ Improper _____

   1 m

   Mixed _____ Improper _____

5. How much greater than a whole is …   a) $\frac{10}{7}$?   b) $\frac{6}{5}$?   c) $\frac{4}{3}$?

jump math
MULTIPLYING POTENTIAL.

Number Sense 2

NS5-70: Investigating Mixed and Improper Fractions

TEACHER:
Your students will need pattern blocks
for this exercise, or a copy of the patterns
block sheet from the Teacher's Guide.

triangle *rhombus* *trapezoid*

hexagon

NOTE: The blocks shown here are not actual size!

Euclid's bakery sells hexagonal pies. They sell pieces shaped like triangles, rhombuses, and trapezoids.

1. a) Shade $2\frac{5}{6}$ pies: b) How many pieces did you shade? _____

   c) Write an improper fraction from the amount of pie shaded: _____

2. Make a model of the pies below with pattern blocks. (Place the smaller shapes on top of the hexagons). Then write a mixed and improper fractions for each pie.

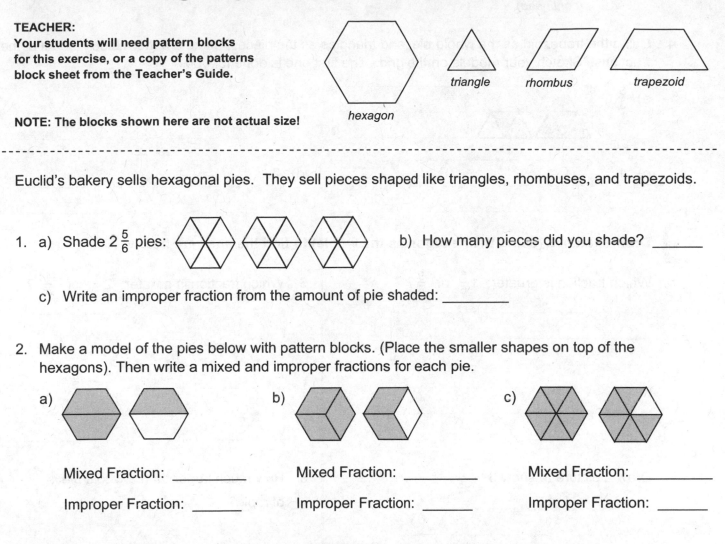

a)

Mixed Fraction: _____

Improper Fraction: _____

b)

Mixed Fraction: _____

Improper Fraction: _____

c)

Mixed Fraction: _____

Improper Fraction: _____

3. Use the hexagon as the whole pie. Use the triangles, rhombuses and trapezoids as the pieces. Make a pattern block model of the fractions below. Then sketch your models on the grid.

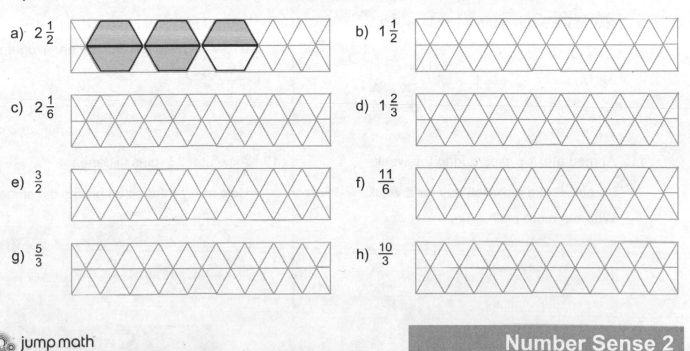

a) $2\frac{1}{2}$

b) $1\frac{1}{2}$

c) $2\frac{1}{6}$

d) $1\frac{2}{3}$

e) $\frac{3}{2}$

f) $\frac{11}{6}$

g) $\frac{5}{3}$

h) $\frac{10}{3}$

jump math
MULTIPLYING POTENTIAL.

Number Sense 2

4. Using the trapezoid as the whole pie, and triangles as the pieces, make a pattern block model of the fractions. Sketch your models on the grid. The first one is done for you.

a) $\frac{5}{3}$

b) $\frac{7}{3}$

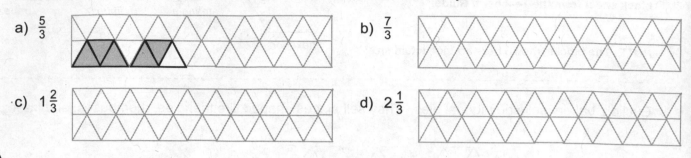

c) $1\frac{2}{3}$

d) $2\frac{1}{3}$

Draw sketches (using the hexagon as the whole) to find the answers below.

5. Which fraction is greater: $1\frac{5}{6}$ or $\frac{9}{6}$?

6. Which fraction is greater: $2\frac{1}{6}$ or $\frac{14}{6}$?

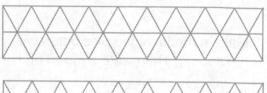

7. Draw a picture to show $3 - \frac{1}{6}$.

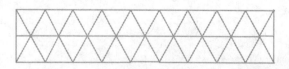

8. How much larger than a whole pie is $\frac{7}{6}$ of a pie?

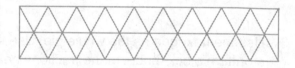

9. How much larger than a whole is $\frac{4}{3}$?

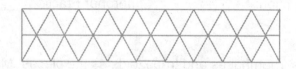

10. Crystal ate $\frac{2}{3}$ of a pie each day for 4 days in a row. How much did she eat altogether?

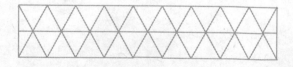

11. Ahmed ate $1\frac{1}{3}$ pies during the week.

   Jill ate $\frac{1}{6}$ of a pie each day for a week. Who ate more pie?

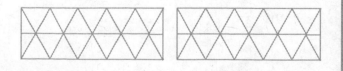

12. Alice ate $3\frac{2}{3}$ pies in January.

   How many third-sized pieces did she eat?

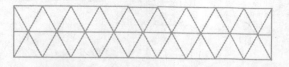

NS5-71: Equivalent Fractions

Aidan shades $\frac{2}{6}$ of the squares in an array:

He then draws heavy lines around the squares to group them into 3 equal groups:

He sees that $\frac{1}{3}$ of the squares are shaded.

The pictures show that two sixths are equal to one third: $\frac{2}{6} = \frac{1}{3}$

Two sixths and one third are **equivalent fractions**.

----

1. Group squares to show an equivalent fraction.

   a)
   $\frac{2}{8} = \frac{}{4}$

   b)
   $\frac{6}{10} = \frac{}{5}$

   c)
   $\frac{3}{9} = \frac{}{3}$

2. Group the squares to show …

   a) Six twelfths equals one half ($\frac{6}{12} = \frac{1}{2}$)

   b) Six twelfths equals three sixths ($\frac{6}{12} = \frac{3}{6}$)

3. Group the squares to make an equivalent fraction.

   a)
   $\frac{8}{10} = \frac{}{5}$

   b)
   $\frac{4}{8} = \frac{}{2}$

   c)
   $\frac{4}{12} = \frac{}{3}$

   d)
   $\frac{9}{15} = \frac{}{}$

   e)
   $\frac{6}{14} = \frac{}{}$

   f)
   $\frac{8}{12} = \frac{}{}$

4. Write four equivalent fractions for the amount shaded here.

   _____ _____ _____ _____

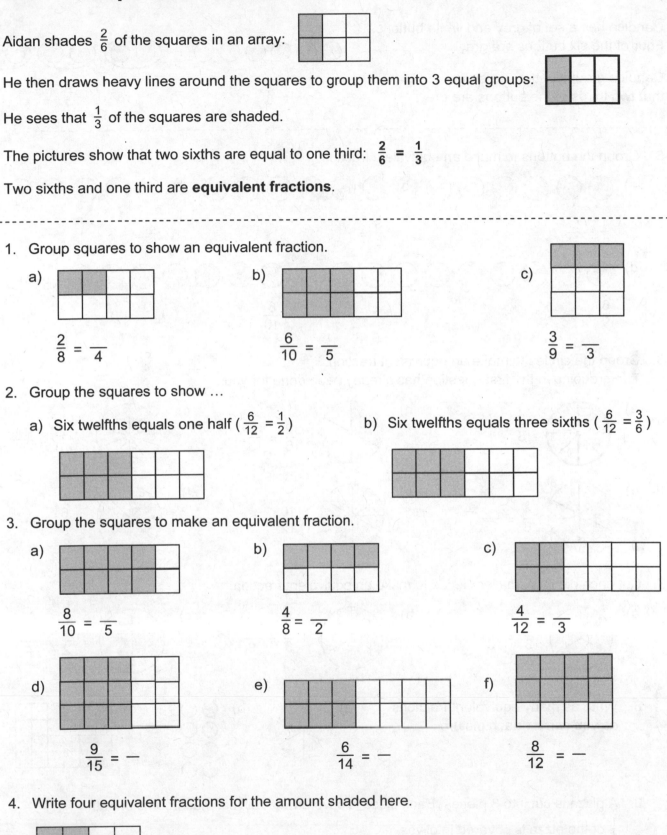

jump math
MULTIPLYING POTENTIAL

Number Sense 2

Candice has a set of grey and white buttons.
Four of the six buttons are grey.

Candice groups buttons to show
that two thirds of the buttons are grey:

$$\frac{4}{6} \qquad = \qquad \frac{2}{3}$$

5. Group the buttons to make an equivalent fraction.

a) $\frac{4}{6} = \underline{}$

b) $\frac{3}{6} = \underline{}$

c) $\frac{2}{6} = \underline{}$

d) $\frac{6}{9} = \underline{}$

e) $\frac{8}{10} = \underline{}$

6. Group the circles to make an equivalent fraction.
    The grouping in the first question has already been done for you.

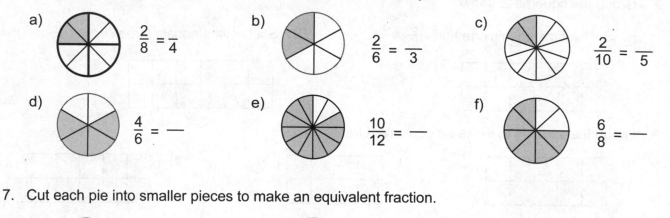

a) $\frac{2}{8} = \frac{}{4}$

b) $\frac{2}{6} = \frac{}{3}$

c) $\frac{2}{10} = \frac{}{5}$

d) $\frac{4}{6} = \underline{}$

e) $\frac{10}{12} = \underline{}$

f) $\frac{6}{8} = \underline{}$

7. Cut each pie into smaller pieces to make an equivalent fraction.

a) $\frac{1}{3} = \frac{}{6}$

b) $\frac{2}{3} = \frac{}{9}$

c) $\frac{1}{2} = \frac{}{4}$

8. Write as many equivalent fractions
    as you can for each picture.

a)   b)   c)

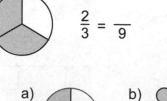

9. A pizza is cut into 8 pieces. Each piece is covered with olives, mushrooms or both.

    $\frac{1}{4}$ of the pizza is covered in olives.

    $\frac{7}{8}$ of the pizza is covered in mushrooms.

    Draw a picture to show how many pieces have both olives and mushrooms on them.

NS5-72: Models of Equivalent Fractions

1. Draw lines to cut the pies into more pieces.

   Then fill in the numerators of the equivalent fractions:

   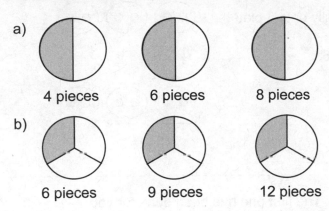

   a)

   4 pieces   6 pieces   8 pieces

   b)

   6 pieces   9 pieces   12 pieces

   $\dfrac{1}{2} = \dfrac{}{4} = \dfrac{}{6} = \dfrac{}{8}$

   $\dfrac{1}{3} = \dfrac{}{6} = \dfrac{}{9} = \dfrac{}{12}$

2. Cut each pie into more pieces. Then fill in the missing numbers.

   a)
   $\dfrac{2}{3} \overset{\times 2}{\underset{\times 2}{=}} \dfrac{}{6}$

   b)
   $\dfrac{3}{4} \overset{\times 2}{\underset{\times 2}{=}} \dfrac{}{8}$

   c)
   $\dfrac{2}{3} \overset{\times}{\underset{\times}{=}} \dfrac{}{9}$

   This number tells you how many pieces to cut each slice into.

3. Use multiplication to find the equivalent fractions below.

   a) $\dfrac{1}{3} \overset{\times 2}{\underset{\times 2}{=}} \dfrac{}{6}$
   b) $\dfrac{1}{2} = \dfrac{}{10}$
   c) $\dfrac{2}{5} = \dfrac{}{10}$
   d) $\dfrac{3}{4} = \dfrac{}{8}$
   e) $\dfrac{1}{4} = \dfrac{}{12}$

4. Use the patterns in the numerators and denominators to find 6 fractions equivalent to …

   a) $\dfrac{1}{2} = \dfrac{2}{4} = \dfrac{3}{} = \dfrac{}{8} = \dfrac{}{10} = \dfrac{}{}$

   b) $\dfrac{3}{5} = \dfrac{6}{} = \dfrac{9}{15} = \dfrac{12}{20} = \dfrac{}{} = \dfrac{}{}$

5. To show that $\dfrac{3}{4}$ is equivalent to $\dfrac{9}{12}$, Brian makes a model of $\dfrac{9}{12}$ using blocks.

   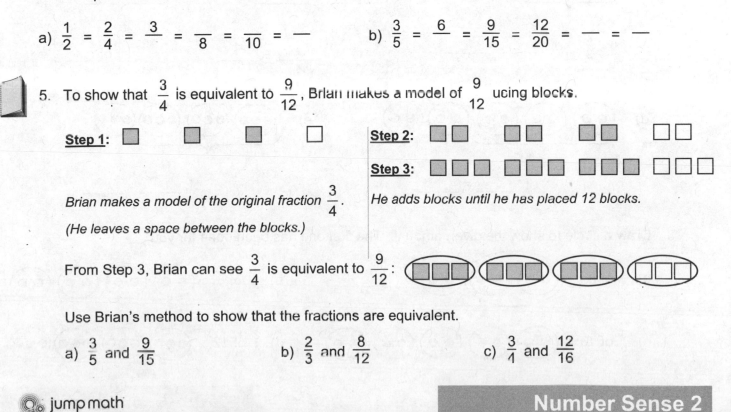

   Step 1:

   Brian makes a model of the original fraction $\dfrac{3}{4}$.
   (He leaves a space between the blocks.)

   Step 2:

   Step 3:

   He adds blocks until he has placed 12 blocks.

   From Step 3, Brian can see $\dfrac{3}{4}$ is equivalent to $\dfrac{9}{12}$:

   Use Brian's method to show that the fractions are equivalent.

   a) $\dfrac{3}{5}$ and $\dfrac{9}{15}$
   b) $\dfrac{2}{3}$ and $\dfrac{8}{12}$
   c) $\dfrac{3}{4}$ and $\dfrac{12}{16}$

Dan has 6 cookies. He wants to give $\frac{2}{3}$ of his cookies to his friends. To do so, he shares the cookies equally onto 3 plates:

There are 3 equal groups, so each group is $\frac{1}{3}$ of 6.

There are 2 cookies in each group, so $\frac{1}{3}$ of 6 is 2.

There are 4 cookies in two groups, so $\frac{2}{3}$ of 6 is 4.

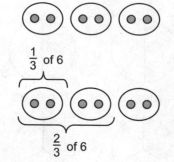

- -

1. Write a fraction for the amount of dots shown. The first one has been done for you.

a)

$\boxed{\dfrac{3}{4}}$ of 8

b)

$\boxed{}$ of 15

2. Fill in the missing numbers.

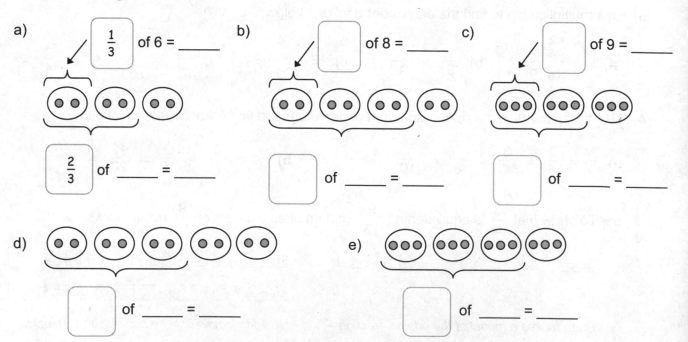

a) $\boxed{\dfrac{1}{3}}$ of 6 = _____

$\boxed{\dfrac{2}{3}}$ of _____ = _____

b) $\boxed{}$ of 8 = _____

$\boxed{}$ of _____ = _____

c) $\boxed{}$ of 9 = _____

$\boxed{}$ of _____ = _____

d)

$\boxed{}$ of _____ = _____

e)

$\boxed{}$ of _____ = _____

3. Draw a circle to show the given amount. The first one has been done for you.

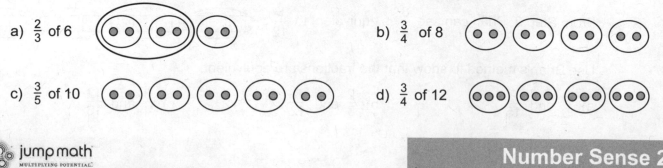

a) $\frac{2}{3}$ of 6

b) $\frac{3}{4}$ of 8

c) $\frac{3}{5}$ of 10

d) $\frac{3}{4}$ of 12

4. Fill in the correct number of dots in each circle, then draw a larger circle to show the given amount.

   a) $\frac{2}{3}$ of 12

   b) $\frac{2}{3}$ of 9

5. Find the fraction of the whole amount by sharing the cookies equally.
   HINT: Draw the correct number of plates then place the cookies one at a time. Then circle the correct amount.

   a) Find $\frac{1}{4}$ of 8 cookies.

   b) Find $\frac{1}{2}$ of 10 cookies.

   $\frac{1}{4}$ of 8 is _____

   $\frac{1}{2}$ of 10 is _____

   c) Find $\frac{2}{3}$ of 6 cookies.

   d) Find $\frac{3}{4}$ of 12 cookies.

   $\frac{2}{3}$ of 6 is _____

   $\frac{3}{4}$ of 12 is _____

6. Andy finds $\frac{2}{3}$ of 12 as follows:

   <u>Step 1</u>:   *He finds $\frac{1}{3}$ of 12 by dividing 12 by 3.*

   12 ÷ 3 = 4 (4 is $\frac{1}{3}$ of 12)

   <u>Step 2</u>:   *Then he multiplies the result by 2.*

   4 × 2 = 8 (8 is $\frac{2}{3}$ of 12)

   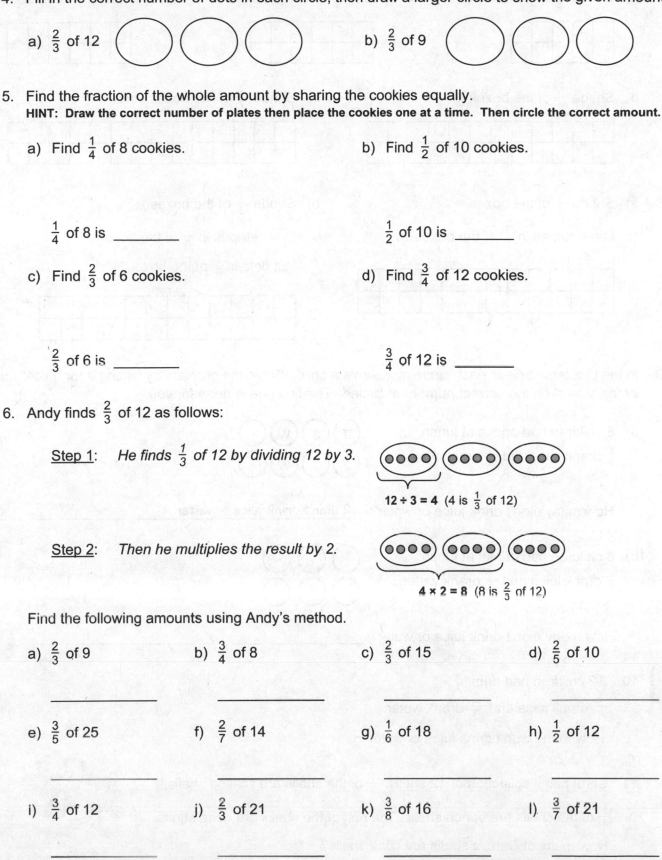

   Find the following amounts using Andy's method.

   a) $\frac{2}{3}$ of 9

   b) $\frac{3}{4}$ of 8

   c) $\frac{2}{3}$ of 15

   d) $\frac{2}{5}$ of 10

   _____

   _____

   _____

   _____

   e) $\frac{3}{5}$ of 25

   f) $\frac{2}{7}$ of 14

   g) $\frac{1}{6}$ of 18

   h) $\frac{1}{2}$ of 12

   _____

   _____

   _____

   _____

   i) $\frac{3}{4}$ of 12

   j) $\frac{2}{3}$ of 21

   k) $\frac{3}{8}$ of 16

   l) $\frac{3}{7}$ of 21

   _____

   _____

   _____

   _____

7. a) Shade $\frac{2}{5}$ of the boxes.   b) Shade $\frac{2}{3}$ of the boxes.   c) Shade $\frac{3}{4}$ of the boxes.

d) Shade $\frac{5}{6}$ of the boxes.   e) Shade $\frac{2}{7}$ of the boxes.

8. a) Shade $\frac{1}{4}$ of the boxes.

   Draw stripes in $\frac{1}{6}$ of the boxes.

   b) Shade $\frac{1}{3}$ of the boxes.

   Draw stripes in $\frac{1}{6}$ of the boxes.

   Put dots in $\frac{1}{8}$ of the boxes.

9. In the problems below, each circle represents a child. Solve the problem by writing **J** for "juice" and **W** for "water" on the correct number of circles. The first one is done for you.

   a) 8 children had drinks at lunch.

   $\frac{1}{2}$ drank juice and $\frac{1}{4}$ drank water.

   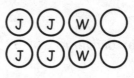

   How many didn't drink juice or water? <u>2 didn't drink juice or water</u>

   b) 6 children had drinks at lunch.

   $\frac{1}{2}$ drank juice and $\frac{1}{3}$ drank water.

   How many didn't drink juice or water? _____

10. 12 children had drinks.

    $\frac{1}{4}$ drank juice and $\frac{2}{3}$ drank water.

    How many didn't drink juice or water?

11. Carol has a collection of 12 shells. $\frac{1}{3}$ of the shells are scallop shells.

    $\frac{1}{4}$ of the shells are conch shells. The rest of the shells are cone shells.

    How many of Carol's shells are cone shells?

conch

1. A kilogram of nuts costs $8.

    How much would $\frac{3}{4}$ of a kilogram cost? _____

2. Gerald has 10 oranges.
    He gives away $\frac{3}{5}$ of the oranges.

    a) How many oranges did he give away? _____   b) How many did he keep? _____

3. Shade $\frac{1}{3}$ of the squares.

    Draw stripes in $\frac{1}{6}$ of the squares.

    How many squares are blank? _____

4. Sapin has 20 marbles.

    $\frac{2}{5}$ are blue. $\frac{1}{4}$ are yellow.

    The rest are green.

    How many are green?

5. Which is longer:

    17 months or $1\frac{3}{4}$ years?

6. How many months are in $\frac{3}{4}$ of a year?

7. How many minutes are in $\frac{2}{3}$ of an hour?

8. Fong had 28 stickers.

    She kept $\frac{1}{7}$ herself and divided the rest
    evenly among 6 friends.

    How many stickers did each friend get?

9. Nancy put 4 of her 10 shells on a shelf.

    Explain how you know
    she put $\frac{2}{5}$ of her shells
    on the shelf.

10. Karl started studying at 7:15.

    He studied for $\frac{3}{5}$ of an hour.

    At what time did he stop
    studying?

11. Linda had 12 apples.

    She gave $\frac{1}{4}$ to Nandita and she gave 2 to Amy.

    She says that she has half left.

    Is she correct?

CHALLENGING:

12. Draw a picture or make a model to solve this problem.

    - $\frac{2}{5}$ of Kim's marbles are yellow
    - $\frac{3}{5}$ are blue
    - 8 are yellow

    How many of Kim's marbles are blue?

Use the fraction strips below to answer Questions 1 to 3.

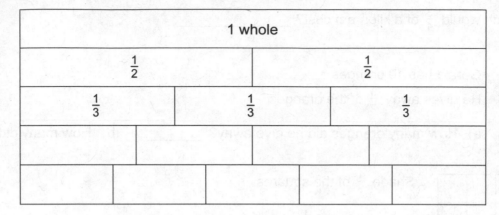

1. Fill in the missing numbers on the fraction strips above. Then write > (greater than) or < (less than) between each pair of numbers below.

   a) $\frac{1}{2}$ ☐ $\frac{2}{3}$ b) $\frac{3}{4}$ ☐ $\frac{2}{3}$ c) $\frac{2}{5}$ ☐ $\frac{3}{4}$ d) $\frac{4}{5}$ ☐ $\frac{3}{4}$

2. Circle the fractions that are greater than $\frac{1}{3}$.

   $\frac{1}{5}$ $\frac{2}{5}$ $\frac{1}{2}$

3. Circle the fractions that are greater than $\frac{1}{2}$.

   $\frac{3}{5}$ $\frac{2}{5}$ $\frac{3}{4}$

4. Draw lines to cut the left-hand pie into the same number of pieces as the right-hand pie. Then circle the greater fraction.

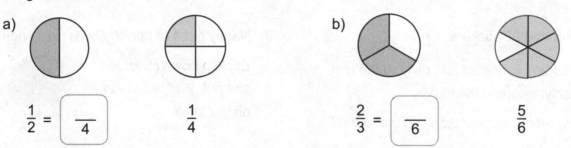

   a) $\frac{1}{2} = \frac{}{4}$ $\frac{1}{4}$ b) $\frac{2}{3} = \frac{}{6}$ $\frac{5}{6}$

5. Turn each fraction on the left into an equivalent fraction with the same denominator as the fraction on the right. Then write > or < to show which fraction is greater.

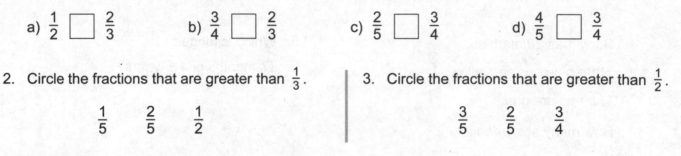

   a) $\frac{1 \times 3}{2 \times 3} = \frac{3}{6}$ [<] $\frac{4}{6}$ b) $\frac{1 \times}{2 \times} = \frac{}{8}$ ☐ $\frac{5}{8}$ c) $\frac{1}{2} = \frac{}{}$ ☐ $\frac{3}{4}$

   d) $\frac{1}{2} = \frac{}{}$ ☐ $\frac{4}{10}$ e) $\frac{1}{2} = \frac{}{}$ ☐ $\frac{3}{12}$ f) $\frac{1}{3} = \frac{}{}$ ☐ $\frac{4}{9}$

   g) $\frac{1}{5} = \frac{}{}$ ☐ $\frac{7}{10}$ h) $\frac{1}{5} = \frac{}{}$ ☐ $\frac{4}{10}$ i) $\frac{1}{4} = \frac{}{}$ ☐ $\frac{7}{16}$

NS5-76: Lowest Common Denominator

1. Cut each pie evenly into the given number of pieces. Then write a fraction for the result.

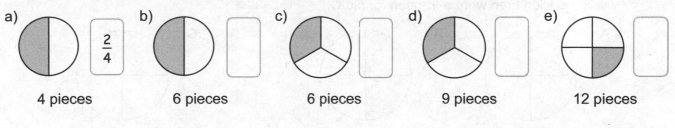

a) $\frac{2}{4}$

4 pieces

b)

6 pieces

c)

6 pieces

d)

9 pieces

e)

12 pieces

2. Recall that to find the **lowest common multiple** (LCM) of a pair of numbers, you first write out the multiples of the number.

Example:

4: 4 8 12

6: 6 12 18

Stop when the same number appears on both lists.

12 *is the LCM of 4 and 6.*

Follow the steps in chart a) below to cut each pair of pies into the same number of pieces.

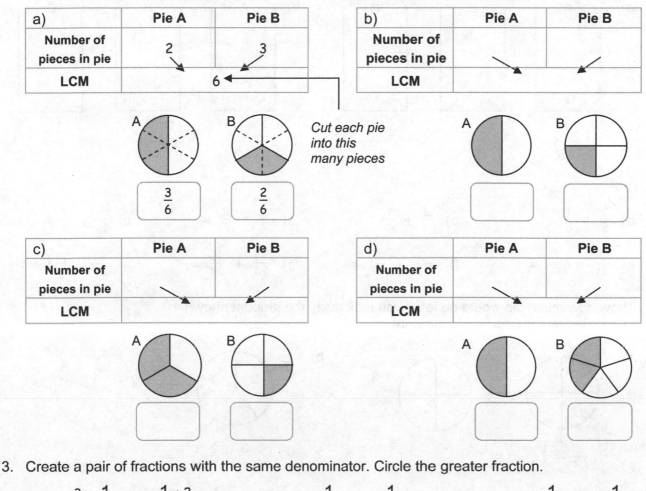

a)	Pie A	Pie B
Number of pieces in pie	2	3
LCM	6	

Cut each pie into this many pieces

$\frac{3}{6}$ $\frac{2}{6}$

b)	Pie A	Pie B
Number of pieces in pie		
LCM		

c)	Pie A	Pie B
Number of pieces in pie		
LCM		

d)	Pie A	Pie B
Number of pieces in pie		
LCM		

3. Create a pair of fractions with the same denominator. Circle the greater fraction.

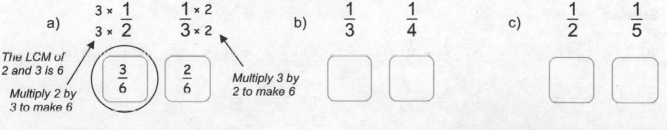

a) $\frac{3 \times 1}{3 \times 2}$ $\frac{1 \times 2}{3 \times 2}$

The LCM of 2 and 3 is 6

Multiply 2 by 3 to make 6

$\frac{3}{6}$ $\frac{2}{6}$

Multiply 3 by 2 to make 6

b) $\frac{1}{3}$ $\frac{1}{4}$

c) $\frac{1}{2}$ $\frac{1}{5}$

1. Imagine moving the shaded pieces from pies A and B onto pie plate C. Show how much of pie C would be filled then write a fraction for pie C.

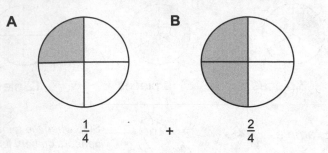 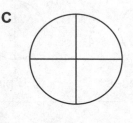

A   B   C

$\frac{1}{4}$ + $\frac{2}{4}$ =   ____

2. Imagine pouring the liquid from cups A and B into cup C.
   Shade the amount of liquid that would be in C.
   Then complete the addition statements.

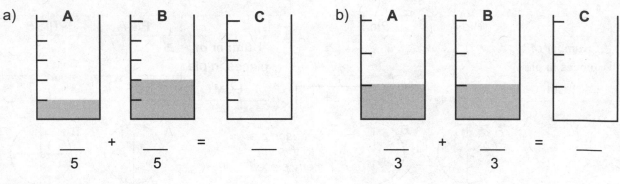

a)   A   B   C
   $\frac{}{5}$ + $\frac{}{5}$ = ____

b)   A   B   C
   $\frac{}{3}$ + $\frac{}{3}$ = ____

3. Add.

a) $\frac{3}{5} + \frac{1}{5} =$ b) $\frac{2}{4} + \frac{1}{4} =$ c) $\frac{3}{7} + \frac{2}{7} =$ d) $\frac{5}{8} + \frac{2}{8} =$

e) $\frac{3}{11} + \frac{7}{11} =$ f) $\frac{5}{17} + \frac{9}{17} =$ g) $\frac{11}{24} + \frac{10}{24} =$ h) $\frac{18}{57} + \frac{13}{57} =$

4. Show how much pie would be left if you took away the amount shown.
   Then complete the fraction statement.

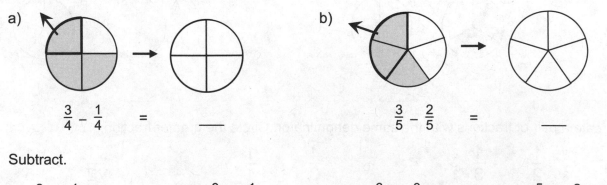

a)
   $\frac{3}{4} - \frac{1}{4}$ = ____

b)
   $\frac{3}{5} - \frac{2}{5}$ = ____

5. Subtract.

a) $\frac{2}{3} - \frac{1}{3} =$ b) $\frac{3}{5} - \frac{1}{5} =$ c) $\frac{6}{7} - \frac{3}{7} =$ d) $\frac{5}{8} - \frac{2}{8} =$

e) $\frac{9}{12} - \frac{2}{12} =$ f) $\frac{6}{19} - \frac{4}{19} =$ g) $\frac{9}{28} - \frac{3}{28} =$ h) $\frac{17}{57} - \frac{12}{57} =$

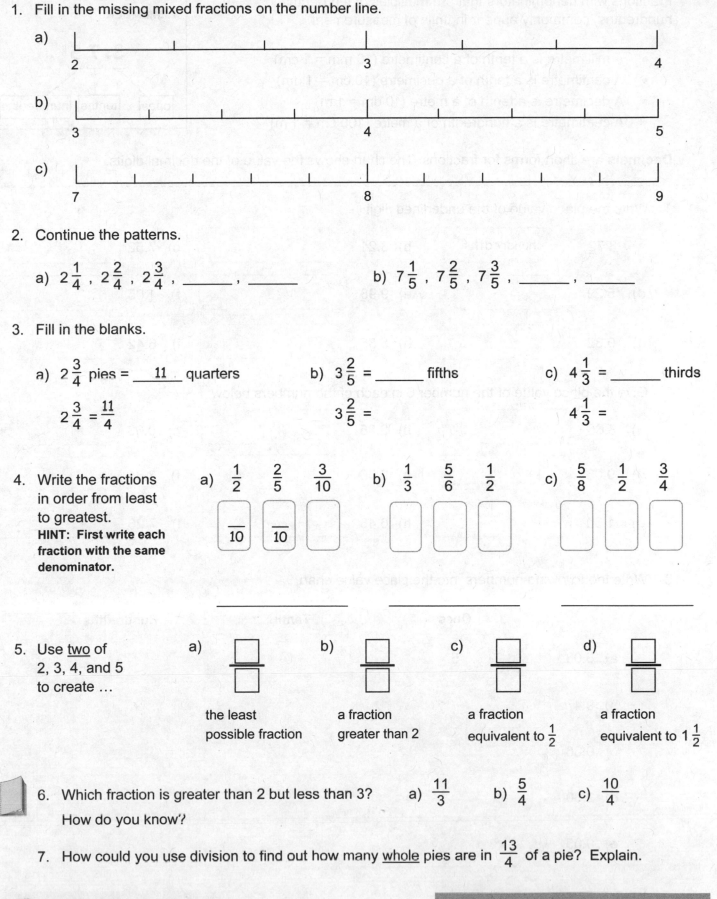

1. Fill in the missing mixed fractions on the number line.

   a)

   2   3   4

   b)

   3   4   5

   c)

   7   8   9

2. Continue the patterns.

   a) $2\frac{1}{4}$, $2\frac{2}{4}$, $2\frac{3}{4}$, _____ , _____

   b) $7\frac{1}{5}$, $7\frac{2}{5}$, $7\frac{3}{5}$, _____ , _____

3. Fill in the blanks.

   a) $2\frac{3}{4}$ pies = ___11___ quarters

      $2\frac{3}{4} = \frac{11}{4}$

   b) $3\frac{2}{5}$ = _____ fifths

      $3\frac{2}{5}$ =

   c) $4\frac{1}{3}$ = _____ thirds

      $4\frac{1}{3}$ =

4. Write the fractions in order from least to greatest.

   HINT: First write each fraction with the same denominator.

   a) $\frac{1}{2}$ $\frac{2}{5}$ $\frac{3}{10}$

   $\frac{}{10}$ $\frac{}{10}$ ☐

   b) $\frac{1}{3}$ $\frac{5}{6}$ $\frac{1}{2}$

   ☐   ☐   ☐

   c) $\frac{5}{8}$ $\frac{1}{2}$ $\frac{3}{4}$

   ☐   ☐   ☐

   _____   _____   _____

5. Use <u>two</u> of 2, 3, 4, and 5 to create …

   a) ☐/☐

   the least possible fraction

   b) ☐/☐

   a fraction greater than 2

   c) ☐/☐

   a fraction equivalent to $\frac{1}{2}$

   d) ☐/☐

   a fraction equivalent to $1\frac{1}{2}$

6. Which fraction is greater than 2 but less than 3?

   a) $\frac{11}{3}$ b) $\frac{5}{4}$ c) $\frac{10}{4}$

   How do you know?

7. How could you use division to find out how many <u>whole</u> pies are in $\frac{13}{4}$ of a pie? Explain.

NS5-79: Place Value Decimals

Fractions with denominators that are multiples of ten (tenths, hundredths) commonly appear in units of measurement.

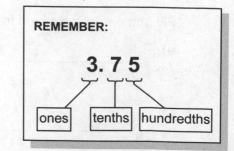

REMEMBER:

- A millimetre is a tenth of a centimetre (10 mm = 1 cm)
- A centimetre is a tenth of a decimetre (10 cm = 1 dm)
- A decimetre is a tenth of a metre (10 dm = 1 m)
- A centimetre is a hundredth of a metre (100 cm = 1 m)

Decimals are short forms for fractions. The chart shows the value of the decimal digits.

---

1. Write the place value of the underlined digit.

   a) 3.7<u>2</u> [hundredths] b) 3.<u>2</u>1 [   ] c) <u>7</u>.52 [   ]

   d) 5.<u>2</u>9 [   ] e) 9.9<u>8</u> [   ] f) <u>1</u>.05 [   ]

   g) <u>0</u>.32 [   ] h) 5.5<u>5</u> [   ] i) 6.<u>4</u>2 [   ]

2. Give the place value of the number 6 in each of the numbers below.

   a) 3.65 [   ] b) 2.36 [   ] c) 0.63 [   ]

   d) 9.06 [   ] e) 0.06 [   ] f) 3.61 [   ]

   g) 1.60 [   ] h) 6.48 [   ] i) 7.26 [   ]

3. Write the following numbers into the place value chart.

	Ones	Tenths	Hundredths
a) 5.03	5	0	3
b) 9.47			
c) 0.36			
d) 2.30			
e) 0.05			

Number Sense 2

1. Count the number of shaded squares. Write a fraction for the shaded part of the hundreds square. Then write the fraction as a decimal.

   HINT: Count by 10s for each column or row that is shaded.

   a)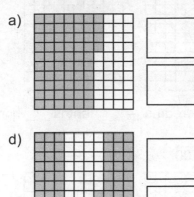

   b)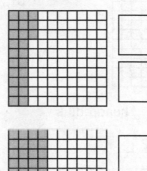

   c)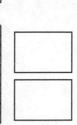

   d)

   e)

   f)

2. Convert the fraction to a decimal. Then shade.

   a) $\dfrac{38}{100}$ = ☐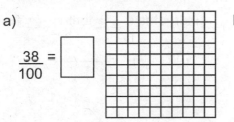

   b) $\dfrac{45}{100}$ = ☐

   c) $\dfrac{5}{100}$ = ☐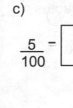

3. The picture shows a floor plan of a museum. Write a fraction and a decimal for each shaded part.

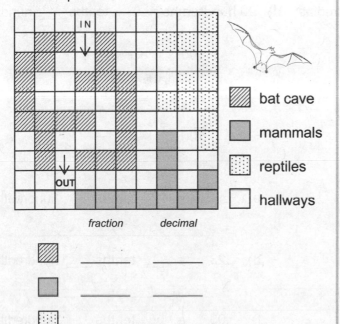

   bat cave

   mammals

   reptiles

   hallways

   fraction   decimal

   ▨ _____ _____

   ▦ _____ _____

   ▨ _____ _____

   ☐ _____ _____

4. Make your own floor plan for a museum. Write a fraction and a decimal for each shaded part.

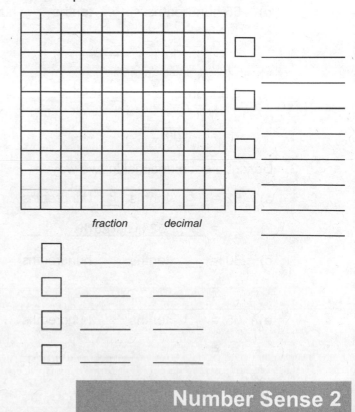

   fraction   decimal

   ☐ _____ _____

   ☐ _____ _____

   ☐ _____ _____

   ☐ _____ _____

NS5-81: Tenths and Hundredths

1. Draw lines around the columns to show tenths as in a). Then, write a fraction and a decimal to represent the number of shaded squares.

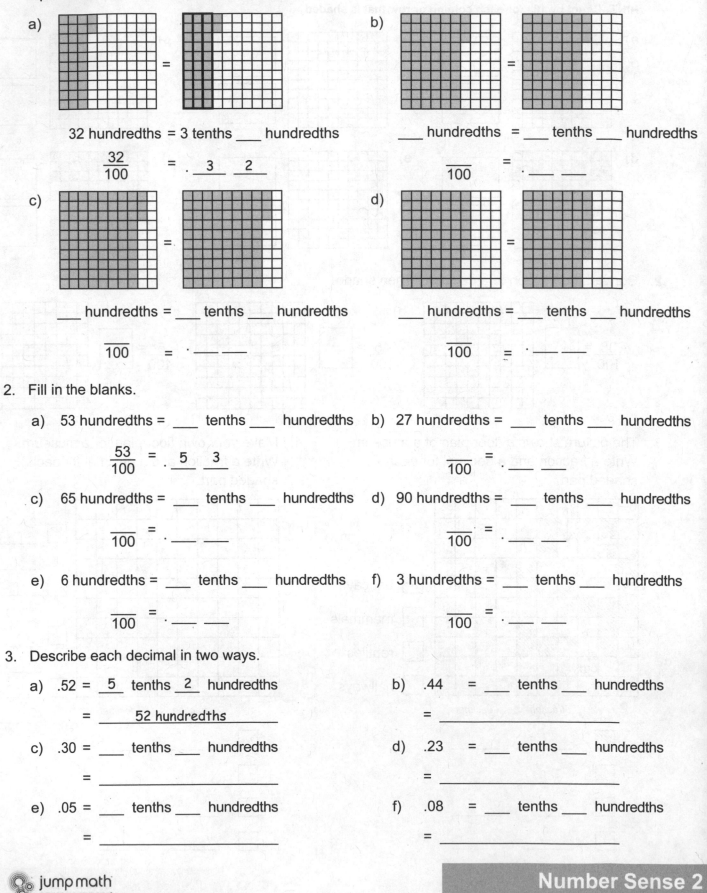

a)

=

32 hundredths = 3 tenths ___ hundredths

$$\frac{32}{100} = \cdot \underline{\ 3\ } \underline{\ 2\ }$$

b)

=

___ hundredths = ___ tenths ___ hundredths

$$\frac{}{100} = \cdot \underline{\ \ } \underline{\ \ }$$

c)

=

___ hundredths = ___ tenths ___ hundredths

$$\frac{}{100} = \cdot \underline{\ \ } \underline{\ \ }$$

d)

=

___ hundredths = ___ tenths ___ hundredths

$$\frac{}{100} = \cdot \underline{\ \ } \underline{\ \ }$$

2. Fill in the blanks.

a) 53 hundredths = ___ tenths ___ hundredths

$$\frac{53}{100} = \cdot \underline{\ 5\ } \underline{\ 3\ }$$

b) 27 hundredths = ___ tenths ___ hundredths

$$\frac{}{100} = \cdot \underline{\ \ } \underline{\ \ }$$

c) 65 hundredths = ___ tenths ___ hundredths

$$\frac{}{100} = \cdot \underline{\ \ } \underline{\ \ }$$

d) 90 hundredths = ___ tenths ___ hundredths

$$\frac{}{100} = \cdot \underline{\ \ } \underline{\ \ }$$

e) 6 hundredths = ___ tenths ___ hundredths

$$\frac{}{100} = \cdot \underline{\ \ } \underline{\ \ }$$

f) 3 hundredths = ___ tenths ___ hundredths

$$\frac{}{100} = \cdot \underline{\ \ } \underline{\ \ }$$

3. Describe each decimal in two ways.

a) .52 = __5__ tenths __2__ hundredths

= _____52 hundredths_____

b) .44 = ___ tenths ___ hundredths

= _____

c) .30 = ___ tenths ___ hundredths

= _____

d) .23 = ___ tenths ___ hundredths

= _____

e) .05 = ___ tenths ___ hundredths

= _____

f) .08 = ___ tenths ___ hundredths

= _____

1. Fill in the chart below. The first one has been done for you.

Drawing	Fraction	Decimal	Equivalent Decimal	Equivalent Fraction	Drawing
	$\frac{4}{10}$	0.4	0.40	$\frac{40}{100}$	

2. Write a fraction for the number of <u>hundredths</u>. Then count the shaded columns and write a fraction for the number of <u>tenths</u>.

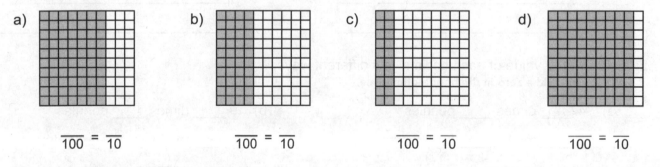

a) $\overline{100} = \overline{10}$

b) $\overline{100} = \overline{10}$

c) $\overline{100} = \overline{10}$

d) $\overline{100} = \overline{10}$

3. Fill in the missing numbers.

REMEMBER: $\frac{10}{100} = \frac{1}{10}$

a) $.8 = \frac{8}{10} = \frac{}{100} = .\underline{\ }\underline{\ }$

b) $.\underline{\ } = \frac{2}{10} = \frac{}{100} = .20$

c) $.\underline{\ } = \frac{6}{10} = \frac{}{100} = .60$

d) $.\underline{\ } = \frac{7}{10} = \frac{}{100} = .\underline{\ }\underline{\ }$

e) $.\underline{\ } = \frac{}{10} = \frac{40}{100} = .\underline{\ }\underline{\ }$

f) $.\underline{\ } = \frac{}{10} = \frac{30}{100} = .\underline{\ }\underline{\ }$

g) $.\underline{\ } = \frac{4}{10} = \frac{}{100} = .\underline{\ }\underline{\ }$

h) $.\underline{\ } = \frac{9}{10} = \frac{}{100} = .\underline{\ }\underline{\ }$

i) $.3 = \frac{}{10} = \frac{}{100} = .\underline{\ }\underline{\ }$

Number Sense 2

NS5-83: Decimals and Money

A **dime** is **one tenth** of a dollar. A **penny** is one **hundredth** of a dollar.

10¢   1¢

1. Express the value of each decimal in four different ways.

a) .64

6 dimes 4 pennies

6 tenths 4 hundredths

64 pennies

64 hundredths

b) .62

_____

_____

_____

_____

c) .57

_____

_____

_____

_____

d) .05

_____

_____

_____

_____

e) .08

_____

_____

_____

_____

f) .13

_____

_____

_____

_____

2. Express the value of each decimal in 4 different ways.
    HINT: First add a zero in the hundredths place.

a) .4 _____ dimes _____ pennies

_____ tenths _____ hundredths

_____ pennies

_____ hundredths

b) .9 _____ dimes _____ pennies

_____ tenths _____ hundredths

_____ pennies

_____ hundredths

3. Express the value of each decimal in four different ways. Then circle the greater number.

.17 _____ dimes _____ pennies

_____ tenths _____ hundredths

_____ pennies

_____ hundredths

.2 _____ dimes _____ pennies

_____ tenths _____ hundredths

_____ pennies

_____ hundredths

4. Tanya says .53 is greater than .7 because 53 is greater than 7. Can you explain her mistake?

1. Fill in the missing numbers.

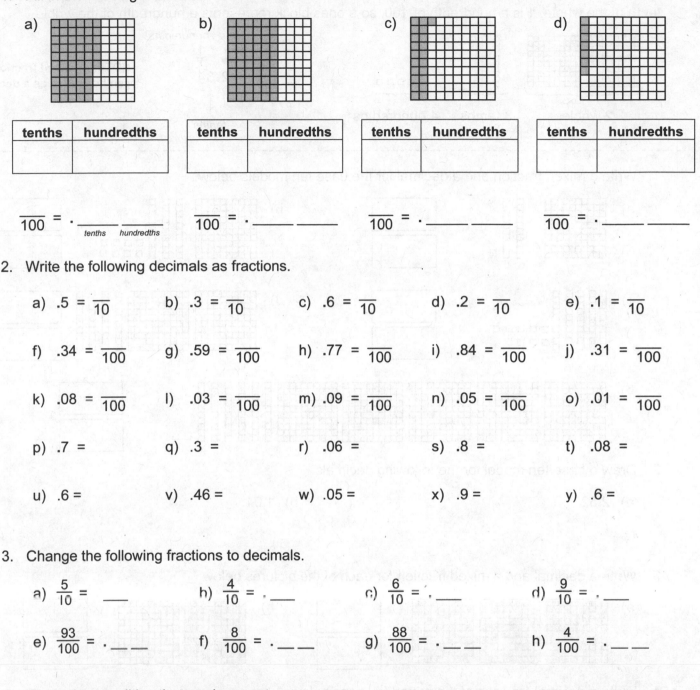

a)

tenths	hundredths

b)

tenths	hundredths

c)

tenths	hundredths

d)

tenths	hundredths

$\overline{100}$ = . $\underline{\hspace{1cm}}$ $\underline{\hspace{1cm}}$
tenths   hundredths

$\overline{100}$ = . $\underline{\hspace{1cm}}$ $\underline{\hspace{1cm}}$

$\overline{100}$ = . $\underline{\hspace{1cm}}$ $\underline{\hspace{1cm}}$

$\overline{100}$ = . $\underline{\hspace{1cm}}$ $\underline{\hspace{1cm}}$

2. Write the following decimals as fractions.

a) .5 = $\overline{10}$ b) .3 = $\overline{10}$ c) .6 = $\overline{10}$ d) .2 = $\overline{10}$ e) .1 = $\overline{10}$

f) .34 = $\overline{100}$ g) .59 = $\overline{100}$ h) .77 = $\overline{100}$ i) .84 = $\overline{100}$ j) .31 = $\overline{100}$

k) .08 = $\overline{100}$ l) .03 = $\overline{100}$ m) .09 = $\overline{100}$ n) .05 = $\overline{100}$ o) .01 = $\overline{100}$

p) .7 =   q) .3 =   r) .06 =   s) .8 =   t) .08 =

u) .6 =   v) .46 =   w) .05 =   x) .9 =   y) .6 =

3. Change the following fractions to decimals.

a) $\frac{5}{10}$ = ___   b) $\frac{4}{10}$ = . ___   c) $\frac{6}{10}$ = . ___   d) $\frac{9}{10}$ = . ___

e) $\frac{93}{100}$ = . __ __   f) $\frac{8}{100}$ = . __ __   g) $\frac{88}{100}$ = . __ __   h) $\frac{4}{100}$ = . __ __

4. Circle the equalities that are incorrect.

a) .63 = $\frac{63}{100}$ b) .9 = $\frac{9}{10}$ c) .6 = $\frac{6}{100}$ d) $\frac{27}{100}$ = .27   e) $\frac{4}{100}$ = .04

f) .7 = $\frac{7}{100}$ g) .64 = $\frac{64}{10}$ h) .75 = $\frac{75}{100}$ i) .06 = $\frac{6}{100}$ j) .03 = $\frac{3}{10}$

5. Explain how you know .7 is equal to .70.

A hundreds block may be used to represent a whole. 10 is a tenth of 100, so a tens block represents a tenth of the whole. 1 is a hundredth of 100, so a ones block represents a hundredth of the whole.

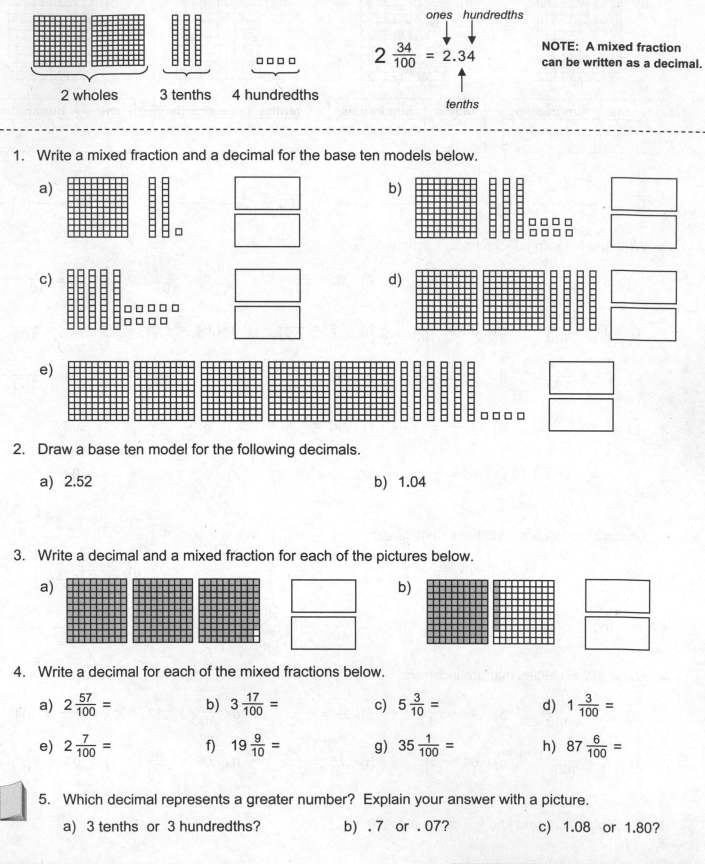

ones   hundredths

$2\frac{34}{100} = 2.34$

tenths

2 wholes   3 tenths   4 hundredths

NOTE: A mixed fraction can be written as a decimal.

---

1. Write a mixed fraction and a decimal for the base ten models below.

a)

b)

c)

d)

e)

2. Draw a base ten model for the following decimals.

a) 2.52   b) 1.04

3. Write a decimal and a mixed fraction for each of the pictures below.

a)   b)

4. Write a decimal for each of the mixed fractions below.

a) $2\frac{57}{100} =$ b) $3\frac{17}{100} =$ c) $5\frac{3}{10} =$ d) $1\frac{3}{100} =$

e) $2\frac{7}{100} =$ f) $19\frac{9}{10} =$ g) $35\frac{1}{100} =$ h) $87\frac{6}{100} =$

5. Which decimal represents a greater number? Explain your answer with a picture.

a) 3 tenths or 3 hundredths?   b) .7 or .07?   c) 1.08 or 1.80?

This number line is divided into tenths. The number represented by Point A is $2\frac{3}{10}$ or 2.3:

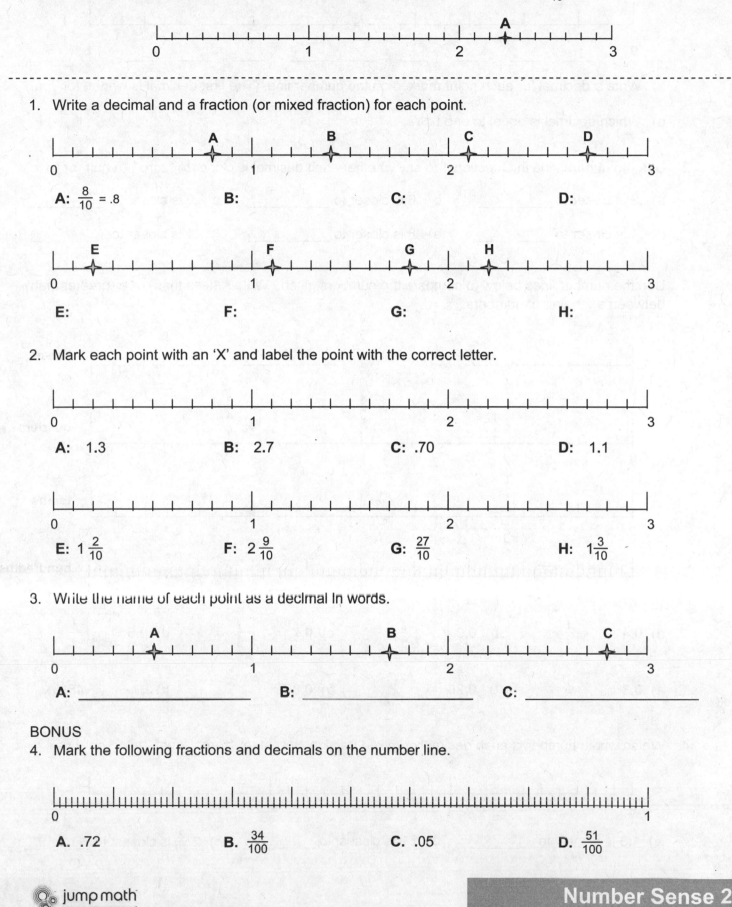

1. Write a decimal and a fraction (or mixed fraction) for each point.

A: $\frac{8}{10}$ = .8   B: C: D:

E: F: G: H:

2. Mark each point with an 'X' and label the point with the correct letter.

A: 1.3   B: 2.7   C: .70   D: 1.1

E: $1\frac{2}{10}$ F: $2\frac{9}{10}$ G: $\frac{27}{10}$ H: $1\frac{3}{10}$

3. Write the name of each point as a decimal in words.

A: _____   B: _____   C: _____

BONUS
4. Mark the following fractions and decimals on the number line.

A. .72   B. $\frac{34}{100}$ C. .05   D. $\frac{51}{100}$

NS5-87: Comparing and Ordering Fractions and Decimals

1.

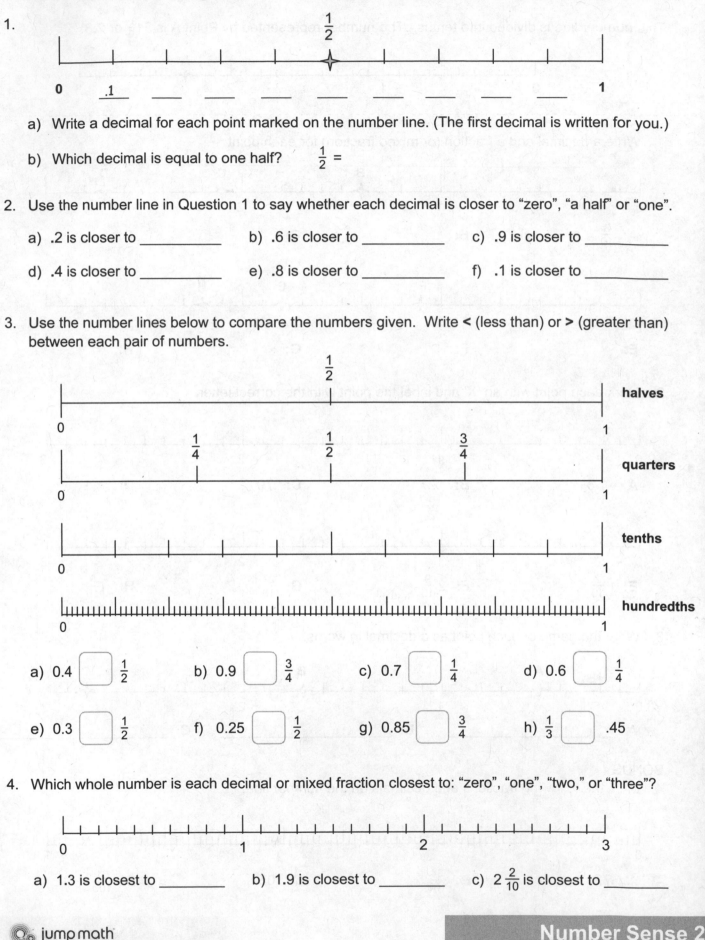

   a) Write a decimal for each point marked on the number line. (The first decimal is written for you.)

   b) Which decimal is equal to one half? $\frac{1}{2}$ =

2. Use the number line in Question 1 to say whether each decimal is closer to "zero", "a half" or "one".

   a) .2 is closer to _____   b) .6 is closer to _____   c) .9 is closer to _____

   d) .4 is closer to _____   e) .8 is closer to _____   f) .1 is closer to _____

3. Use the number lines below to compare the numbers given. Write < (less than) or > (greater than) between each pair of numbers.

   a) 0.4 ☐ $\frac{1}{2}$ b) 0.9 ☐ $\frac{3}{4}$ c) 0.7 ☐ $\frac{1}{4}$ d) 0.6 ☐ $\frac{1}{4}$

   e) 0.3 ☐ $\frac{1}{2}$ f) 0.25 ☐ $\frac{1}{2}$ g) 0.85 ☐ $\frac{3}{4}$ h) $\frac{1}{3}$ ☐ .45

4. Which whole number is each decimal or mixed fraction closest to: "zero", "one", "two," or "three"?

   a) 1.3 is closest to _____   b) 1.9 is closest to _____   c) $2\frac{2}{10}$ is closest to _____

1. Write the numbers in order by first changing each decimal to a fraction with a denominator of 10.
   NOTE: Show your work below each number.

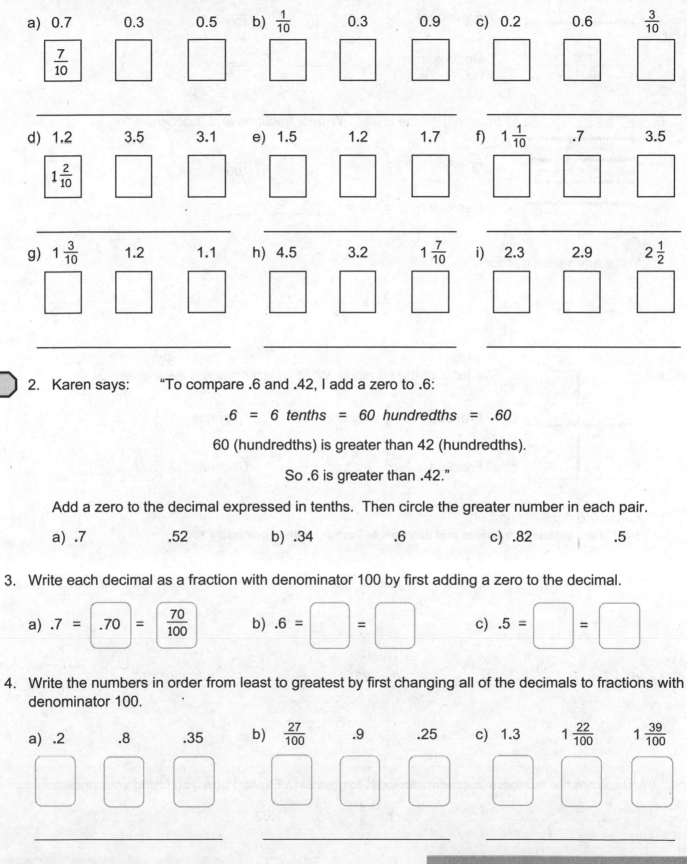

a) 0.7   0.3   0.5   b) $\frac{1}{10}$ 0.3   0.9   c) 0.2   0.6 $\frac{3}{10}$

$\frac{7}{10}$

d) 1.2   3.5   3.1   e) 1.5   1.2   1.7   f) $1\frac{1}{10}$ .7   3.5

$1\frac{2}{10}$

g) $1\frac{3}{10}$ 1.2   1.1   h) 4.5   3.2 $1\frac{7}{10}$ i) 2.3   2.9 $2\frac{1}{2}$

2. Karen says: "To compare .6 and .42, I add a zero to .6:

    .6 = 6 tenths = 60 hundredths = .60

    60 (hundredths) is greater than 42 (hundredths).

    So .6 is greater than .42."

   Add a zero to the decimal expressed in tenths. Then circle the greater number in each pair.

   a) .7   .52   b) .34   .6   c) .82   .5

3. Write each decimal as a fraction with denominator 100 by first adding a zero to the decimal.

   a) .7 = .70 = $\frac{70}{100}$ b) .6 = ☐ = ☐   c) .5 = ☐ = ☐

4. Write the numbers in order from least to greatest by first changing all of the decimals to fractions with denominator 100.

   a) .2   .8   .35   b) $\frac{27}{100}$ .9   .25   c) 1.3 $1\frac{22}{100}$ $1\frac{39}{100}$

5. 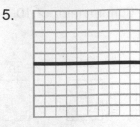   Shade $\frac{1}{2}$ of the squares. Write 2 fractions and 2 decimals for $\frac{1}{2}$.

Fractions: $\frac{1}{2}$ = $\frac{}{10}$ = $\frac{}{100}$

Decimals: $\frac{1}{2}$ = .____ = .____

6. 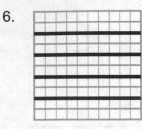   Shade $\frac{1}{5}$ of the boxes. Write 2 fractions and 2 decimals for $\frac{1}{5}$.

Fractions: $\frac{1}{5}$ = $\frac{}{10}$ = $\frac{}{100}$

Decimals: $\frac{1}{5}$ = .____ = .____

7. Write equivalent fractions.

a) $\frac{2}{5}$ = $\frac{}{10}$ = $\frac{}{100}$ b) $\frac{3}{5}$ = $\frac{}{10}$ = $\frac{}{100}$ c) $\frac{4}{5}$ = $\frac{}{10}$ = $\frac{}{100}$

8. [grid image]   Shade $\frac{1}{4}$ of the squares. Write a fraction and a decimal for $\frac{1}{4}$.

Fraction: $\frac{1}{4}$ = $\frac{}{100}$ Decimal: $\frac{1}{4}$ = .____

Fraction: $\frac{3}{4}$ = $\frac{}{100}$ Decimal: $\frac{3}{4}$ = .____

9. Circle the greater number.
   HINT: First change all fractions and decimals to fractions with denominator 100.

a) $\frac{1}{2}$ .37   b) $\frac{1}{4}$ .52   c) $\frac{2}{5}$ .42

$\boxed{\frac{50}{100}}$ $\boxed{}$ $\boxed{}$ $\boxed{}$ $\boxed{}$ $\boxed{}$

d) .7 $\frac{3}{5}$ e) .23 $\frac{1}{5}$ f) .52 $\frac{1}{2}$

$\boxed{}$ $\boxed{}$ $\boxed{}$ $\boxed{}$ $\boxed{}$ $\boxed{}$

10. Write the numbers in order from least to greatest. Explain how you found your answers.

a) .7   .32 $\frac{1}{2}$ b) $\frac{1}{4}$ $\frac{3}{5}$ .63   c) $\frac{2}{5}$ .35 $\frac{1}{2}$

NS5-89: Adding and Subtracting Tenths

1. 1.3 is one whole and 3 tenths. How many tenths is that altogether? _____

2. a) 4.7 = _____ tenths   b) 7. 1 = _____ tenths   c) 3. 0 = _____ tenths

   d) _____ = 38 tenths   e) _____ = 42 tenths   f) _____ = 7 tenths

3. Add or subtract the decimals by first writing them as whole numbers of tenths.

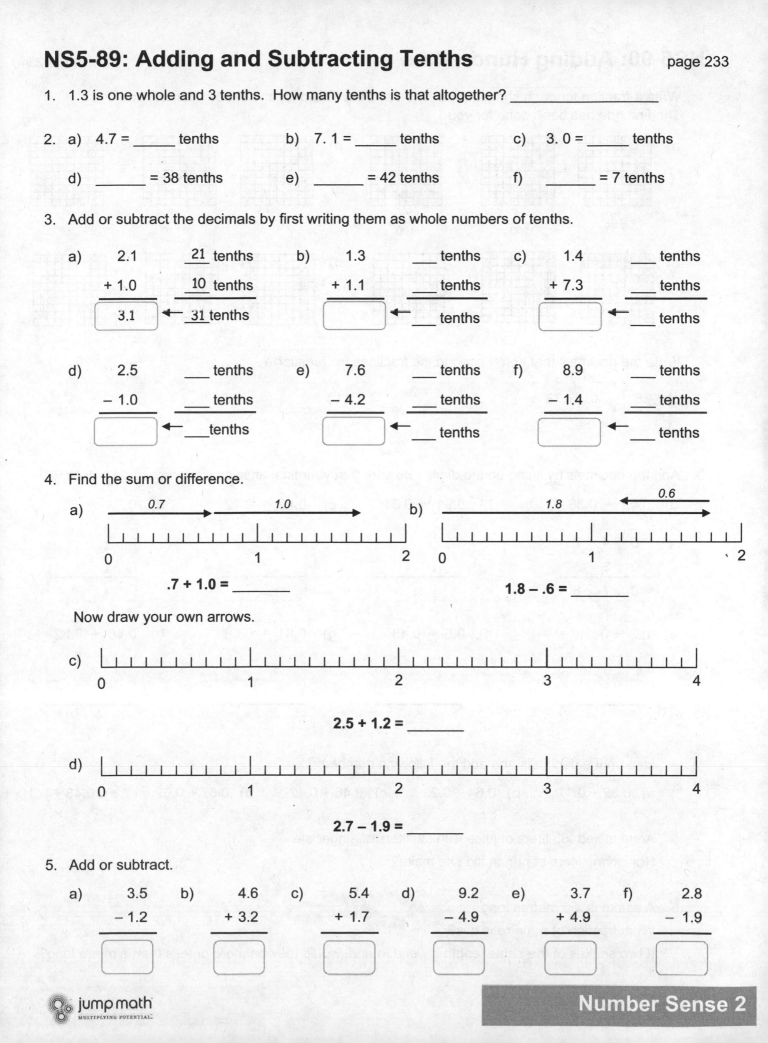

   a)   2.1   _21_ tenths   b)   1.3   ___ tenths   c)   1.4   ___ tenths
         + 1.0   _10_ tenths   + 1.1   ___ tenths   + 7.3   ___ tenths
         ┌─────┐   ┌─────┐   ┌─────┐
         │ 3.1 │ ◄── _31_ tenths   │   │ ◄── ___ tenths   │   │ ◄── ___ tenths
         └─────┘   └─────┘   └─────┘

   d)   2.5   ___ tenths   e)   7.6   ___ tenths   f)   8.9   ___ tenths
         – 1.0   ___ tenths   – 4.2   ___ tenths   – 1.4   ___ tenths
         ┌─────┐   ┌─────┐   ┌─────┐
         │   │ ◄── ___ tenths   │   │ ◄── ___ tenths   │   │ ◄── ___ tenths
         └─────┘   └─────┘   └─────┘

4. Find the sum or difference.

   a)   b)

   .7 + 1.0 = _____   1.8 – .6 = _____

   Now draw your own arrows.

   c)

   2.5 + 1.2 = _____

   d)

   2.7 – 1.9 = _____

5. Add or subtract.

   a)   3.5   b)   4.6   c)   5.4   d)   9.2   e)   3.7   f)   2.8
         – 1.2   + 3.2   + 1.7   – 4.9   + 4.9   – 1.9

jump math
MULTIPLYING POTENTIAL

Number Sense 2

NS5-90: Adding Hundredths

1. Write a fraction for each shaded part. Then add the fractions, and shade your answer. The first one has been done for you.

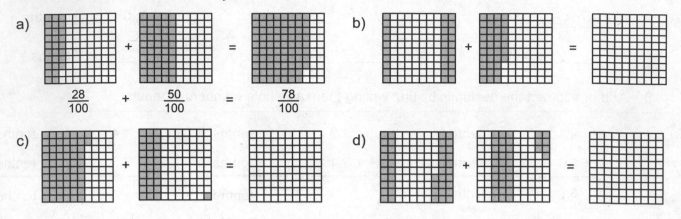

a) $\dfrac{28}{100}$ + $\dfrac{50}{100}$ = $\dfrac{78}{100}$ b)

c) + =   d) + =

2. Write the decimals that correspond to the fractions in Question 1.

a) .28 + .50 = .78	b)
c)	d)

3. Add the decimals by lining up the digits. Be sure that your final answer is expressed as a decimal.

   a) 0.42 + 0.36   b) 0.91 + 0.04   c) 0.42 + 0.72   d) 0.22 + 0.57

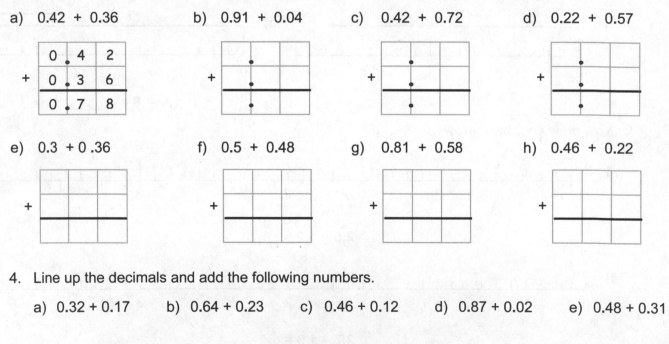

	0	4	2
+	0	3	6
	0	7	8

   e) 0.3 + 0 .36   f) 0.5 + 0.48   g) 0.81 + 0.58   h) 0.46 + 0.22

4. Line up the decimals and add the following numbers.

   a) 0.32 + 0.17   b) 0.64 + 0.23   c) 0.46 + 0.12   d) 0.87 + 0.02   e) 0.48 + 0.31

5. Anne mixed .63 liters of juice with .36 liters of ginger ale.
   How many liters of punch did she make?

6. A snake is .56 metres long.

   What fraction of a metre is this?
   If two snakes of the same length lay end to end, would they be more or less than a metre long?

1. Subtract by crossing out the correct number of boxes.

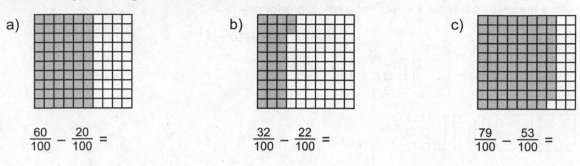

a) $\frac{60}{100} - \frac{20}{100} =$

b) $\frac{32}{100} - \frac{22}{100} =$

c) $\frac{79}{100} - \frac{53}{100} =$

2. Write the decimals that correspond to the fractions in Question 1.

a) .60 - .20 = .40   b)   c)

3. Subtract the decimals by lining up the digits.

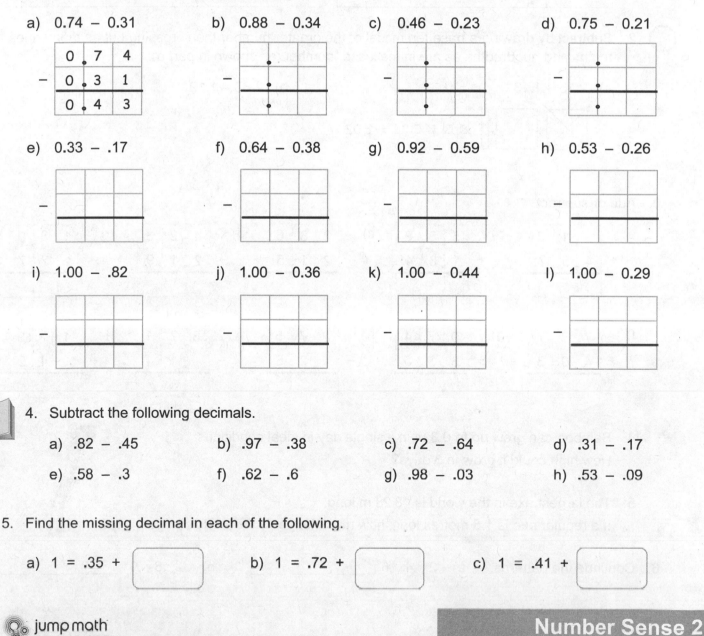

a) 0.74 − 0.31   b) 0.88 − 0.34   c) 0.46 − 0.23   d) 0.75 − 0.21

	0	7	4
−	0	3	1
	0	4	3

e) 0.33 − .17   f) 0.64 − 0.38   g) 0.92 − 0.59   h) 0.53 − 0.26

i) 1.00 − .82   j) 1.00 − 0.36   k) 1.00 − 0.44   l) 1.00 − 0.29

4. Subtract the following decimals.

a) .82 − .45   b) .97 − .38   c) .72 − .64   d) .31 − .17

e) .58 − .3   f) .62 − .6   g) .98 − .03   h) .53 − .09

5. Find the missing decimal in each of the following.

a) 1 = .35 + [   ]   b) 1 = .72 + [   ]   c) 1 = .41 + [   ]

1. Add by drawing a base ten model. Then, using the chart provided, line up the decimal points and add.
   NOTE: Use a hundreds block for a whole and a tens block for one tenth.

   a) 1.32 + 1.15

   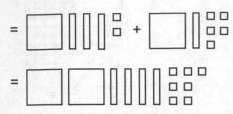

   b) 1.46 + 1.33

	ones	tenths	hundredths
+			

	ones	tenths	hundredths
+			

2. Subtract by drawing a base ten model of the greater number then crossing out as many ones, tenths and hundredths as are in the lesser number, as shown in part a).

   a) 2.15 – 1.13

   b) 2.33 – 1.12

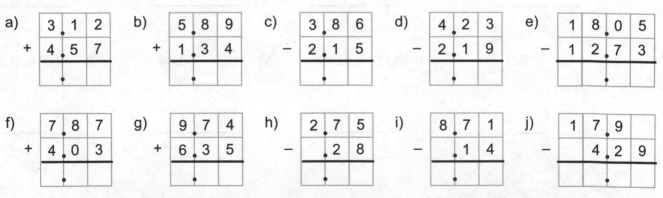

3. Add or subtract.

   a)
	3	1	2
+	4	5	7

   b)
	5	8	9
+	1	3	4

   c)
	3	8	6
–	2	1	5

   d)
	4	2	3
–	2	1	9

   e)
1	8	0	5
1	2	7	3

   f)
	7	8	7
+	4	0	3

   g)
	9	7	4
+	6	3	5

   h)
	2	7	5
–		2	8

   i)
	8	7	1
–		1	4

   j)
1	7	9	
	4	2	9

4. Bamboo can grow up to 0.3 m in a single day in ideal conditions.
   How high could it grow in 3 days?

5. The largest axe in the world is 18.28 m long.
   If a regular axe is 1.5 metres long, how much longer is the world's largest axe?

6. Continue the patterns.   a) .2 , .4 , .6 , _____ , _____ , _____   b) .3 , .6 , .9 , _____ , _____ , _____

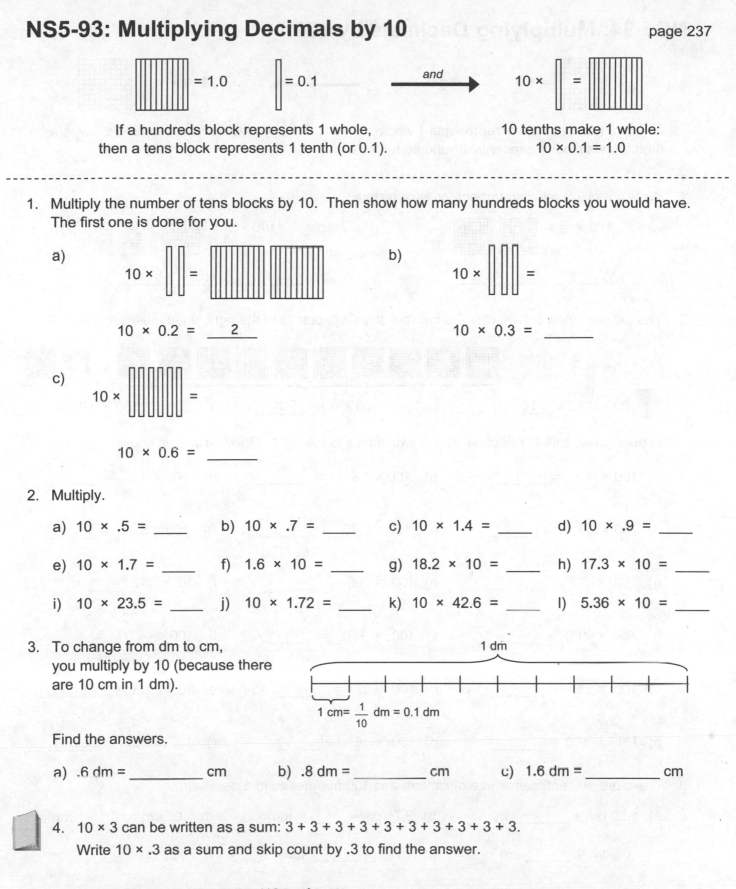

If a hundreds block represents 1 whole,
then a tens block represents 1 tenth (or 0.1).

10 tenths make 1 whole:
10 × 0.1 = 1.0

----

1. Multiply the number of tens blocks by 10. Then show how many hundreds blocks you would have.
    The first one is done for you.

    a) 10 × ⎮⎮ =

        10 × 0.2 = ___2___

    b) 10 × ⎮⎮⎮ =

        10 × 0.3 = _____

    c) 10 × ⎮⎮⎮⎮⎮⎮ =

        10 × 0.6 = _____

2. Multiply.

    a) 10 × .5 = ____   b) 10 × .7 = ____   c) 10 × 1.4 = ____   d) 10 × .9 = ____

    e) 10 × 1.7 = ____   f) 1.6 × 10 = ____   g) 18.2 × 10 = ____   h) 17.3 × 10 = ____

    i) 10 × 23.5 = ____ j) 10 × 1.72 = ____ k) 10 × 42.6 = ____   l) 5.36 × 10 = ____

3. To change from dm to cm,
    you multiply by 10 (because there
    are 10 cm in 1 dm).

    1 cm= $\frac{1}{10}$ dm = 0.1 dm

    Find the answers.

    a) .6 dm = _____ cm   b) .8 dm = _____ cm   c) 1.6 dm = _____ cm

4. 10 × 3 can be written as a sum: 3 + 3 + 3 + 3 + 3 + 3 + 3 + 3 + 3 + 3.
    Write 10 × .3 as a sum and skip count by .3 to find the answer.

5. A dime is a tenth of a dollar (10¢ = $0.10).
    Draw a picture or use play money to show that 10 × $0.20 = $2.00.

NS5-94: Multiplying Decimals by 100

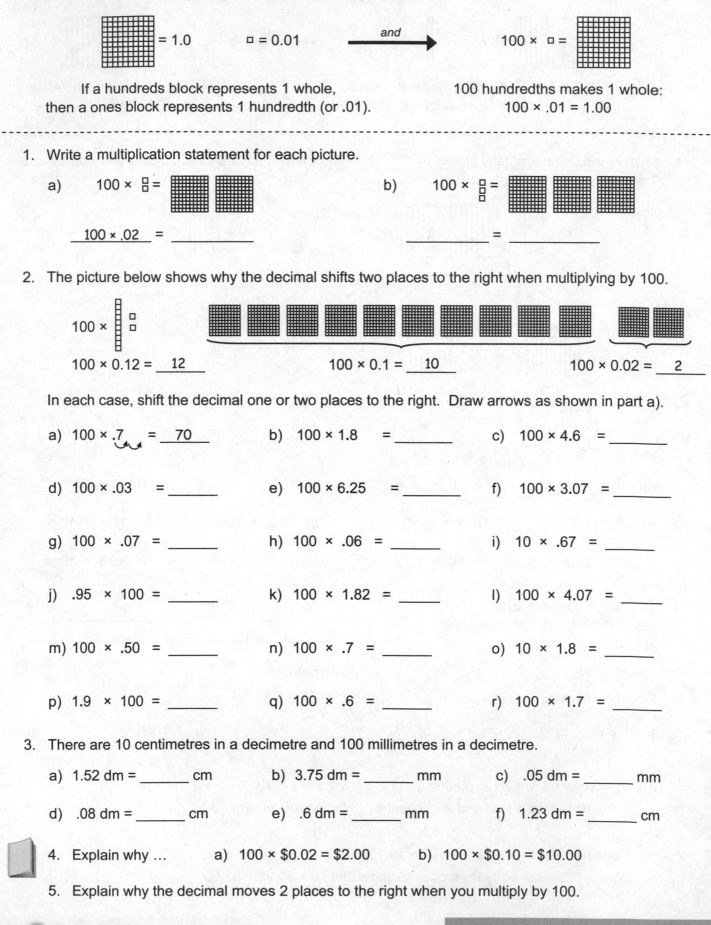

= 1.0   □ = 0.01   *and* →   100 × □ =

If a hundreds block represents 1 whole,
then a ones block represents 1 hundredth (or .01).

100 hundredths makes 1 whole:
100 × .01 = 1.00

----

1. Write a multiplication statement for each picture.

   a)   100 × □/□ =

   <u> 100 × .02 </u> = _____

   b)   100 × □/□ =

   _____ = _____

2. The picture below shows why the decimal shifts two places to the right when multiplying by 100.

   100 × □/□

   100 × 0.12 = <u> 12 </u>   100 × 0.1 = <u> 10 </u>   100 × 0.02 = <u> 2 </u>

   In each case, shift the decimal one or two places to the right. Draw arrows as shown in part a).

   a) 100 × .7 = <u> 70 </u>   b) 100 × 1.8 = _____   c) 100 × 4.6 = _____

   d) 100 × .03 = _____   e) 100 × 6.25 = _____   f) 100 × 3.07 = _____

   g) 100 × .07 = _____   h) 100 × .06 = _____   i) 10 × .67 = _____

   j) .95 × 100 = _____   k) 100 × 1.82 = _____   l) 100 × 4.07 = _____

   m) 100 × .50 = _____   n) 100 × .7 = _____   o) 10 × 1.8 = _____

   p) 1.9 × 100 = _____   q) 100 × .6 = _____   r) 100 × 1.7 = _____

3. There are 10 centimetres in a decimetre and 100 millimetres in a decimetre.

   a) 1.52 dm = _____ cm   b) 3.75 dm = _____ mm   c) .05 dm = _____ mm

   d) .08 dm = _____ cm   e) .6 dm = _____ mm   f) 1.23 dm = _____ cm

4. Explain why ...   a) 100 × $0.02 = $2.00   b) 100 × $0.10 = $10.00

5. Explain why the decimal moves 2 places to the right when you multiply by 100.

jump math
MULTIPLYING POTENTIAL.

Number Sense 2

The picture shows how to multiply a decimal by a whole number.

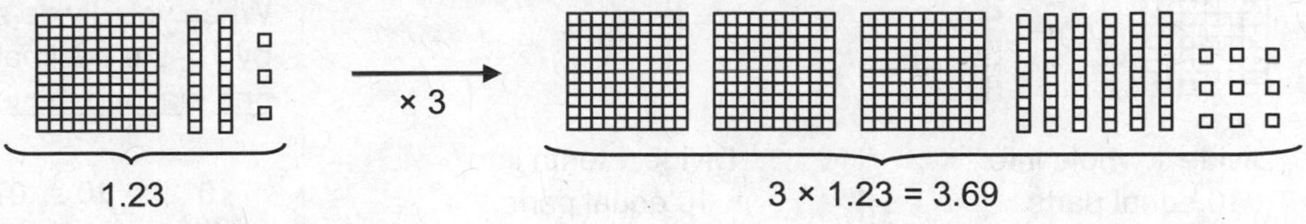

1.23   × 3   3 × 1.23 = 3.69

HINT: Simply multiply each digit separately.

----

1. Multiply mentally.

   a) 2 × 1.43 = _____   b) 3 × 1.2 = _____   c) 5 × 1.01 = _____   d) 4 × 2.1 = _____

   e) 2 × 5.34 = _____   f) 4 × 2.1 = _____   g) 3 × 3.12 = _____   h) 3 × 4.32 = _____

2. Multiply by regrouping tenths as ones (the first one is done for you).

   a) 6 × 1.4 = __6__ ones + __24__ tenths = __8__ ones + __4__ tenths = __8.4__

   b) 3 × 2.5 = _____ ones + _____ tenths = _____ ones + _____ tenths = _____

   c) 3 × 2.7 = _____ ones + _____ tenths = _____ ones + _____ tenths = _____

   d) 4 × 2.6 = _____

3. Multiply by regrouping tenths as ones or hundredths as tenths.

   a) 3 × 2.51 = _____ ones + _____ tenths + _____ hundredths

      = _____ ones + _____ tenths + _____ hundredths = _____

   b) 4 × 2.14 = _____ ones + _____ tenths + _____ hundredths

      = _____ ones + _____ tenths + _____ hundredths = _____

   c) 5 × 1.41 = _____ ones + _____ tenths + _____ hundredths

      = _____ ones + _____ tenths + _____ hundredths = _____

4. Multiply. In some questions you will have to regroup twice.

   a)   3 4 5   × 3

   b)   7 6 2   × 4

   c)   4 3 1   × 6

   d)   3 2 5   × 3

5. Find the products.

   a) 5 × 2.1   b) 3 × 8.3   c) 5 × 7.5   d) 9 × 2.81   e) 7 × 3.6   f) 6 × 3.4

   g) 4 × 3.2   h) 5 × 6.35   i) 6 × 3.95   j) 8 × 2.63   k) 3 × 31.21   l) 4 × 12.32

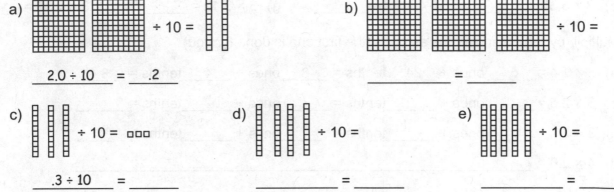

Divide 1 whole into
10 equal parts.

Each part is 1 tenth:
1.0 ÷ 10 = 0.1

Divide 1 tenth into
10 equal parts.

Each part is 1 hundredth:
0.1 ÷ 10 = 0.01.

When you divide a decimal
by 10, the decimal shifts
<u>one place to the left</u>:

0 . 7 ÷ 10 = .07

7 . 0 ÷ 10 = .7

1. Complete the picture and write a division statement for each picture.

   a) ÷ 10 =

      <u>2.0 ÷ 10</u>   =   <u>.2</u>

   b) ÷ 10 =

      _____   = _____

   c) ÷ 10 = ▫▫▫

      <u>.3 ÷ 10</u>   = _____

   d) ÷ 10 =

      _____   = _____

   e) ÷ 10 =

      _____   = _____

2. Complete the picture and write a division statement (the first one is done for you).

   a) ÷ 10 =

      <u>2.3 ÷ 10</u>   =   <u>.23</u>

   b) ÷ 10 =

      _____   = _____

3. Shift the decimal one place to the left by drawing an arrow. (If there is no decimal, add one.)

   a) 0.3 ÷ 10 = ___.03___   b) 0.5 ÷ 10 = _____   c) 0.7 ÷ 10 = _____   d) 1.3 ÷ 10 = _____

   e) 7.6 ÷ 10 = _____   f) 12.0 ÷ 10 = _____   g) 9 ÷ 10 = _____   h) 6 ÷ 10 = _____

   i) 42 ÷ 10 = _____   j) 17 ÷ 10 = _____   k) .9 ÷ 10 = _____   l) 27.3 ÷ 10 = _____

4. Change the following measurements by dividing by 10.

   a) 5 cm = _____ dm   b) 1.7 cm = _____ dm   c) 3.5 mm = _____ cm   d) 2mm = _____ cm

5. Sarah has 2.7 m of ribbon. She wants to cut the ribbon into 10 equal lengths.
   How long will each piece be (in metres)?

6. A swimming pool is 25 m wide. It is divided into 10 lanes.
   How wide is each lane (in metres)?

NS5-97: Dividing Decimals by Whole Numbers

You can divide a decimal by a whole number using base ten blocks. Keep track of your work using long division. Use the hundreds block to represent 1 whole, the tens block to represent 1 tenth and a ones block to represent 1 hundredth.

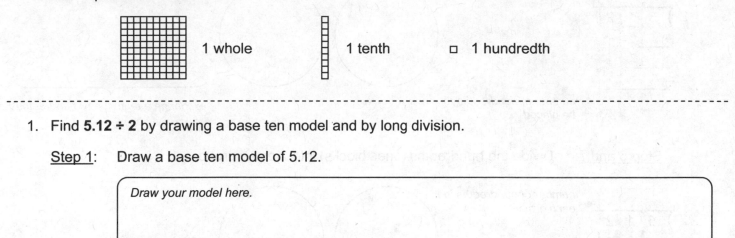

1 whole   1 tenth   □ 1 hundredth

---

1. Find **5.12 ÷ 2** by drawing a base ten model and by long division.

   Step 1:   Draw a base ten model of 5.12.

   Draw your model here.

   Step 2:   Divide the ones (hundreds blocks) into 2 equal groups.

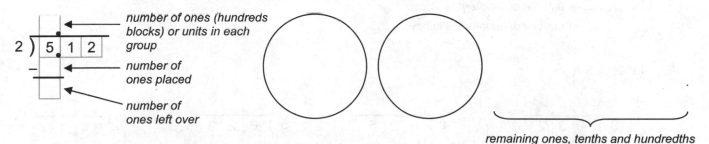

   Step 3:   Exchange the left over one (hundreds blocks) for 10 tenths (tens blocks).

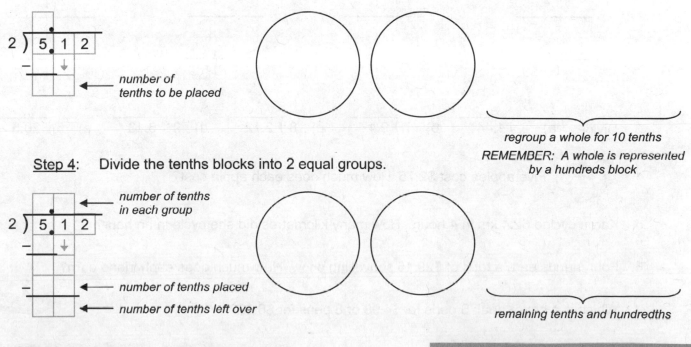

   Step 4:   Divide the tenths blocks into 2 equal groups.

Step 5:   Regroup the leftover tenths (tens blocks) as 10 hundredths (ones blocks).

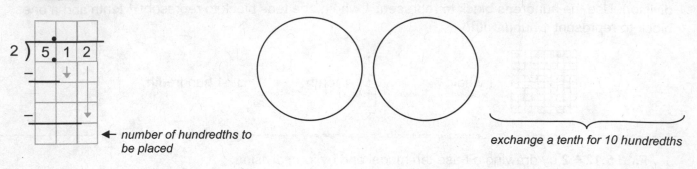

← number of hundredths to be placed

exchange a tenth for 10 hundredths

Step 6 and 7:   Divide the hundredths (ones blocks) into 2 equal groups.

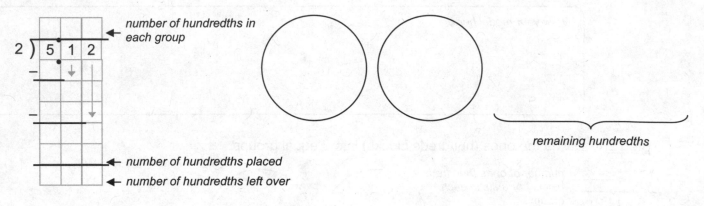

← number of hundredths in each group

remaining hundredths

← number of hundredths placed
← number of hundredths left over

2. Divide.

a)   b)   c)   d)

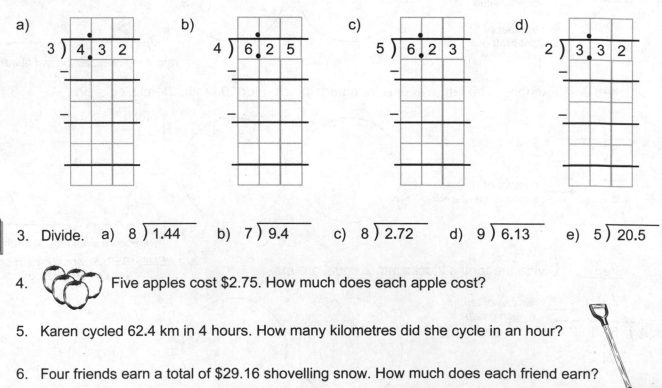

3. Divide. a) $8\overline{)1.44}$ b) $7\overline{)9.4}$ c) $8\overline{)2.72}$ d) $9\overline{)6.13}$ e) $5\overline{)20.5}$

4.   Five apples cost $2.75. How much does each apple cost?

5. Karen cycled 62.4 km in 4 hours. How many kilometres did she cycle in an hour?

6. Four friends earn a total of $29.16 shovelling snow. How much does each friend earn?

7. Which is a better deal: 6 pens for $4.98 or 8 pens for $6.96?

NS5-98: Thousandths

If a thousands cube is used to represent a whole number, then a hundreds block represents a tenth, a tens block represents a hundredth, and a ones block represents a thousandth of a whole.

1 whole   **1 tenth**   **1 hundredth**   **1 thousandth**

REMEMBER:

tenths   thousandths

ones { 6.146

hundredths

----

1. Beside each number, write the place value of the underlined digit.

    a) 3.8<u>1</u>9   b) 9.78<u>2</u>   c) 4.<u>5</u>14

    d) 7.15<u>9</u>   e) <u>2</u>.541   f) 3.8<u>9</u>8

2. Write the following numbers into the place value chart. The first one has been done for you.

	ones	tenths	hundredths	thousandths
a) 6.512	6	5	1	2
c) 2.83				
e) 1.763				
g) 9.02				
i) 4.081				

	ones	tenths	hundredths	thousandths
b) 4.081				
d) 1.306				
f) .53				
h) 8				
j) 2.011				

3. Write the following decimals as fractions.

    a) .725 =   b) .237 =   c) .052 =   d) .006 =

4. Write each decimal in expanded form.

    a) .237 = _2 tenths + 3 hundredths + 7 thousandths_

    b) .523 = _____

    c) 6.253 = _____

5. Write the following fractions as decimals.

    a) $\frac{94}{100}$ =   b) $\frac{5}{100}$ =   c) $\frac{875}{1000}$ =   d) $\frac{25}{1000}$ =

6. Compare each pair of decimals by writing < or > in the box.
   HINT: Add zeroes wherever necessary to give each number the same number of digits.

    a) .275 ☐ .273   b) .332 ☐ .47   c) .596 ☐ .7

    d) .27 ☐ .123   e) .7 ☐ .32   f) .8 ☐ .526

Number Sense 2

NS5-99: Differences of 0.1 and 0.01

1. Fill in the blanks.

   a) .64 + .1 = _____

   b) .35 + .1 = _____

   c) .06 + .1 = _____

   d) .89 + .1 = _____

   e) .73 + .01 = _____

   f) .40 + .01 = _____

   g) 4.23 + .01 = _____

   h) 2.87 + .1 = _____

   i) 11.95 + .01 = _____

2. Fill in the blanks.

   a) _____ is .1 more than .7

   b) _____ is .1 more than 2.6

   c) _____ is .1 more than 1.32

   d) _____ is .1 more than .63

   e) _____ is .01 more than .35

   f) _____ is .01 more than .2

3. Fill in the blanks.

   a) 1.35 + _____ = 1.36

   b) 2.3 + _____ = 2.4

   c) 3.06 − _____ = 3.05

   d) 4.95 − _____ = 4.94

   e) 3.7 + _____ = 4.7

   f) 7.85 + _____ = 7.95

4. Fill in the missing numbers on the number lines.

   a)

   5.0 ———————————————————— 6.0

   b)

   3.8 ———————————————————— 4.8

   c)

   4.14 ———————————————————— 4.24

5. Continue the patterns.

   a) .2, .3, .4, _____, _____, _____

   b) 6.6, 6.7, 6.8, _____, _____, _____

   c) 3.5, 3.6, 3.7, _____, _____, _____

   d) 9.6, 9.7, 9.8, _____, _____, _____

   e) 4.71, 4.72, 4.73, _____, _____, _____

   f) 5.96, 5.97, 5.98, _____, _____, _____

6. Fill in the blanks.

   a) 3.9 + .1 = _____

   b) 4.9 + .1 = _____

   c) 8.93 + .1 = _____

   d) 3.79 + .01 = _____

   e) 6.09 + .01 = _____

   f) 7.99 + .01 = _____

NS5-100: Decimals (Review)

The size of a unit of measurement depends on which unit has been selected as the **whole**.

A millimetre is a **tenth** of a centimetre, but it is only a **hundredth** of a decimetre.

1 cm   1 mm

1 dm

----

1. Draw a picture in the space provided to show 1 tenth of each whole.

a)   1 whole   1 tenth

b)   1 whole   1 tenth

c)   1 whole   1 tenth

2. Write each measurement as a fraction then as a decimal.

a) 1 cm = $\frac{1}{10}$ dm = ___.1___ dm

b) 100 cm = ☐ dm = _____ dm

c) 1 mm = ☐ cm = _____ cm

d) 16 mm = ☐ cm = _____ cm

e) 77 mm = ☐ dm = _____ dm

f) 83 cm = ☐ m = _____ m

3. Add by first changing the smaller unit into a decimal in the larger unit.

a) 4 cm + 9.2 dm = ___0.4 dm + 9.2 dm = 9.6 dm___   b) 6 cm + 2.9 dm = _____

c) 9 mm + 8.4 cm = _____   d) 33 cm + 1.64 m = _____

4. What amount is represented by the tenths digits?

a) 7.52 m ___5 dm___   b) $6.29 _____   c) 2.32 m _____

d) 3.7 million _____   e) 2.8 thousand _____   f) 5.35 dm _____

5. Round each decimal to the nearest tenth.
   HINT: Underline the hundredths digit first. It will tell you whether you round up or down.

a) .2<u>5</u> _____   b) .32 _____   c) .68 _____   d) 1.35 _____

6. Round each decimal to the nearest whole number. **HINT: Underline the tenths digit first.**

a) 3.<u>2</u>5 _____   b) 4.13 _____   c) 2.95 _____   d) 8.3 _____

jump math
MULTIPLYING POTENTIAL.

Number Sense 2

7. The diagram shows a section of measuring tape.

    Round each measurement to the nearest tenth of a metre.
    Write your answer in words.

    ```
        A                          B                    C                D
    |++++|++++|++++|++++|++++|++++|++++|++++|++++|++++|++++|++++|++++|++++|
    5 m                          6 m                                    7 m
    ```

    A: ___Five and two tenths___   **B:** _____

    C: _____   **D:** _____

8. Write a decimal for each description.

    a) Between 3.52 and 3.57:   ___ . ___ ___   b) Between 1.70 and 1.80:   ___ . ___ ___

    c) Between 12.65 and 12.7:   ___ ___ . ___ ___   d) Between 2.6 and 2.7:   ___ . ___ ___

9. Add.

    a) $3\,000 + 200 + 7 + 0.02 =$ _____   b) $10\,000 + 500 + 20 + 0.1 + 0.05 =$ _____

    c) $6\,000 + 300 + 8 + 0.1 =$ _____   d) $400 + 7 + .02 =$ _____

10. Write < or > to show which decimal is greater.

    a) 3.7 ☐ 3.5   b) 2.32 ☐ 2.37   c) 1.7 ☐ 1.69   d) 0.5 ☐ 0.55

11. If you divide a number by 10, the result is 12.9.
    What was the original number? Explain.

12. The Olympic gold medal throw for the shot put in 2004 was 21.16 m.
    The bronze throw was 21.07 m.

    a) Was the difference in the throws more or less than 0.1 m?

    b) Round both throws to the nearest tenth.
        What is the difference in the rounded amounts?

    c) Make up two throws which would round to the same number (when rounded to the tenths).

    d) Why are Olympic shot put throws measured so precisely?

NS5-101: Word Problems with Decimals

Answer the following questions in your notebook.

1. Giant Kelp is the fastest growing ocean plant.
   It can grow 0.67 m in a day.
   How much could it grow in a week?

2. Lichen grows slowly at a rate of 3.4 mm a year.
   Could it grow 1 cm in 3 years?

3. How much do 7 books cost at $8.99 per book?

4. Under which deal do you pay less for 1 pen:
   4 pens for $2.96 or 6 pens for $4.99?

5. On a map, 1 cm represents 15 km.

   Two towns are 2.3 cm apart on the map.

   How far apart are the towns?

6.
   $$\begin{array}{r} 6.42 \\ +\ 7.19 \\ \hline 78.32 \end{array}$$

   Tim added the numbers on his calculator.

   What mistake do you think Tim made pressing the buttons on the calculator?

7. $0.45 means 4 dimes and 5 pennies.
   Why do we use decimal notation for money?
   What is a dime a tenth of?
   What is a penny a hundredth of?

8. Here are the greatest lengths of some sea creatures.

   a) How much longer than the great white shark is the blue whale?

   b) About how many times longer than the turtle is the great white shark?

   c) About how long would 3 ocean sunfish be if they swam in a row?

Animal	Length (m)
Blue Whale	34
Great White Shark	7.9
Pacific Leather Back Turtle	2.1
Ocean Sun Fish	2.9

Number Sense 2

NS5-102: Unit Rates

A **rate** is a comparison of two quantities in different units.

In a **unit rate**, one of the quantities is equal to one.
For instance, "1 apple costs 30¢" is a unit rate.

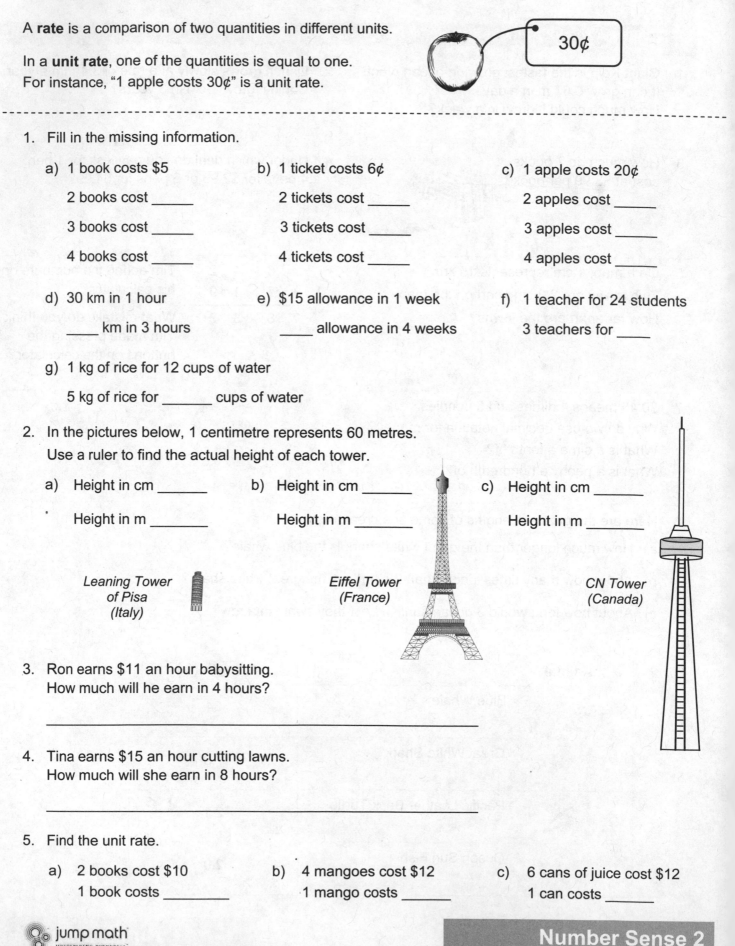

30¢

----

1. Fill in the missing information.

   a) 1 book costs $5

      2 books cost _____

      3 books cost _____

      4 books cost _____

   b) 1 ticket costs 6¢

      2 tickets cost _____

      3 tickets cost _____

      4 tickets cost _____

   c) 1 apple costs 20¢

      2 apples cost _____

      3 apples cost _____

      4 apples cost _____

   d) 30 km in 1 hour

      ____ km in 3 hours

   e) $15 allowance in 1 week

      ____ allowance in 4 weeks

   f) 1 teacher for 24 students

      3 teachers for ____

   g) 1 kg of rice for 12 cups of water

      5 kg of rice for _____ cups of water

2. In the pictures below, 1 centimetre represents 60 metres.
   Use a ruler to find the actual height of each tower.

   a) Height in cm _____

      Height in m _____

   b) Height in cm _____

      Height in m _____

   c) Height in cm _____

      Height in m _____

   *Leaning Tower
   of Pisa
   (Italy)*

   *Eiffel Tower
   (France)*

   *CN Tower
   (Canada)*

3. Ron earns $11 an hour babysitting.
   How much will he earn in 4 hours?

   _____

4. Tina earns $15 an hour cutting lawns.
   How much will she earn in 8 hours?

   _____

5. Find the unit rate.

   a) 2 books cost $10
      1 book costs _____

   b) 4 mangoes cost $12
      1 mango costs _____

   c) 6 cans of juice cost $12
      1 can costs _____

jump math
MULTIPLYING POTENTIAL.

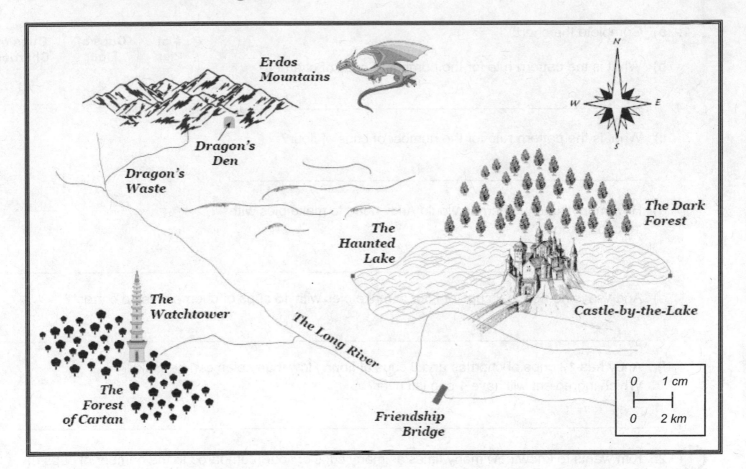

1. Sharon has drawn a map of a fantasy world. Use the scale to answer the questions below.

    a) How many kilometres must the dragon fly from its den to reach Castle-by-the-Lake's entrance?

    _____

    b) How long is the Haunted Lake (from East to West)?

    _____

    c) How wide is the Dark Forest (from North to South)?

    _____

    d) How far must a knight ride to get from the Watchtower to the entrance of Castle-by-the-Lake?
        (Assume the only way across the river is by Friendship Bridge.)

    _____

2. On a map that Jacob drew, 2 cm = 50 km.
    How many kilometres would each of the following distances on the map represent?

    a) 8 cm: _____   b) 10 cm: _____   c) 1 cm: _____   d) 5 cm: _____   e) 9 cm: _____

1. a) Complete the chart.

    b) What is the pattern rule for the number of cups of cherries?

    _____

    c) What is the pattern rule for the number of cups of flour?

    _____

    d) How many cups of cherries would Andy need to make pies with
        10 cups of flour?

    _____

    e) Andy says he needs 8 cups of flour to make pies with 15 cups of cherries. Is he correct?

    _____

    f) Andy has 12 cups of cherries and 9 cups of flour. How many pies can he make?
        Which ingredient will have 1 cup left over?

    _____

# of Pies	Cups of Flour	Cups of Cherries
1	2	3
2		

2. Kim wants to know how many times as many cups of flour (compared to the number of cups of
    fruit) she needs for each pancake recipe.

    Fill in the chart.

	Ratio of cups of flour to cups of fruit	Unit ratio	Ratio (mixed fraction)	Ratio (decimal)	How many times as many cups of flour?
a) 10 cups flour 8 cups bananas	10 to 8	$\frac{10}{8}$ to 1 or $\frac{5}{4}$ to 1	$1\frac{1}{4}$ to 1	1.25 to 1	___1.25___ times as many cups of flour
b) 6 cups flour 4 cups apples		or			_____ times as many cups of flour
c) 13 cups flour 4 cups peaches		or			_____ times as many cups of flour

    d) 20 cups of flour to 8 cups of cherries   e) 15 cups of flour to 6 cups of blueberries

Answer the following questions in your notebook.

DAILY NEWS

During explosive growth spurts, teenage Tyrannosaurus rexes gained almost 2.1 kilograms a day.

Scientists have discovered that T. rex added 2.07 kilograms a day during a four-year growth spurt between the ages of 14 and 18 years, but experienced little or no growth after that. An adult T. rex could weigh up to five and a half tonnes.

A blue whale gains 90 kilograms a day for the first seven months of its life and can reach 136 tonnes.

1. a) In the newspaper article above, two different measures are given for the amount of weight a Tyrannosaurus could gain in a day.

   i) What are the two measures?

   ii) Which measure is more precise?

   iii) Which measure is greater?

   iv) What is the difference between the two measures?

   b) About how many times more kilograms does a baby blue whale gain per day?

   c) A human newborn weighs about 3 kg.
      If the baby grew as fast as a T. rex, how much would it weigh after a month?

2. The graph (from a newspaper) shows how many new planets have been discovered by astronomers.

   a) How many more planets were discovered in 2002 than in 2004?

   b) In which years were more than 15 planets discovered?

   c) Between which years were at least 5 planets discovered each year?

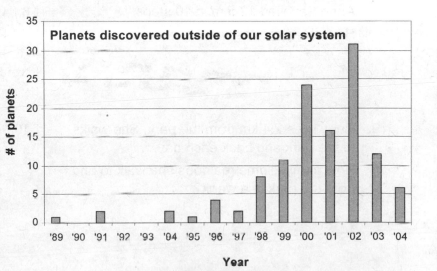

Planets discovered outside of our solar system

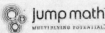

Answer the following questions in your notebook.

1. On a 3-day canoe trip, Pamela canoed 25.5 km on the first day, 32.6 km on the second, and 17.25 km on the third.

a) How far did she canoe in total?

b) What was the average distance she paddled each day?

c) If she canoes for 6 hours each day, about how many kilometres does she travel each hour?

d) Pamela's canoe can hold 100 kg. Pamela weighs 45 kg, her tent weighs 10 kg and her supplies weigh 15 kg. How much more weight can the canoe carry?

2. Jessica has 78 beads.
She gave her 3 friends 23 beads each.
How many did she have left over?

3. James bought a slice of pizza for $3.21, a video game for $15.87, a bottle of pop for $1.56, and a bag of chips for $1.37.
How much change did he get from $25.00?

4. Six classes went skating.
There are 24 students in each class.
Each bus holds 30 students.
The teachers ordered 4 buses.
Will there be enough room?
Explain.

5. Janice earned $28.35 on Monday. On Thursday, she spent $17.52 for a shirt.
She now has $32.23.
How much money did she have before she started work Monday?
HINT: Work backwards. How much money did she have before she bought the shirt?

6. Sue spent half of her money on a book. Then she spent $1.25 on a pen. She has $3.20 left.
How much did she start with?

7. Anne travelled 12.5 m in 10 steps.
How many metres was each step?

8. Gravity on Jupiter is 2.3 times as strong as the gravity on Earth.
How much more would a 7 kg dog weigh on Jupiter than on Earth?

9. Ruby lives 2.4 km from the park. She walks to the park and back each day.
How many kilometres does she walk to and from the park in a week?

10. Encke's Comet appears in our sky every 3.3 years. It was first seen in 1786.
When was the last time the comet was seen in the 1700s (i.e. before 1800)?
Show your work.

NS5-107: Organized Lists

Many problems in mathematics and science have more than one solution.

If a problem involves two quantities, list the values of one quantity in increasing order. Then you won't miss any solutions.

For instance, to find all the ways you can make 35¢ with dimes and nickels, start by assuming you have no dimes, then 1 dime, and so on up to 3 dimes (4 would be too many).

In each case, count on by 5s to 35 to find out how many nickels you need to make 35¢.

Step 1:

dimes	nickels
0	
1	
2	
3	

Step 2:

dimes	nickels
0	7
1	5
2	3
3	1

----

1. Fill in the amount of pennies, nickels, or dimes you need to …

a) make 17¢.

nickels	pennies
0	
1	
2	
3	

b) make 45¢.

dimes	nickels
0	
1	
2	
3	
4	

c) make 23¢.

nickels	pennies
0	
1	
2	
3	
4	

d) make 32¢.

dimes	pennies
0	
1	
2	
3	

e) make 65¢.

quarters	nickels
0	
1	
2	

f) make 85¢.

quarters	nickels
0	
1	
2	
3	

2.

quarters	nickels
0	
1	
2	

Ben wants to find all the ways he can make 60¢ using quarters and nickels. He lists the number of quarters in increasing order. Why did he stop at 2 quarters?

_____

_____

3. Make a chart to show all the ways you can make the given amount.

a) Make 27¢ using nickels and pennies.

b) Make 70¢ using quarters and nickels.

c) Make 65¢ using dimes and nickels.

d) Make $13 using loonies and toonies.

Alana wants to find all pairs of numbers that multiply to give 15.

There are no numbers that will multiply by 2 or 4 to give 15, so Alana leaves those rows in her chart blank.

The numbers in the last row of the chart are the same as those in the 3rd row so Alana knows she has found all possible pairs of numbers that multiply to give 15: 1 × 15 = 15 and 3 × 5 = 15.

1st Number	2nd Number
1	15
2	---
3	5
4	---
5	3

----

4. Find all pairs of numbers that multiply to give the number provided.

a) **6**

First Number	Second Number

b) **8**

First Number	Second Number

5.

quarters	dimes
0	
1	
2	

Alicia wants to find all the ways she can make 70¢ using quarters and dimes.

One of the entries on her chart won't work. Which one is it?

6. Find all the ways to make the amounts using quarters and dimes. (Some entries on your chart may not work.)

a) 80¢

quarters	dimes
0	
1	
2	
3	

b) 105¢

quarters	dimes

7.

Width	1	2	3	4
Length				

Find all rectangles with side lengths that are whole numbers that have area 16 square units.

8. Make a chart to find all the pairs of numbers that multiply to give …

    a) 12   b) 14   c) 20   d) 24

9. Find all the rectangles with side lengths that are whole numbers and with a perimeter of 14 units.

10. Find all the rectangles with side lengths that are whole numbers and with an area of 10 square units.

1. The numbers 2 and 5 have a **product** of 10 (they **multiply** to give 10).
   They have a **sum** of 7 (they **add** to give 7).

   Can you find two numbers that have ...

   a) a <u>product</u> of 8, and a <u>sum</u> of 6? ____ ____   b) a <u>product</u> of 9, and a <u>sum</u> of 6? ____ ____

   c) a <u>product</u> of 12, and a <u>sum</u> of 7? ____ ____   d) a <u>product</u> of 12, and a <u>sum</u> of 8? ____ ____

2. Fill in the blanks using digits from 0 to 9. (In each question, use each digit only once.)

   Make ...

   a) the greatest number:

   ____ ____ ____ ____

   b) the lowest odd number:

   ____ ____ ____ ____

   c) the greatest number with 9 in the tens place:

   ____ ____ __ ____

   d) the greatest even number with 6 in the hundreds place:

   ____ ____ ____ ____

3. Place the numbers 1, 2, 3, 4, 5, and 6 so that the three numbers along each edge add to ...

   a) 10 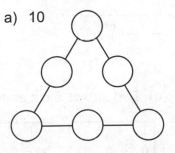   b) 11 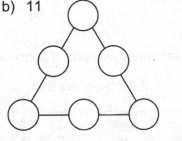   c) 12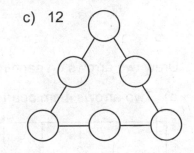

4. Crayons come in boxes of 4 or 5.
   Can you buy a combination of boxes that will give you each number exactly?
   NOTE: For some questions, you needn't buy boxes of both types.

   a) 8 crayons   b) 10 crayons   c) 11 crayons   d) 14 crayons

   e) 17 crayons   f) 18 crayons   g) 19 crayons   h) 21 crayons

5. The number 188 has the same ones and tens digits.
   How many numbers from 100 to 200 have the same ones and tens digits?

6. "I am a <u>4-digit</u> number ..."

   a) "I am less than 2000. My first three digits are all the same. The sum of my digits is 7."

   b) "All of my digits are the same. The sum of my digits is 20."

   c) "I am less than 4000. All of my digits are multiples of 3. The sum of my digits is 21.

A **centimetre** is a unit of measurement for <u>length</u> (or <u>height</u>, or <u>thickness</u>).

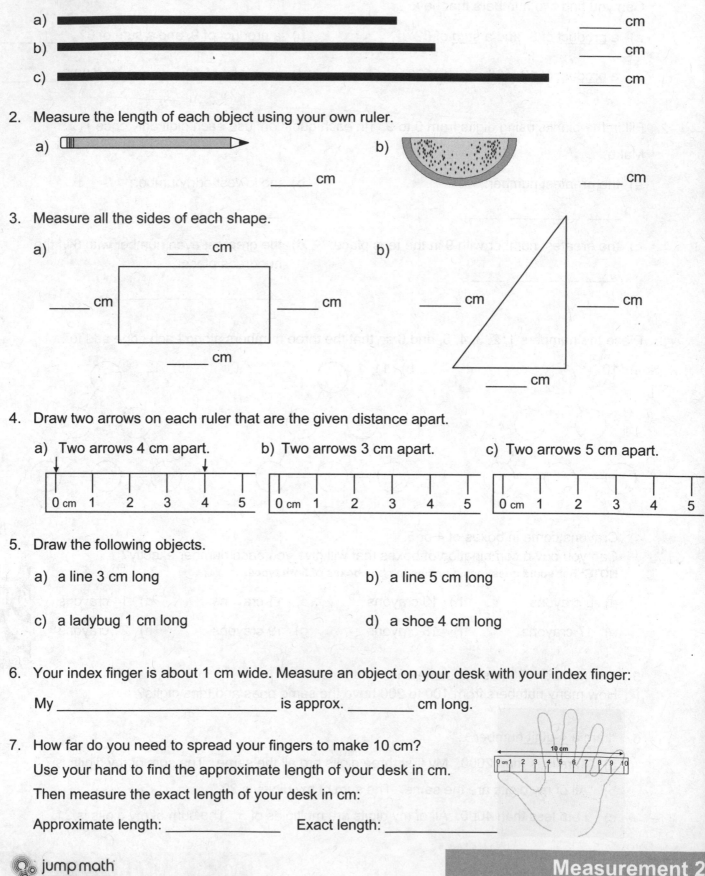

1. Measure the length of each line using your ruler.

    a) _____ cm

    b) _____ cm

    c) _____ cm

2. Measure the length of each object using your own ruler.

    a)   _____ cm

    b)   _____ cm

3. Measure all the sides of each shape.

    a) _____ cm

    _____ cm   _____ cm

    _____ cm

    b) _____ cm   _____ cm

    _____ cm

4. Draw two arrows on each ruler that are the given distance apart.

    a) Two arrows 4 cm apart.   b) Two arrows 3 cm apart.   c) Two arrows 5 cm apart.

    0 cm 1   2   3   4   5   0 cm 1   2   3   4   5   0 cm 1   2   3   4   5

5. Draw the following objects.

    a) a line 3 cm long   b) a line 5 cm long

    c) a ladybug 1 cm long   d) a shoe 4 cm long

6. Your index finger is about 1 cm wide. Measure an object on your desk with your index finger:

    My _____ is approx. _____ cm long.

7. How far do you need to spread your fingers to make 10 cm?

    Use your hand to find the approximate length of your desk in cm.

    Then measure the exact length of your desk in cm:

    Approximate length: _____   Exact length: _____

ME5-9: Millimetres and Centimetres

If you look at a ruler with **millimetre** markings, you can see that 1 cm is equal to 10 mm.

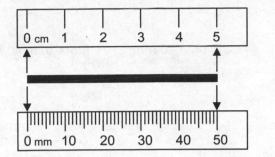

How long is the line in cm? How long is it in mm?

The line is _____ cm long, or _____ mm long.

To convert a measurement from cm to mm,
we have to multiply the measurement by _____.

----

1. Your index finger is about 1 cm or 10 mm wide.
    Measure the objects below using your index finger.
    Then convert your measurement to mm.

    a)

    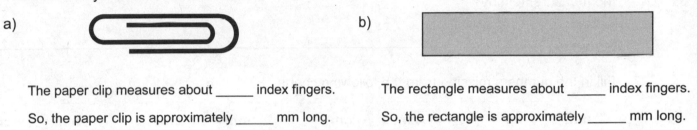

    The paper clip measures about _____ index fingers.

    So, the paper clip is approximately _____ mm long.

    b)

    The rectangle measures about _____ index fingers.

    So, the rectangle is approximately _____ mm long.

2. Measure the distance between the two arrows on each ruler.

    a)

    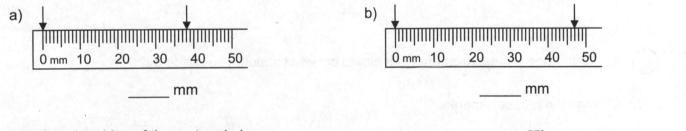

    _____ mm

    b)

    _____ mm

3. Measure the sides of the rectangle in cm.
    Then measure the distance between the two diagonal
    corners in cm and mm.
    NOTE: Your answer in cm will be a decimal.

    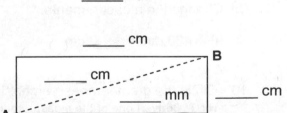

    _____ cm

    _____ cm

    _____ mm   _____ cm

4. Use a ruler to draw the following objects to the exact millimetre.

    a) A line 20 mm long.

    b) Draw a line 52 mm long.

    c) A beetle 35 mm long.

    d) A pencil 70 mm long.

5. Estimate whether each line is <u>less</u> than 40 mm or <u>more</u> than 40 mm.
    Place a checkmark in the appropriate column.
    Then measure the actual length.

		Less than 40 mm	More than 40 mm
a)			
b)			
c)			

a) _____ mm   b) _____ mm   c) _____ mm

6. To change a measurement from centimetres (cm) into millimetres (mm), what should you <u>multiply</u> the measurement by?

_____

7. Fill in the numbers missing from the following charts.

mm	cm
	13
	32

mm	cm
	8
	18

mm	cm
	213
	170

mm	cm
	9
	567

8. To change a measurement from mm to cm what should you <u>divide</u> by? _____

9. Change the measurements.

    a) 460 mm = ____ cm   b) 60 mm = ____ cm   c) 580 mm = ____ cm

10. Circle the greater measurement in each pair.
    HINT: Convert one of the measurements so that both units are the same. Show your work.

    a) 5 cm   70 mm

    b) 83 cm   910 mm

    c) 45 cm   53 mm

    d) 2 cm   12 mm

    e) 60 cm   6200 mm

11. Draw a rectangle 2 cm high and 50 mm long.

12. Using your ruler, draw a second line so that the pair of lines are the given distance apart. Complete the chart.

	Distance apart	
	in cm	in mm
  | |	4	40
  |	3	
  |		80

13. In the space provided, draw a line that is between …

    a) 4 and 5 cm.

        How long is your line in mm? _____

    b) 6 and 7 cm.

        How long is your line in mm? _____

14. Write a measurement in mm that is between …

    a) 7 and 8 cm: _____ mm   b) 27 and 28 cm: _____ mm

15. Write a measurement in a whole number of cm that is between …

    a) 67 mm and 75 mm: _____ cm   b) 27 mm and 39 mm: _____   c) 52 mm and 7 cm: _____

16. Draw a line that is a whole number of centimetres long and is between …

    a) 35 and 45 mm   b) 55 and 65 mm   c) 27 and 33 mm

17. Carl has a set of sticks: some are 5 cm long and some are 3 cm long.

    The picture (not drawn to scale) shows how he could line up the sticks to measure 14 cm:

    <u>5 cm</u>   <u>3 cm</u>   <u>3 cm</u>   <u>3 cm</u>

    Draw a sketch to show how Carl could measure each length by lining the sticks up end to end.

    a) 8 cm   b) 11 cm   c) 13 cm   d) 26 cm   e) 19 cm   f) 17 cm

    BONUS
    g) Use two 5 cm sticks and one 3 cm stick to draw a line 7 cm long.

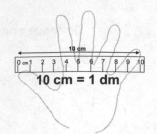

10 cm = 1 dm

If you spread your fingers wide, your hand is about 10 cm wide: 10 centimetres are equal to 1 **decimetre** (dm).

So there are 10 **cm** in 1 **dm**.

(Similarly, 10 **mm** is equal to 1 **cm**.)

----

1. Place a checkmark in the correct column.
   HINT: Remember that 1 dm = 10 cm.

	Less than 1 dm	More than 1 dm
My arm		
A paperclip		
My pencil		
The height of the classroom door		

2. To change a measurement from decimetres (dm) to centimetres (cm), what should you multiply by?

   _____

3. To change a measurement from cm to dm what should you divide by? _____

4. Find the numbers missing from the following charts.

   a)

cm	dm
150	15
	23
	32

   b)

cm	dm
90	
	510
400	

   c)

cm	dm
610	
	1
780	

5. Draw a line that is between 1 and 2 decimetres long.

   a) How long is your line in cm? _____   b) How long is your line in mm? _____

6. Write a measurement in cm that is between …

   a) 4 and 5 dm _____   b) 3 and 4 dm _____   c) 7 and 8 dm _____

7. Write a measurement in dm that is between …

   a) 72 and 82 cm _____   b) 27 and 35 cm _____   c) 68 and 74 cm _____

8. There are 10 mm in 1 cm. There are 10 cm in 1 dm. How many mm are in 1 dm? Explain.

ME5-11: Metres and Kilometres

A **metre** is a unit of measurement for **length** (or **height** or **thickness**) equal to 100 cm.

A metre stick is 100 cm long.

A **kilometre** is a unit of measurement for length equal to 1000 metres.

Here are some measurements you can use for estimating in metres.

about 2 metres	*about 2 metres*	*about 10 metres*	*about 100 metres*
The height of a (tall) adult	The length of an adult's bicycle	The length of a school bus	The length of a football field

1. How many adults do you think could lie head to foot across your classroom? _____

2. a) About how many school buses high is your school? _____

   b) About how high is your school? _____

3. A small city block is about 100 m long.

   Name a place you can walk to from your school. _____

   Approximately how many metres away from the school is the place you named? _____

4. Change these measurements into metres.

   a) 3 km = _____   b) 6 km = _____   c) 7 km = _____   d) 12 km = _____

5. A football field is about 100 m long. About how many football fields long is a kilometre?

   _____

6. You can travel 1 km if you walk for 15 minutes at a regular speed.
   Name a place that is about 1 km from your school.

   _____

7. The CN Tower is 531 metres high.
   About how many CN Towers, laid end to end, would make a kilometre?
   Explain.

1. Complete the following King St. streetcar schedule, using the pattern in the numbers.

	Streetcar 1	Streetcar 2	Streetcar 3	Streetcar 4	Streetcar 5
Jameson Ave.	7:00	7:15	7:30		
Dunn Ave.	7:05	7:20	7:35		
Dufferin St.	7:10	7:25	7:40		
Strachan Ave.	7:15	7:30	7:45		

a) How long does it take to travel from Jameson Ave. to …

Dunn Ave.? _____   Dufferin St.? _____   Strachan Ave.? _____

b) When should you leave from Jameson Ave. to be at Strachan Ave. …

at 7:40? _____   at 8:15? _____   at 11:10? _____

2. Jameson Ave. and Dufferin St. are 1 km apart.
It takes the streetcar 10 minutes to travel that distance.

a) How far will a streetcar travel in 1 hour, moving at an average speed of 1 km every 10 minutes?

_____

b) How far would a streetcar travel in an hour if it was moving at an average speed of …

3 km every 20 minutes?   5 km every half hour?   2 km every 15 minutes?

_____   _____   _____

3. If a streetcar was moving at an average speed of 12 km every hour, how far would it travel in …

a) 2 hours?   b) 7 hours?   c) $2\frac{1}{2}$ hours?   d) $\frac{1}{4}$ hour?

_____   _____   _____   _____

4. If a streetcar travels at an average speed of 15 km per hour, does that mean it is always moving at the same speed?

_____

ME5-13: Changing Units

1. Finish the table by following the pattern.

m	1	2	3	4	5	6
dm	10	20				
cm	100	200				
mm	1000	2000				

2. What would you multiply by to change each measurement?

   a) m to cm _____   b) m to mm _____   c) cm to mm _____

3. Convert the following measurements.

m	cm
8	
70	

m	mm
5	
17	

cm	mm
4	
121	

dm	cm
32	
5	

4. Kathy measured her bedroom door with both a metre stick and a measuring tape.

   • When she measured with the metre stick, the height of the door was 2 m with 25 cm.

   • When she measured with the measuring tape, she got a measurement of 225 cm.

   Was there a difference in the two measurements? Explain.

   _____

   _____

   _____

5. Convert the measurement given in cm to a measurement using multiple units.

   a) 423 cm = _4_ m _23_ cm   b) 514 cm = ___ m ____ cm   c) 627 cm = ___ m ____ cm

   d) 673 cm = ___ m _____ cm   e) 381 cm = ___ m _____ cm   f) 203 cm = ___ m ____ cm

6. Convert the following multiple units of measurements to a single unit.

   a) 2 m 83 cm = _283_ cm   b) 3 m 65 cm = _____ cm   c) 4 m 85 cm = _____ cm

   d) 9 m 47 cm = _____ cm   e) 7 m 4 cm = _____ cm   f) 6 m 40 cm = _____ cm

7. Change the following measurements to multiple units then to decimal notation.

   a) 546 cm = _5_ m _46_ cm = _5.46_ m   b) 217 cm = _____ m _____ cm = _____ m

   c) 783 cm = _____ m _____ cm = _____ m   d) 648 cm = _____ m _____ cm = _____ m

8. Why do we use the same decimal notation for dollars and cents and for metres and centimetres?

ME5-14: Problem Solving with Kilometres

The Demster highway is a **736 km** long gravel road that crosses the Arctic Circle.

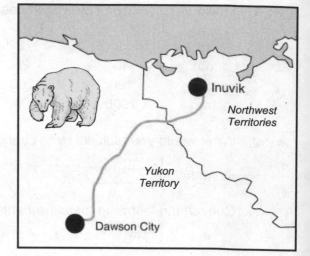

1. Round the length of the highway to the nearest 100 km.

_____

2. About how long would it take you to drive from Dawson City to Inuvik driving at an average speed of ...

   a) 100 km per hour? _____

   b) 50 km per hour? _____

   c) 25 km per hour? _____

3. The Eagle's Nest Hotel is half-way between Dawson City and Inuvik.

   a) How far from Dawson City is the Eagle's Nest? _____ km

   b) Draw a point on the map about where you would think the Eagle's Nest is located.

4. If you drive from Inuvik towards Dawson City ...

   A. you will cross the Arctic Circle after driving 331 km.

   B. you will reach the border between the Yukon and the Northwest Territories 60 km before you reach the Arctic Circle.

   a) How far is the drive from the Arctic Circle to ...

   Dawson City? _____   The Eagle's Nest? _____

   b) How far is Inuvik from the Yukon border? _____ km

   c) How far is Dawson City from the Northwest Territories border? _____ km

   d) Driving at 100 km per hour, about how long would it take to get from Dawson City to the border?

_____

ME5-15: Changing Units (Advanced)

1. Measure the line below in mm, cm, and dm.

_____

_____ mm   _____ cm   _____ dm

a) Which of the units (mm, cm, or dm) is largest? _____ smallest? _____

b) Which unit did you need more of to measure the line, the <u>larger</u> unit or the <u>smaller</u> unit?

_____

c) To change a measurement from a **larger** to a **smaller** unit, do you need ...

more of the smaller units   or   **fewer** of the smaller units?

_____

2. Fill in the missing numbers.

a) 1 cm = _____ mm   b) 1 dm = _____ cm

c) 1 dm = _____ mm   d) 1 m = _____ dm

e) 1 m = _____ cm   f) 1 m = _____ mm

> Units **decrease** in size going **down** the stairway:
>
>   m
>   ⌐dm
>   ⌐cm
>   ⌐mm
>
> - 1 step down = 10 × smaller
> - 2 steps down = 100 × smaller
> - 3 steps down = 1 000 × smaller

3. Change the measurements below by following the steps. The first one has been done for you.

a) Change 3.5 cm to mm

   i) The new units are ___10___ times _smaller_

   ii) So I need _10_ times _more_ units

   iii) So I _multiply_ by __10__

   3.5 cm = ___35___ mm

b) Change 2.7 cm to mm

   i) The new units are _____ times _____

   ii) So I need _____ times _____ units

   iii) So I _____ by _____

   2.7 cm = _____ mm

c) Change 6.3 dm to cm

   i) The new units are _____ times _____

   ii) So I need _____ times _____ units

   iii) So I _multiply_ by _____

   6.3 dm = _____ cm

d) Change 3 m to cm

   i) The new units are _____ times _____

   ii) So I need _____ times _____ units

   iii) So I _____ by _____

   3 m = _____ cm

e) Change 4 m to dm

   i)   The new units are _____ times _____

   ii) So I need _____ times _____ units

   iii) So I _____ by _____

        4 m = _____ dm

f) Change 17.3 cm to mm

   i)   The new units are _____ times _____

   ii) So I need _____ times _____ units

   iii) So I _____ by _____

        17.3 cm = _____ mm

g) Change 5.2 cm to mm

   i)   The new units are _____ times _____

   ii) So I need _____ times _____ units

   iii) So I _____ by _____

        5.2 cm = _____ mm

h) Change 2.14 dm to mm

   i)   The new units are _____ times _____

   ii) So I need _____ times _____ units

   iii) So I _____ by _____

        2.14 dm = _____ mm

4. Change the units by following the steps in Question 3 mentally.

   a) 4 m = _____ dm   b) 1.3 dm = _____ mm   c) 20 cm = _____ mm

5. Order the fern leaves from longest to shortest.
   (Express each measurement in the smallest unit first.)

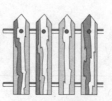

Fern	Length of leaf	In smallest units
Oak Fern	18 cm	
Ostrich Fern	1.5 m	
Bracken Fern	90 cm	
Royal Fern	1.30 m	

1. _____

2. _____

3. _____

4. _____

6. Is 362 mm longer or shorter than 20 cm?
   How do you know?

7. A fence is made of 4 parts each 32 cm long.
   Is the fence longer or shorter than a metre?

8. A decimetre of ribbon costs 5¢.
   How much will 90 cm cost?

9. Michelle says that to change 6 m 80 cm to centimetres, you multiply the 6 by 100 and then add 80.
   Is Michelle correct? Why does Michelle multiply by 100?

ME5-16: Ordering & Assigning Appropriate Units

1. Match the word with the symbol. Then match the object with the appropriate unit of measurement.

   a)

mm	kilometre	thickness of a fingernail
cm	centimetre	length of a finger
m	millimetre	height of a door
km	metre	distance to Moscow

   b)

km	metre	length of a canoe
cm	millimetre	distance to the moon
m	kilometre	length of a pen
mm	centimetre	length of a flea

2. Circle the unit of measurement that makes the statement correct:

   a) A very tall adult is about 2 **dm** / **m** high.

   b) The width of your hand is close to 1 **dm** / **cm**.

   c) The Calgary Tower is 191 **cm** / **m** high.

3. Julie measured some objects, but she forgot to include the units. Add the appropriate unit.

   a) bed: 180 _____   b) car: 2 _____   c) hat: 25 _____

   d) toothbrush: 16 _____   e) driveway: 11 _____

4. Which unit of measurement (mm, cm, m or km) would make the statement correct?

   a) A fast walker can walk 1 _____ in 10 minutes.

   b) The length of your leg is about 70 _____ .

   c) A great white shark can grow up to 4 _____ long.

   d) A postcard is about 150 _____ long.

   e) The Trans-Canada Highway from Newfoundland to British Columbia is 7604 _____ long.

   f) Niagara Falls is 56 _____ high.

   g) A porcupine can grow up to 80 _____ long.

5. Name an object in your classroom that has ...

   a) a thickness of about 20 mm: _____

   b) a height of about 2 m: _____

6. Order the lengths of the tails from <u>longest</u> to <u>shortest</u>.

Animal	Length of tail	In smallest units
Red Fox	5.5 dm	
Beaver	40 cm	
Black Bear	12 cm	
Grey Squirrel	2.3 dm	

1. _____

2. _____

3. _____

4. _____

7. The number line is a decimetre long. Mark each measurement on the number line with an arrow as shown.

A

0 dm || 1 dm

A 12 mm   **B** 35 mm   **C** 2.0 cm   **D** 49 mm   **E** 9.9 cm   **F** 5.7 cm   **G** 6.3 cm

8. Mark the approximate location of each measurement with an X.

0 dm |___|___|___|___|___|___|___|___|___|___| 1 dm

A 3 cm   **B** 5 cm   **C** 25 mm   **D** 9 cm   **E** 4.5 cm   **F** 8.2 cm   **G** .7 cm

0 km |___|___|___|___|___|___|___|___|___|___| 1 km

H 200 m   **I** 500 m   **J** 700 m   **K** 350 m   **L** 850 m   **M** 630 m   **N** 90 m

9. Fill in the numbers in the box in the correct places.

a) The CN Tower is _____ **m** high.

It is located about _____ **km** from the nearest subway stop.

It was built more than _____ **years** ago.

20	553	2

b) Toronto is about _____ **km** from Vancouver.

It takes _____ **hours** to fly between the cities.

Planes flying between the cities can

cruise as high as _____ **km**.

5.5	11	3500

Measurement 2

ME5-17: Mathematics and Architecture

Mathematics has been used to design many beautiful buildings, including the pyramids of Egypt.
Each pyramid is drawn to a scale: **1 millimetre** on the diagram represents **5 metres** on the actual pyramid.

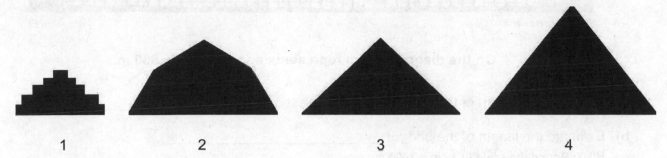

| 1 | 2 | 3 | 4 |

1. Measure the diagrams above in mm, then calculate the <u>actual</u> measurements of the pyramids.
   NOTE: 1mm = 5 m.

No.	Name	Height of diagram in mm	Actual height of pyramid in m	Length of base of diagram in mm	Actual length of base in m
1.	Step Pyramid of Djoser				
2.	Bent Pyramid at Dashur				
3.	Red Pyramid of Snefru				
4.	Great Pyramid at Giza				

2. The bricks used to build the Pyramid of Giza measure 0.66 m high and 1.00 m long.

   a) How <u>high</u> are the bricks in: i) centimetres _____ ii) decimetres _____

   b) How <u>long</u> are the bricks in: i) centimetres _____ ii) decimetres _____

   c) If a pyramid was 100 bricks high, how high would it be in metres? _____

   d) How many bricks are along the bottom of one side of the Pyramid of Giza? _____ bricks.

3. Fill in the chart. Then, in your notebook, draw a scale diagram of each pyramid below using the scale
   1 mm = 5 m. (Each pyramid looks like a triangle from the side).

No.	Name	Height in mm	Approx. height in m	Base length in mm	Approx. base Length in m
1.	Black Pyramid		80 m		105 m
2.	Pyramid at Meidum		90 m		145 m
3.	Pyramid of Kharfe		145 m		230 m

jump math
MULTIPLYING POTENTIAL

Measurement 2

The Confederation Bridge, which links New Brunswick and Prince Edward Island, was finished in 1997.

New Brunswick   *PEI*

On the diagram, 1 cm represents approximately 860 m.

1. a) Measure the length of the diagram to the nearest cm: _____

    b) Estimate the length of the bridge: _____
        HINT: Round the scale to 1 cm = 1000 m.

2. The actual length of the bridge is 12.9 km.
    How many metres long is the bridge?

3. A school bus is about 10 m long.
    About how many school buses would span the
    bridge if they were parked end to end?

4. The bridge is made of three segments:

    *   the East Approach Bridge, which is 600 m long
    *   the West Approach Bridge, which is 1300 m long
    *   and the Main Bridge (which connects the two).

    How long is the Main Bridge in metres?

5. The distance between the bridge piers is 250 m.
    A boat 20 m wide passes between the two piers in the middle
    of the channel.
    How far is the pier from the side of the boat?

6. Emergency telephones are placed every 750 m along the bridge.
    About how many telephones are on the bridge?

 jump math
MULTIPLYING POTENTIAL.

Measurement 2

ME5-19: Perimeter

1. Each edge is 1 cm long. Write the total length of each side in cm as shown in figure a). Then write an addition statement and find the perimeter.

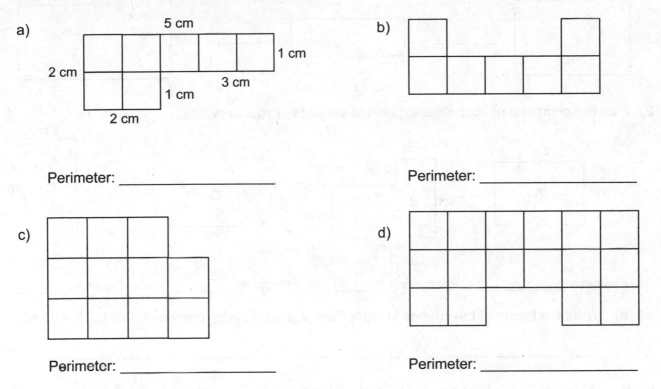

a)

5 cm
2 cm
1 cm
1 cm
3 cm
2 cm

Perimeter: _____

b)

Perimeter: _____

c)

Perimeter: _____

d)

Perimeter: _____

2. Each edge is 1 unit long. Write the length of each side beside the figure (don't miss any edges!). Then use the side lengths to find the perimeter.

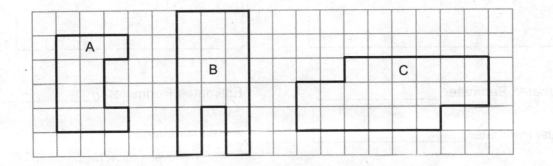

A

B

C

3. Draw your own figure and find the perimeter.

4. On grid paper, draw your own figures and find their perimeters. Try making letters or other shapes.

jump math
MULTIPLYING POTENTIAL

Measurement 2

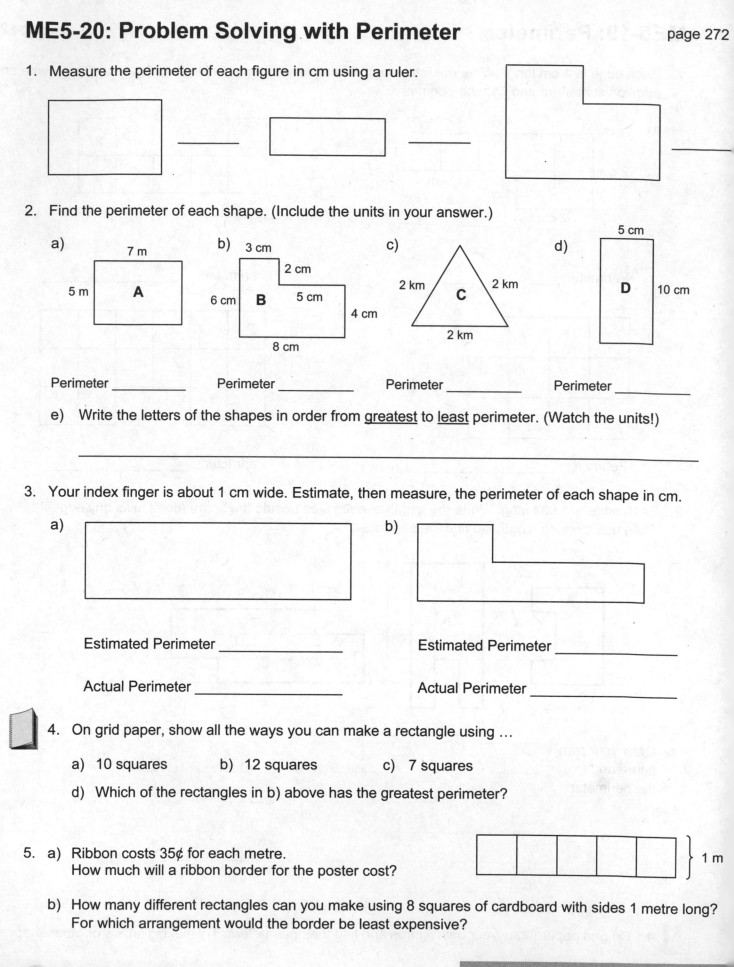

1. Measure the perimeter of each figure in cm using a ruler.

2. Find the perimeter of each shape. (Include the units in your answer.)

    a) **A** 7 m 5 m

    b) **B** 3 cm 2 cm 6 cm 5 cm 4 cm 8 cm

    c) **C** 2 km 2 km 2 km

    d) **D** 5 cm 10 cm

    Perimeter _____   Perimeter _____   Perimeter _____   Perimeter _____

    e) Write the letters of the shapes in order from <u>greatest</u> to <u>least</u> perimeter. (Watch the units!)

    _____

3. Your index finger is about 1 cm wide. Estimate, then measure, the perimeter of each shape in cm.

    a)

    b)

    Estimated Perimeter _____   Estimated Perimeter _____

    Actual Perimeter _____   Actual Perimeter _____

4. On grid paper, show all the ways you can make a rectangle using ...

    a) 10 squares   b) 12 squares   c) 7 squares

    d) Which of the rectangles in b) above has the greatest perimeter?

5. a) Ribbon costs 35¢ for each metre.
        How much will a ribbon border for the poster cost?

    } 1 m

    b) How many different rectangles can you make using 8 squares of cardboard with sides 1 metre long?
        For which arrangement would the border be least expensive?

ME5-21: Exploring Perimeters

Serge buys 12 metres of fence to make a rectangular garden.
Each section of fence is 1 m long.
What dimensions can Serge's garden have?

Serge tries widths 1 m, 2 m, and 3 m.

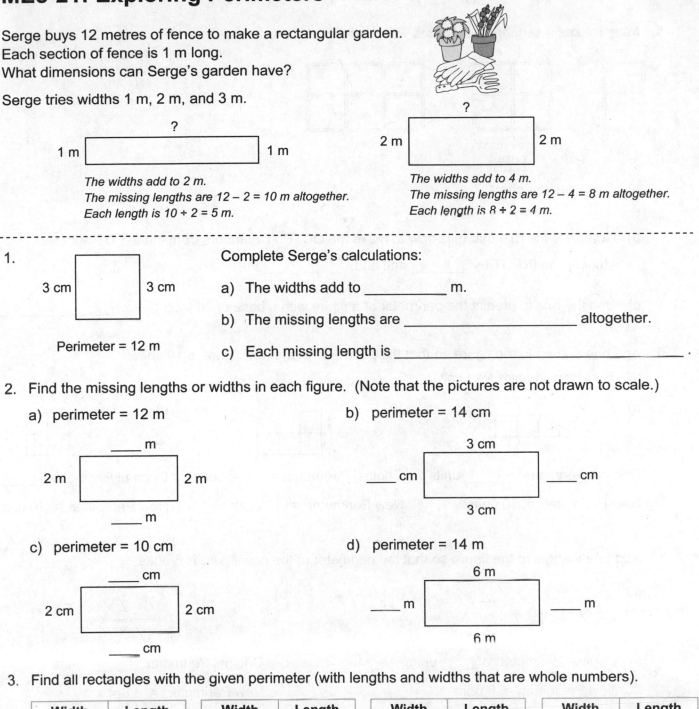

The widths add to 2 m.
The missing lengths are 12 – 2 = 10 m altogether.
Each length is 10 ÷ 2 = 5 m.

The widths add to 4 m.
The missing lengths are 12 – 4 = 8 m altogether.
Each length is 8 ÷ 2 = 4 m.

1. Complete Serge's calculations:

   Perimeter = 12 m

   a) The widths add to _____ m.

   b) The missing lengths are _____ altogether.

   c) Each missing length is _____.

2. Find the missing lengths or widths in each figure. (Note that the pictures are not drawn to scale.)

   a) perimeter = 12 m

   b) perimeter = 14 cm

   c) perimeter = 10 cm

   d) perimeter = 14 m

3. Find all rectangles with the given perimeter (with lengths and widths that are whole numbers).

Width	Length
Perimeter = 6 units	

Width	Length
Perimeter = 12 units	

Width	Length
Perimeter = 16 units	

Width	Length
Perimeter = 18 units	

4. Write a rule for finding the perimeter of a rectangle from its width and length. _____

5. Mark makes a sequence of figures with toothpicks.

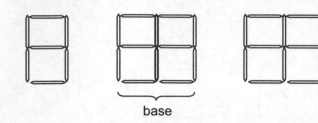

base

INPUT Number of toothpicks in base	OUTPUT Perimeter
1	6

a) Complete the chart.

b) Complete the rule that tells how to make the OUTPUT numbers from the INPUT numbers:

Multiply the INPUT by _____ and add _____.

c) Use the rule to predict the perimeter of a figure with a base of 10 toothpicks. _____

6. Add one square to the figure so that the perimeter of the new figure is 10 units.

NOTE: Assume all edges are 1 unit.

a)

Original Perimeter = ____ units

New Perimeter = 10 units

b)

Original Perimeter = ____ units

New Perimeter = 10 units

c)

Original Perimeter = ____ units

New Perimeter = 10 units

7. Add one triangle to the figure so that the perimeter of the new figure is 6 units.

a)

Original Perimeter = ____ units

New Perimeter = 6 units

b)

Original Perimeter = ____ units

New Perimeter = 6 units

8. Repeat steps a) to c) of question 5 for the following patterns.

a)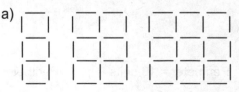

b)

9. Emma says the formula 2 x (length + width) gives the perimeter of a rectangle. Is she correct?

ME5-22: Circles and Irregular Polygons

1. The horizontal and vertical distance between adjacent pairs of dots is 1 cm.
   The diagonal distance is about 1.4 cm.

   1.4 cm

   Find the approximate perimeter of each figure by counting diagonal sides
   as 1.4 cm. (How can multiplication help you sum the sides of length 1.4 cm?)

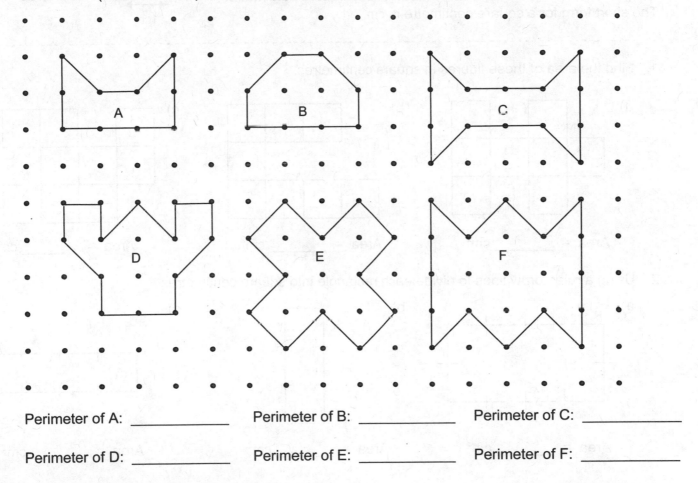

Perimeter of A: _____   Perimeter of B: _____   Perimeter of C: _____

Perimeter of D: _____   Perimeter of E: _____   Perimeter of F: _____

2. The distance around the outside of a circle is called
   the **circumference**.

   mark the distance
   around the circle
   on the strip

   a) Measure the circumference of each circle to the
   nearest **cm** using a strip of rolled up paper and a ruler.
   Record the width and circumference in the chart.

Width	Circumference

   b) About how many times greater than the width is the circumference? _____

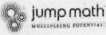

ME5-23: Area in Square Centimetres

Shapes that are flat are called **two-dimensional** (2-D) shapes.
The area of a 2-dimensional shape is the amount of space it takes up.

A square centimetre is a unit for measuring area.
A square with sides of 1 cm has an area of one square centimetre.
The short form for a square centimetre is cm².

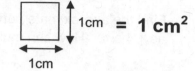

1cm = **1 cm²**

---

1. Find the area of these figures in square centimetres.

   a)

   Area = _____ cm²

   b)

   Area = _____ cm²

   c)

   Area = _____ cm²

2. Using a ruler, draw lines to divide each rectangle into square centimetres.

   a)

   Area = _____ cm²

   b)

   Area = _____ cm²

   c)

   Area = _____ cm²

3. How can you find the area (in square units) of each of the given shapes?

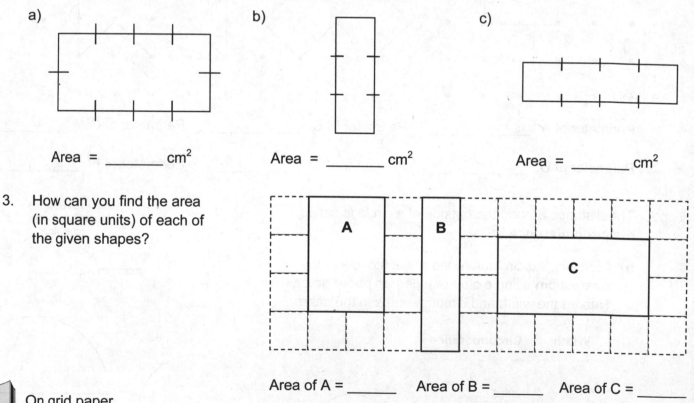

   Area of A = _____   Area of B = _____   Area of C = _____

On grid paper …

4. Draw 3 different shapes that have an area of 10 cm² (the shapes don't have to be rectangles).

5. Draw several shapes and find their area and perimeter.

6. Draw a rectangle with an area of 12 cm² and perimeter of 14 cm.

jump math
MULTIPLYING POTENTIAL.

Measurement 2

ME5-24: Area of Rectangles

1. Write a multiplication statement for each array.

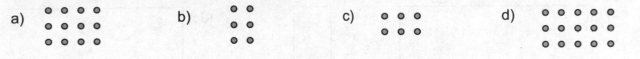

a)   b)   c)   d)

_____   _____   _____   _____

2. Draw a dot in each box.
    Then write a multiplication statement that tells you the number of boxes in the rectangle.

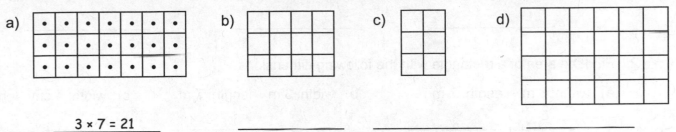

a)   b)   c)   d)

___3 × 7 = 21___   _____   _____   _____

3. Write the number of boxes along the width and length of each rectangle.
    Then write a multiplication statement for the area of the rectangle (in square units).

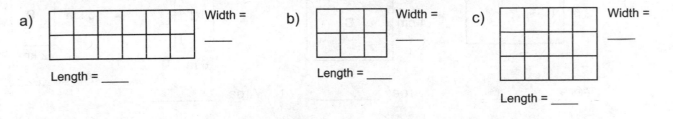

a)   Width =   b)   Width =   c)   Width =
            ____   ____   ____
    Length = ____   Length = ____   Length = ____

_____   _____   _____

4. The sides of the rectangles have been marked in centimetres. Using a ruler, draw lines to divide
    each rectangle into squares. Write a multiplication statement for the area of the boxes in cm².
    NOTE: You will have to mark the last row of boxes yourself using a ruler.

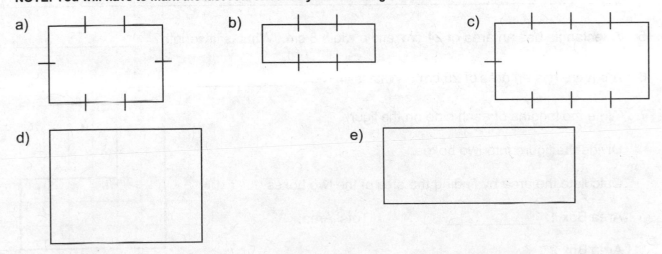

a)   b)   c)

d)   e)

5. If you know the length and width of a rectangle, how can you find its area?

ME5-25: Exploring Area

1. Measure the length and width of the figures, then find the area.

    a)   b)   c)

    _____   _____   _____

2. Find the area of a rectangle with the following dimensions:

    a) width: 6 m   length: 7 m   b) width: 3 m   length: 7 m   c) width: 4 cm   length: 8 cm

    _____   _____   _____

3. a) Calculate the area of each rectangle (be sure to include the units).

    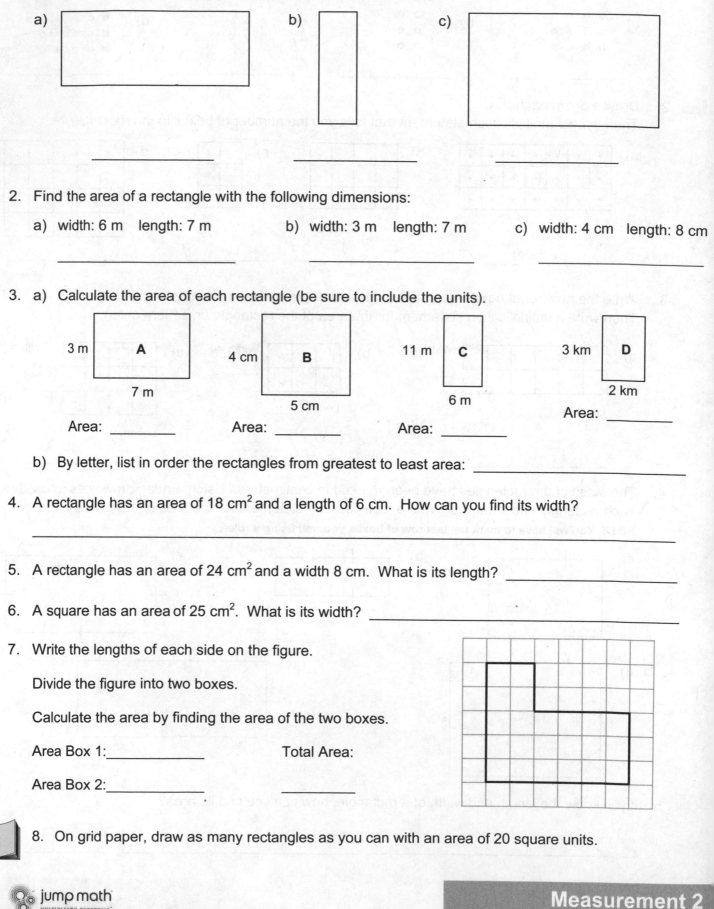

    3 m   **A**   4 cm   **B**   11 m   **C**   3 km   **D**
           7 m   5 cm   6 m   2 km

    Area: _____   Area: _____   Area: _____   Area: _____

    b) By letter, list in order the rectangles from greatest to least area: _____

4. A rectangle has an area of 18 cm² and a length of 6 cm. How can you find its width?

    _____

5. A rectangle has an area of 24 cm² and a width 8 cm. What is its length? _____

6. A square has an area of 25 cm². What is its width? _____

7. Write the lengths of each side on the figure.

    Divide the figure into two boxes.

    Calculate the area by finding the area of the two boxes.

    Area Box 1:_____   Total Area:

    Area Box 2:_____   _____

8. On grid paper, draw as many rectangles as you can with an area of 20 square units.

ME5-26: Area of Polygons

1. Two half squares 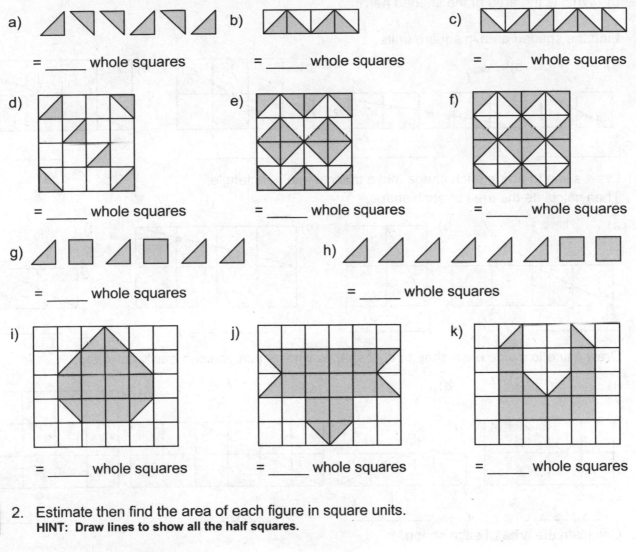 cover the same area as a whole square .

    Count each <u>pair</u> of half squares as a whole square to find the area shaded.

a)

= _____ whole squares

b)

= _____ whole squares

c)

= _____ whole squares

d)

= _____ whole squares

e)

= _____ whole squares

f)

= _____ whole squares

g)

= _____ whole squares

h)

= _____ whole squares

i)

= _____ whole squares

j)

= _____ whole squares

k)

= _____ whole squares

2. Estimate then find the area of each figure in square units.
    HINT: Draw lines to show all the half squares.

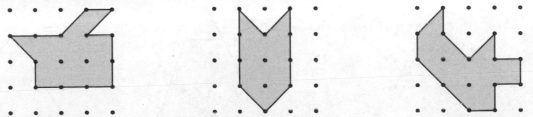

3. For each picture say whether the shaded area is <u>more</u> than, <u>less</u> than or <u>equal</u> to the unshaded area.
    Explain how you know in your notebook.

a)

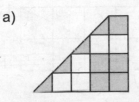

b)

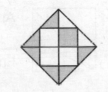

c)

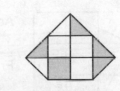

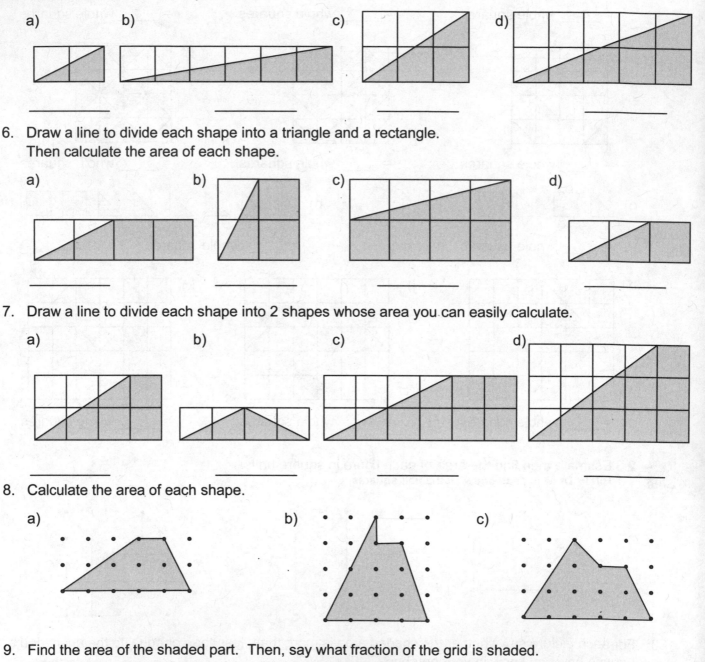

4. a) What fraction of the rectangle is the shaded part?_____

    b) What is the area of the rectangle in square units?_____

    c) What is the area of the shaded part?_____

5. Find the shaded area in square units.

    a)   b)   c)   d)

    _____   _____   _____   _____

6. Draw a line to divide each shape into a triangle and a rectangle.
    Then calculate the area of each shape.

    a)   b)   c)   d)

    _____   _____   _____   _____

7. Draw a line to divide each shape into 2 shapes whose area you can easily calculate.

    a)   b)   c)   d)

    _____   _____   _____   _____

8. Calculate the area of each shape.

    a)   b)   c)

9. Find the area of the shaded part. Then, say what fraction of the grid is shaded.
    HINT: How can you use the area of the unshaded part and the area of the grid?

    a)   Area: b)   Area: c)   Area:

                        _____   _____   _____

                        Fraction: Fraction: Fraction:

                        _____   _____   _____

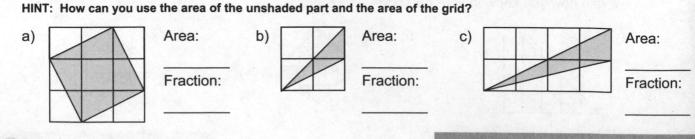

ME5-27: Area of Irregular Shapes and Polygons

1. Each of the shaded shapes below represents ½ a square (whether divided diagonally, vertically or horizontally).
   How many total squares do they add up to? **REMEMBER: Two ½ squares = 1 full square**

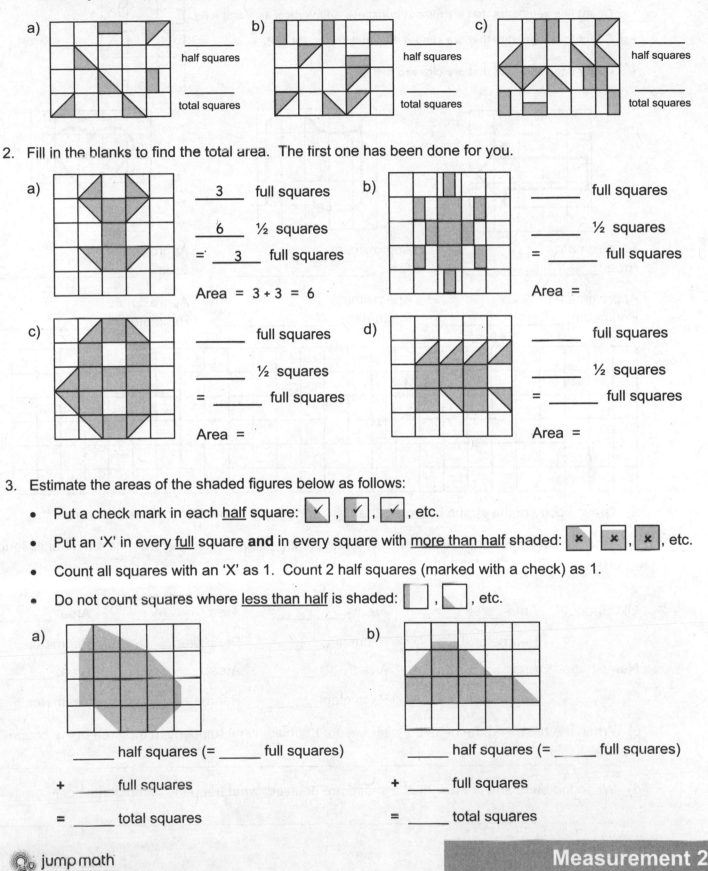

a) _____ half squares

_____ total squares

b) _____ half squares

_____ total squares

c) _____ half squares

_____ total squares

2. Fill in the blanks to find the total area. The first one has been done for you.

a)
_____3_____ full squares

_____6_____ ½ squares

= _____3_____ full squares

Area = 3 + 3 = 6

b)
_____ full squares

_____ ½ squares

= _____ full squares

Area =

c)
_____ full squares

_____ ½ squares

= _____ full squares

Area =

d)
_____ full squares

_____ ½ squares

= _____ full squares

Area =

3. Estimate the areas of the shaded figures below as follows:

- Put a check mark in each <u>half</u> square: ✓ , ✓ , ✓ , etc.

- Put an 'X' in every <u>full</u> square **and** in every square with <u>more than half</u> shaded: ✗ ✗ , ✗ , etc.

- Count all squares with an 'X' as 1. Count 2 half squares (marked with a check) as 1.

- Do not count squares where <u>less than half</u> is shaded: , , etc.

a)
_____ half squares (= _____ full squares)

+ _____ full squares

= _____ total squares

b)
_____ half squares (= _____ full squares)

+ _____ full squares

= _____ total squares

1. Estimate the area (in square units) and perimeter of the shapes below.

    HINT (For Estimating Perimeter):

    *   Count line segments that are almost horizontal and vertical as 1 unit long.

    *   Count line segments that are almost diagonal as $1\frac{1}{2}$ (or 1.5).

    *   Count line segments that are close to half as $\frac{1}{2}$.

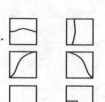

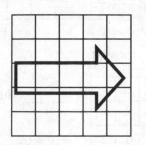
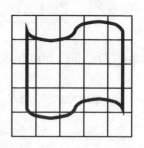

Approximate
Area:_____

Approximate
Area:_____

Approximate
Area:_____

Approximate
Perimeter: _____

Approximate
Perimeter: _____

Approximate
Perimeter: _____

2.

| A | | B | | C | | D |

a) Draw a copy of the shape but make the <u>base</u> and <u>height</u> 2 times as long as the original.

b) Find the perimeter and area of each original shape. (Count each diagonal line as 1.4 units long.)
    Then find the perimeter and area of the new shapes.

	A	B	C	D
Old Shape	Area: _____	Area: _____	Area: _____	Area: _____
	Perimeter: _____	Perimeter: _____	Perimeter: _____	Perimeter: _____
New Shape	Area: _____	Area: _____	Area: _____	Area: _____
	Perimeter: _____	Perimeter: _____	Perimeter: _____	Perimeter: _____

c) When the base and the height of a shape are doubled, what happens to the area of the shape?

    _____

d) When the base and the height of a shape are doubled, what happens to the perimeter?

    _____

ME5-29: Comparing Area and Perimeter

1. For each shape below, calculate the perimeter and area of each shape, and write your answers in the chart below. The first one has been done for you. **NOTE: Each square represents a centimetre.**

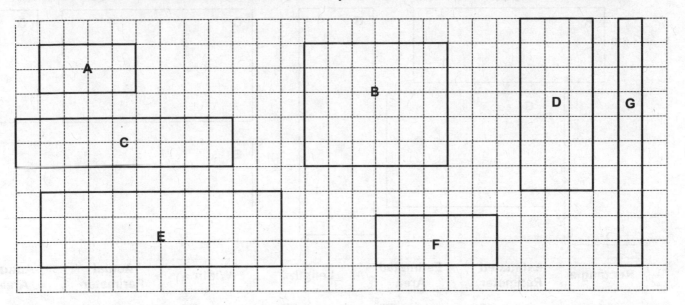

Shape	Perimeter	Area
A	2 + 4 + 4 + 2 = 12 cm	2 x 4 = 8 cm²
B		
C		
D		
E		
F		
G		

2. Shape C has a greater perimeter than shape D. Does it also have greater area? _____

3. Name two other shapes where one has a greater perimeter and the other, a greater area.

   _____

4. Write the shapes in order from greatest to least perimeter: _____

5. Write the shapes in order from greatest to least area: _____

6. Are the orders in Questions 4 and 5 the same? _____

7. What is the difference between PERIMETER and AREA? _____

   _____

   _____

ME5-30: Area and Perimeter

1. Measure the length and width of each rectangle, and then record your answers in the chart below.

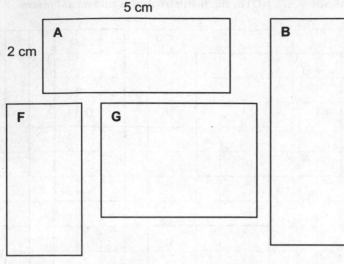

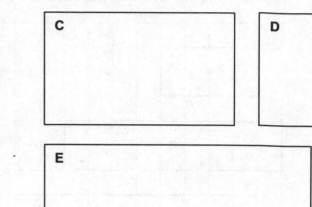

Rectangle	Estimated Perimeter	Estimated Area	Length	Width	Actual Perimeter	Actual Area
A	cm	cm^2	cm	cm	cm	cm^2
B						
C						
D						
E						
F						
G						

2. Find the area of the rectangle using the clues.

    a) Width = 2 cm   Perimeter = 10 cm
       Area = ?

    b) Width = 4 cm   Perimeter = 18 cm
       Area = ?

3. Draw a square on grid paper with the given perimeter. Then find the area of the square.

    a) Perimeter = 12 cm   Area = ?

    b) Perimeter = 20 cm   Area = ?

4. On grid paper or a geoboard, create a rectangle with …

    a) … an area of 10 square units and
       a perimeter of 14 units.

    b) … an area of 8 square units and
       a perimeter of 12 units.

5. The length of a rectangle is increased by 1 and its width is decreased by 1.
    What happens to the perimeter?

Measurement 2

ME5-31: Problems and Puzzles

1. George wants to build a rectangular flower bed in his garden.
    The width of the flower bed will be 3 m and the perimeter will be 14 m.

    a) What is the length of the bed? _____

    b) Show the shape of the flower bed in the grid.

    c) If fencing is $12 a metre, how much will a fence cost?

    _____

    d) George will plant 16 flowers on each square metre of land.
        Each flower is 5¢. How much will the flowers cost?

    _____

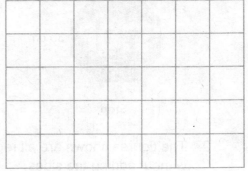

Each edge on the grid represents 1 metre.

    e) If George pays for the flowers with a twenty dollar bill, how much change will he get back?

    _____

2. A rectangle has sides whose lengths are whole numbers.
    Find all the possible lengths and widths for the given area.

Area = 8 cm²	
Width	Length

Area = 14 cm²	
Width	Length

Area = 18 cm²	
Width	Length

3. Name something you would measure in …

    a) square metres _____   b) square kilometres _____

4. Crystal wants to make a rectangular garden with 12 m of fencing.
    What width and length will give the greatest area?

5. Paul wants to make a rectangular patio with 20 square tiles (each of area 1 m²)
    What length and width will give the least perimeter?

6. The length of a rabbit hut is twice its width.
    How could you calculate the perimeter without adding the lengths of the sides?

Answer the following questions in your notebook.

1. What is the perimeter of these signs?

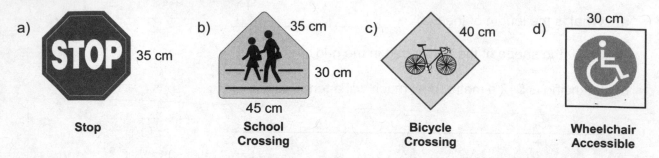

a)

35 cm

Stop

b)

35 cm

30 cm

45 cm

School Crossing

c)

40 cm

Bicycle Crossing

d)

30 cm

Wheelchair Accessible

2. The figures shown are all regular (all sides are the same length). Find the perimeter of each figure without adding the sides.

a)

5 cm

b)

6 cm

c)

8 cm

3.

1 m

50 cm   1 m

a) What is the area of each red rectangle on the flag?
   HINT: Change the measurements to the same unit.

b) What is the area of the flag?

c) What is the perimeter of the flag?

d) About how many flags would cover the blackboard in your classroom?

4. *Example:*

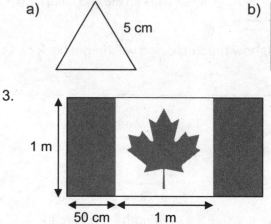

dresser

chair

bed

1 cm { table

1 cm represents 1 m

The diagram shows a floor plan for a bedroom. Find:

a) The perimeter and area of the room.

b) The area of the room covered by furniture.

c) Draw your own floor plan for a room and answer parts a) and b).

5. A square garden has sides of length 6 m.
   Fence posts are placed every 2 metres along the sides of the garden.
   How many fence posts are in the garden?

6. Your thumbnail has an area of about 1 cm².
   Find something in your class or at home that has area about 1 cm².
   Justify your answer.

7. Your arm span has a length of about 1 m.
   Find something in your class with area about 1 m².

ME5-33: Volume

Volume is the amount of space taken up by a three dimensional object.

To measure volume, we can use 1 cm blocks. These blocks are uniform squares with length, width, and height all 1 cm long.

1 cm block
height = 1 cm
length = 1 cm
width = 1 cm

The volume of a container is based on how many of these 1 cm blocks will fit inside the container.

This object, made of centimetre cubes, has a volume of 4 cubes or 4 cubic centimetres (written 4 cm³).

---

1. Using "centicubes" as your unit of measurement, write the <u>volume</u> of each object.

   a)

   Volume = _____ cubes

   b)

   Volume = _____ cubes

   c)

   Volume = _____ cubes

2. Given a structure made of cubes, you can draw a "mat plan" as shown.

3	1	2
1		

   ← The numbers tell you how many cubes are stacked in each position.

   For each figure below, fill in the missing numbers in the mat plan.

   a)

   b)

   c)

   d)

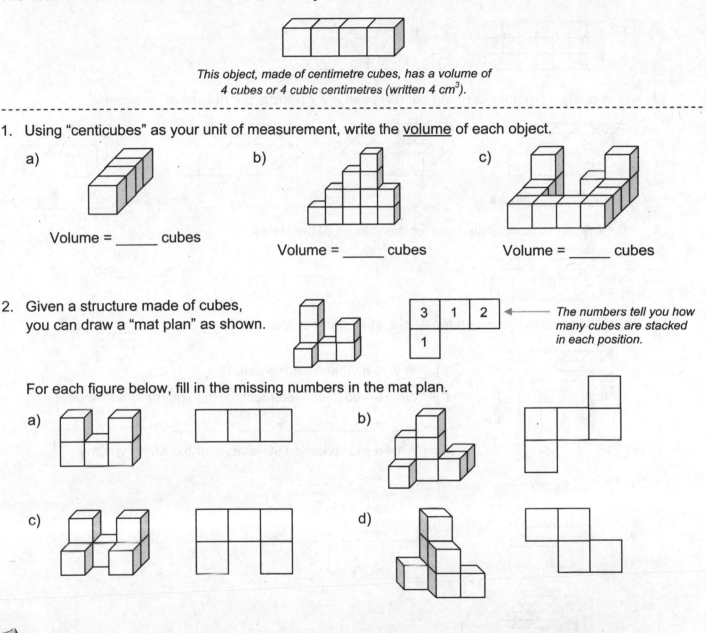

3. On grid paper, draw a mat plan for each of the following structures (use cubes to help).

   a)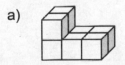

   b)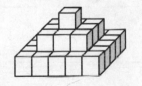

   c)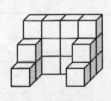

ME5-34: Volume of Rectangular Prisms

1. Use the number of blocks in the shaded column to write an addition statement and a multiplication statement for each area.

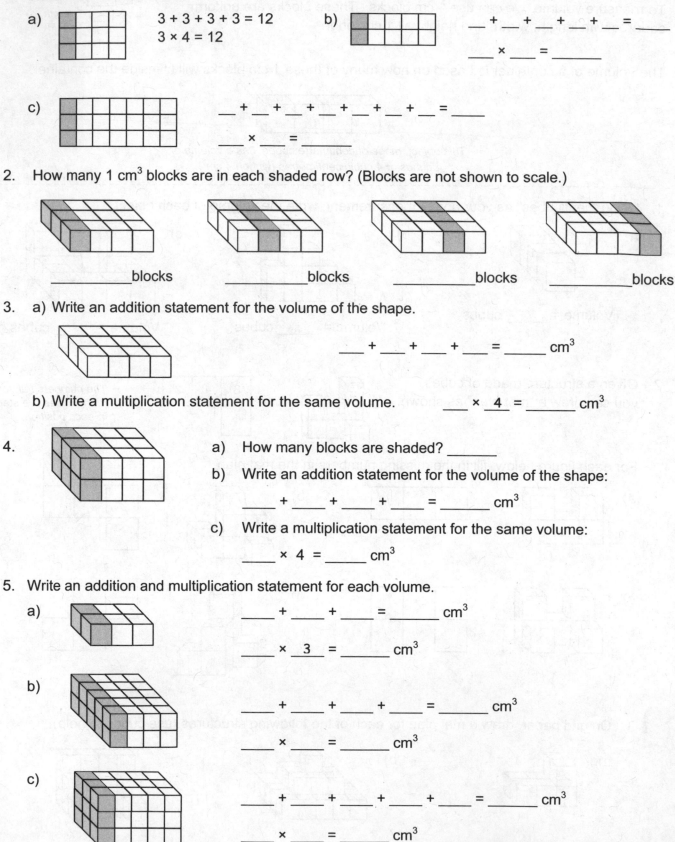

    a)   3 + 3 + 3 + 3 = 12
                3 × 4 = 12

    b)   __ + __ + __ + __ + __ = _____
                ___ × ___ = _____

    c)   __ + __ + __ + __ + __ + __ + __ = _____
                ___ × ___ = _____

2. How many 1 cm³ blocks are in each shaded row? (Blocks are not shown to scale.)

    _____blocks   _____blocks   _____blocks   _____blocks

3. a) Write an addition statement for the volume of the shape.

                ___ + ___ + ___ + ___ = _____ cm³

    b) Write a multiplication statement for the same volume.   ___ × 4 = _____ cm³

4.
    a) How many blocks are shaded? _____

    b) Write an addition statement for the volume of the shape:
        ____ + ____ + ____ + ____ = _____ cm³

    c) Write a multiplication statement for the same volume:
        ____ × 4 = _____ cm³

5. Write an addition and multiplication statement for each volume.

    a)   ____ + ____ + ____ = _____ cm³
                ____ × 3 = _____ cm³

    b)   ____ + ____ + ____ + ____ = _____ cm³
                ____ × ___ = _____ cm³

    c)   ____ + ____ + ____ + ____ + ____ = _____ cm³
                ____ × ___ = _____ cm³

ME5-34: Volume of Rectangular Prisms (continued)

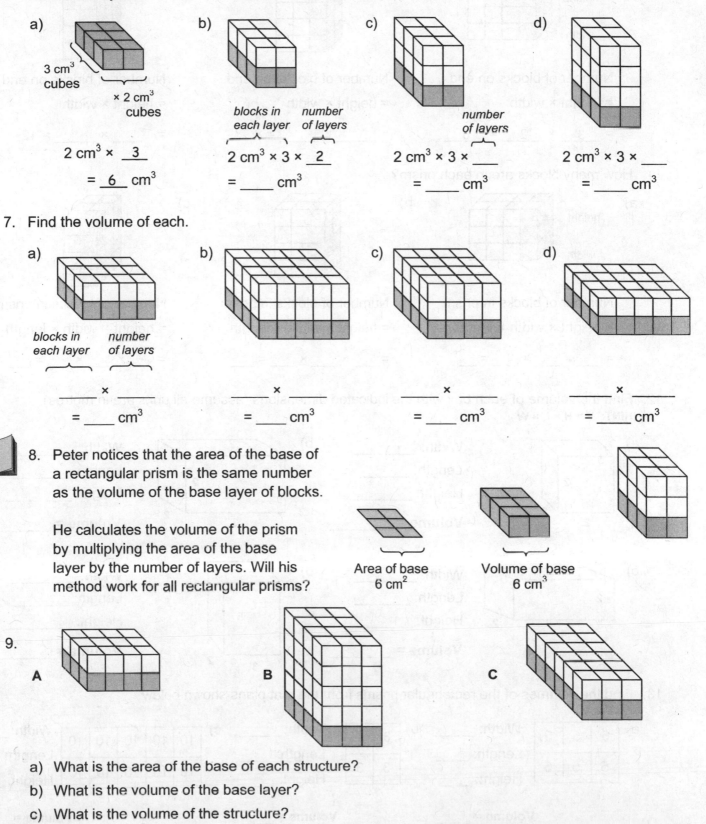

6. Claire stacks blocks to make a tower.

    She finds the number of cubes in each tower by multiplying the number of cubes in the base by the number of layers.

    a)
    3 cm³ cubes

    × 2 cm³ cubes

    $2 \text{ cm}^3 \times \underline{\ 3\ }$
    $= \underline{\ 6\ } \text{ cm}^3$

    b)
    blocks in   number
    each layer   of layers

    $2 \text{ cm}^3 \times 3 \times \underline{\ 2\ }$
    $= \underline{\ \ \ \ } \text{ cm}^3$

    c)
    number
    of layers

    $2 \text{ cm}^3 \times 3 \times \underline{\ \ \ \ }$
    $= \underline{\ \ \ \ } \text{ cm}^3$

    d)
    $2 \text{ cm}^3 \times 3 \times \underline{\ \ \ \ }$
    $= \underline{\ \ \ \ } \text{ cm}^3$

7. Find the volume of each.

    a)
    blocks in   number
    each layer   of layers

    $\underline{\ \ \ } \times \underline{\ \ \ }$
    $= \underline{\ \ \ } \text{ cm}^3$

    b)
    $\underline{\ \ \ } \times \underline{\ \ \ }$
    $= \underline{\ \ \ } \text{ cm}^3$

    c)
    $\underline{\ \ \ } \times \underline{\ \ \ }$
    $= \underline{\ \ \ } \text{ cm}^3$

    d)
    $\underline{\ \ \ } \times \underline{\ \ \ }$
    $= \underline{\ \ \ } \text{ cm}^3$

8. Peter notices that the area of the base of a rectangular prism is the same number as the volume of the base layer of blocks.

    He calculates the volume of the prism by multiplying the area of the base layer by the number of layers. Will his method work for all rectangular prisms?

    Area of base
    6 cm²

    Volume of base
    6 cm³

9.

    A   B   C

    a) What is the area of the base of each structure?
    b) What is the volume of the base layer?
    c) What is the volume of the structure?

jump math
MULTIPLYING POTENTIAL

ME5-34: Volume of Rectangular Prisms (continued)

10. How many blocks are on the end of each prism?

a)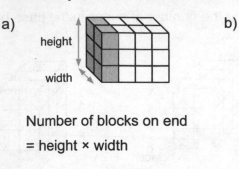

Number of blocks on end

= height × width

= __3__ × __2__ = __6__

b)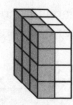

Number of blocks on end

= height × width

= ____ × ____ = 8

c)

Number of blocks on end

= height × width

= ____ × ____ = 12

11. How many blocks are in each prism?

a)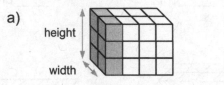

Number of blocks in prism

= height × width × length

= ___ × ___ × ___ = ___

b)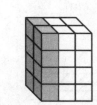

Number of blocks in prism

= height × width × length

= ___ × ___ × ___ = ___

c)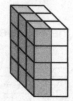

Number of blocks in prism

= height × width × length

= ___ × ___ × ___ = ___

12. Find the volume of each box with the indicated dimensions (assume all units are in metres).
    HINT: V = H × L × W

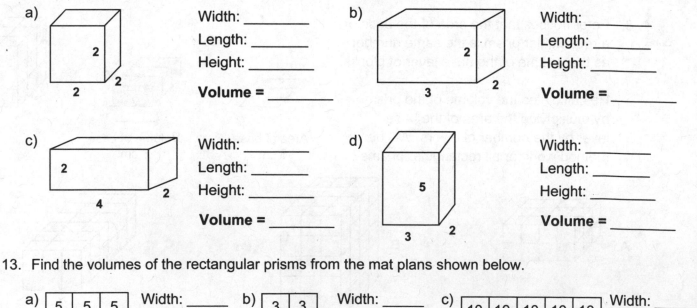

a)

2
2
2

Width: _____
Length: _____
Height: _____
Volume = _____

b)

2
3
2

Width: _____
Length: _____
Height: _____
Volume = _____

c)

2
4
2

Width: _____
Length: _____
Height: _____
Volume = _____

d)

5
3   2

Width: _____
Length: _____
Height: _____
Volume = _____

13. Find the volumes of the rectangular prisms from the mat plans shown below.

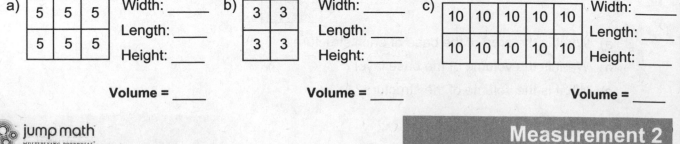

a)

5	5	5
5	5	5

Width: _____
Length: ____
Height: ____

Volume = ____

b)

3	3
3	3

Width: _____
Length: ____
Height: ____

Volume = ____

c)

10	10	10	10	10
10	10	10	10	10

Width: _____
Length: ____
Height: ____

Volume = ____

ME5-35: Mass

Mass measures the amount of substance in a thing. Grams (g) and kilograms (kg) are units for measuring weight or mass.

One kilogram is equal to 1 000 grams.

Things that weigh about one <u>gram</u>:
✓ A paper clip
✓ A dime
✓ A chocolate chip

Things that weigh about one <u>kilogram</u>:
✓ A one litre bottle of water
✓ A bag of 200 nickels
✓ A squirrel

---

1. Estimate the weight of the following things, in grams.
    REMEMBER: A 1 litre bottle of water weighs 1 kg or 1000 g.

    a) a pencil _____   b) an orange _____   c) this workbook _____

2. Can you name an object that weighs about one gram? _____

3.

Penny	2.5 grams
Nickel	4 grams
Dime	2 gram
Quarter	4.5 grams
Loonie	7 grams

a) How much would 35¢ in nickels weigh? _____

b) How much would 12 dimes weigh? _____

c) How much would $1.00 in quarters weigh? _____

d) How much would 50 loonies weigh? _____

e) How many quarters weigh as much as 12 nickels? _____

f) How many pennies would weigh as much as 2 nickels? _____

4. Estimate the weight of the following things in kilograms:

    a) your math book _____   b) your desk _____   c) a bicycle _____

What unit is more appropriate to measure each item? Circle the appropriate unit.

5.

grams or kilograms?

grams or kilograms?

grams or kilograms?

6.

grams or kilograms?

grams or kilograms?

grams or kilograms?

7. Order (by letter) the following from <u>greatest to least</u> mass.

A. dog   **B.** mouse   **C.** giraffe   _____ , _____ , _____

8. Check off the appropriate box. Would you use grams or kilograms to weigh ...

a) a computer?   ☐ **g** ☐ **kg**   b) a bed?   ☐ **g** ☐ **kg**

c) a piece of bread?   ☐ **g** ☐ **kg**   d) a frog?   ☐ **g** ☐ **kg**

e) a pen?   ☐ **g** ☐ **kg**   f) an apple?   ☐ **g** ☐ **kg**

9. Write in the missing masses to balance the scales.

a)
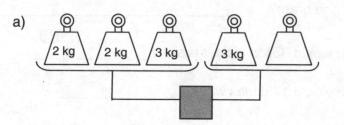

b)
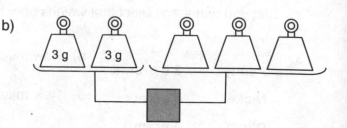

10. 1 kilogram = 1 000 grams

    1 kilometre = 1 000 metres

    Looking at the equations above, what do you think the Greek word "kilo" means?

11. a) The cost of shipping a package is $3.00 for each kilogram shipped.

    How much does it cost to ship a package that weighs 14 kilograms?

    b) A rat has a mass of about 60 grams. What is the mass of 5 rats?

12. What do you need to multiply a measurement in kilograms by to change it to grams?

    c) There are 260 trout in the pond, and each weighs approximately two kilograms.

    What is the total weight of all the trout in the pond?

13. Write an estimate of your weight ...

    a) in kilograms

    b) in grams

14. A baby has a mass of 4 500 grams, which is the same as 4.5 kg.

    Another baby has a mass of 3 500 grams. What is its mass in kg?

15. A matchbox has a mass of 20 g.

    The mass of the match box alone is 8 g.

    If there are 6 matches in the box, what is the mass of each match?

The **capacity** of a container is how much it can hold.
The capacity of a regular carton of milk is 1 L.

Litres (L) and millilitres (mL) are the basic units for measuring capacity → 1 litre (L) = 1000 millilitres (mL)

Some sample capacities:

1 teaspoon = 5 mL	1 can of pop = 350 mL	1 regular carton of juice = 1 L
1 tube of toothpaste = 75 mL	1 large bottle of shampoo = 750 mL	1 large can of paint = 3 to 5 L

- -

1. Check off the appropriate box. Would you use millilitres (mL) or litres (L) to measure ...

    a) a glass of water?   ☐ **mL**   ☐ **L**   b) a rain drop?   ☐ **mL**   ☐ **L**

    c) a bath tub?   ☐ **mL**   ☐ **L**   d) a bucket of ice cream?   ☐ **mL**   ☐ **L**

    e) a swimming pool?   ☐ **mL**   ☐ **L**   f) a medicine bottle?   ☐ **mL**   ☐ **L**

2. Circle the appropriate unit to measure the capacity of each container. Is it litres (L) or millilitres (mL)?

    a)   L or mL?   b)   L or mL?

    c)   L or mL?   d)   L or mL?

3.

2 L — A
3 L — B
5 L — C

   a) How many containers of size C would hold 20 L?

   b) How many containers of size A would hold as much
       water as 4 containers of size B?

   c) Which will hold more, 4 containers of size B or
       3 containers of size C?

4. For each of the following capacities, how many containers would be needed to make a litre? Explain.

    a) 100 mL   b) 200 mL   c) 500 mL   d) 250 mL

5. Jenna bought:

    - 2 L of juice   - a 500 mL bottle of canola oil   - a 1.5 L bottle of soda

    What is the total capacity of the items in mL?

ME5-37: Volume and Capacity

A **centicube** has height, length, and width of 1 cm. Its volume is 1 cm³.

A centicube will displace 1 mL of liquid.

1 cm   1 cm cubed **OR** 1 cm³

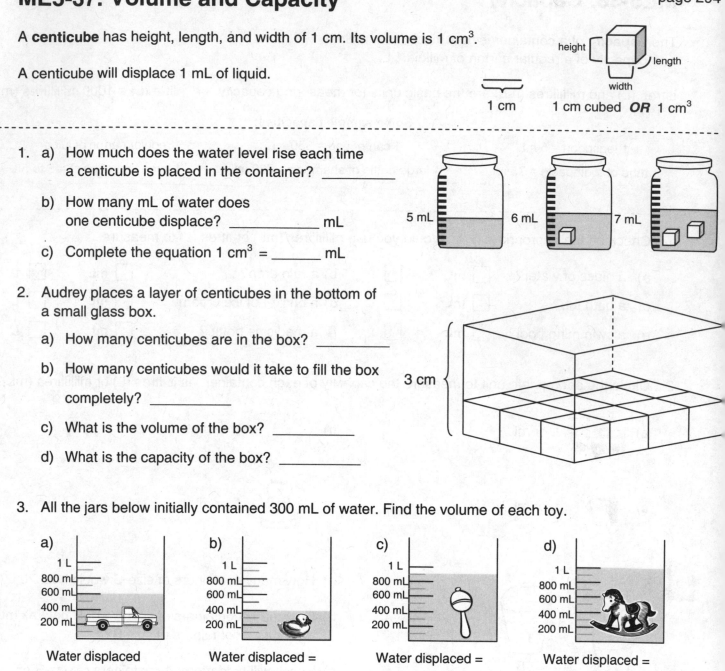

1. a) How much does the water level rise each time
   a centicube is placed in the container? _____

   b) How many mL of water does
   one centicube displace? _____ mL

   c) Complete the equation 1 cm³ = _____ mL

   5 mL   6 mL   7 mL

2. Audrey places a layer of centicubes in the bottom of
   a small glass box.

   a) How many centicubes are in the box? _____

   b) How many centicubes would it take to fill the box
   completely? _____

   c) What is the volume of the box? _____

   d) What is the capacity of the box? _____

   3 cm

3. All the jars below initially contained 300 mL of water. Find the volume of each toy.

   a)

   1 L
   800 mL
   600 mL
   400 mL
   200 mL

   Water displaced

   _____300 mL_____

   Volume of toy =

   _____300 cm³_____

   b)

   1 L
   800 mL
   600 mL
   400 mL
   200 mL

   Water displaced =

   _____

   Volume of toy =

   _____

   c)

   1 L
   800 mL
   600 mL
   400 mL
   200 mL

   Water displaced =

   _____

   Volume of toy =

   _____

   d)

   1 L
   800 mL
   600 mL
   400 mL
   200 mL

   Water displaced =

   _____

   Volume of toy =

   _____

4. Why would it be difficult to measure the volume of the container
   shown using Audrey's method in Question 2?

5. The water level in a jar rises from 200 mL to 500 mL when some strawberries are immersed in it.
   What is the strawberries' volume?

jump math
MULTIPLYING POTENTIAL

Measurement 2

ME5-38: Changing Units of Measurement

1. Change the amount given from dollars and cents to cents.

   a) 3 dollars 27 cents = _____327 cents_____   b) 8 dollars 16 cents = _____

   c) 9 dollars 2 cents = _____   d) 3 dollars 7 cents = _____

2. Change the measurement from metres and centimetres to centimetres.

   a) 5 m 1 cm = _____501 cm_____   b) 3 m 8 cm = _____   c) 7 m 14 cm = _____

   d) 9 m 48 cm = _____   e) 16 m 10 cm = _____   f) 1 m 2 cm = _____

3. Change the measurement from kilometres and metres to metres.

   a) 8 km 5 m = ____8005 m____   b) 3 km 62 m = _____   c) 9 km 6 m = _____

   d) 5 km 7 m = _____   e) 12 km 327 m = _____   f) 19 km 1 m = _____

4. Change from hours and minutes to minutes. Remember, there are 60 minutes in an hour.

   a) 2 h 2 min = ____122 min____   b) 1 h 5 min = _____   c) 2 h 10 min = _____

   d) 3 h 15 min = _____   e) 3 h 48 min = _____   f) 4 h 25 min = _____

BONUS
5. Change each amount to a decimal in the larger unit.

   a) $9 and 2¢ = ____$9.02____   b) $18 and 3¢ = _____   c) $57 and 2¢ = _____

   d) 9 m 7 cm = _____   e) 5 m 27 cm = _____   f) 5 cm 2 mm = _____

   g) 6 dm 1 cm = _____   h) 7 L 2 mL = _____   i) 8 kg 27 g = _____

6. A sunflower can grow about 3 cm in a day.
   About how many months will it take to reach 3 metres?

1. Move enough blocks so that all stacks have the same number of blocks in each stack.
   The **mean** is the number of blocks in each stack.

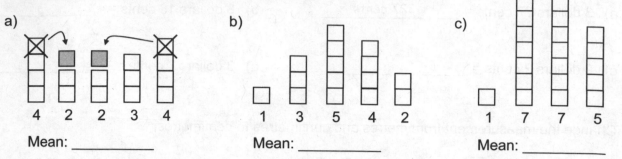

a) 4 2 2 3 4

Mean: _____

b) 1 3 5 4 2

Mean: _____

c) 1 7 7 5

Mean: _____

2. Shade the number of blocks given.
   Move blocks to find the mean. (Show your work with a different shading.)

a) 1 6 4 1

Mean: ____3____

b) 2 7 4 5 7

Mean: _____

c) 7 5 0 3 4 5

Mean: _____

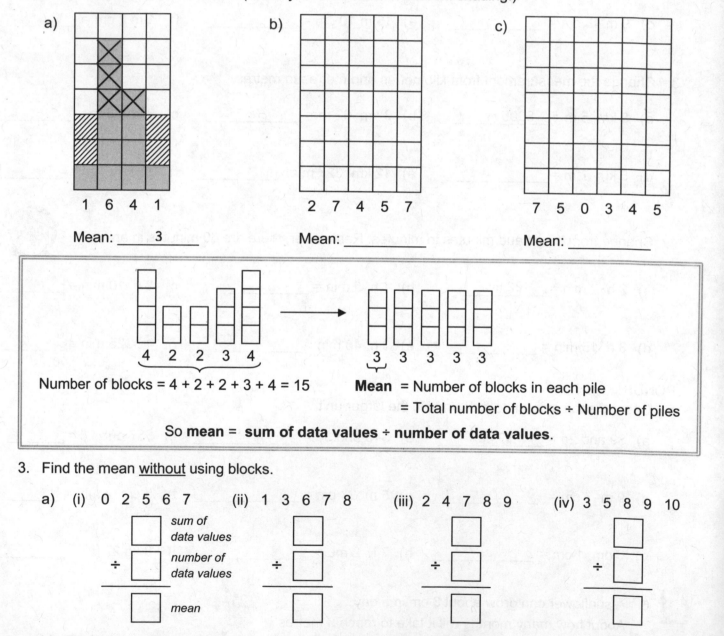

4 2 2 3 4

Number of blocks = 4 + 2 + 2 + 3 + 4 = 15

3 3 3 3 3

Mean = Number of blocks in each pile
       = Total number of blocks ÷ Number of piles

So **mean = sum of data values ÷ number of data values**.

3. Find the mean <u>without</u> using blocks.

a) (i) 0 2 5 6 7   (ii) 1 3 6 7 8   (iii) 2 4 7 8 9   (iv) 3 5 8 9 10

[ ] *sum of data values*

÷ [ ] *number of data values*

———

[ ] *mean*

b) Explain how the mean changes when you add 1 to each data value.

PDM5-14: Finding the Mean

1. Find the mean and draw a horizontal line to show it.

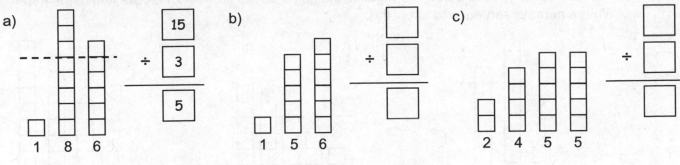

2. Count the blocks above the mean and the spaces below the mean.

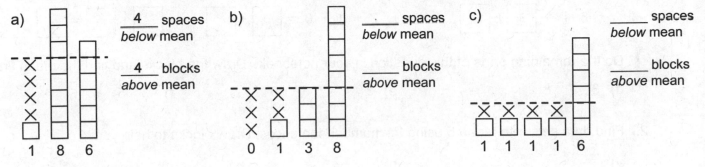

a) __4__ spaces *below* mean

__4__ blocks *above* mean

b) ____ spaces *below* mean

____ blocks *above* mean

c) ____ spaces *below* mean

____ blocks *above* mean

3. Look at your answers to Question 2. What do you notice? Explain.

_____

4. Naima draws a line to guess where the mean is. Is her guess too high or too low?

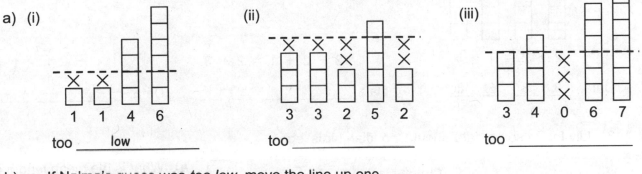

a) (i) too ___low___

(ii) too _____

(iii) too _____

b) • If Naima's guess was *too low*, move the line up one.
   • If her guess was *too high*, move the line down one.
   • Then check to see if you have found the mean.

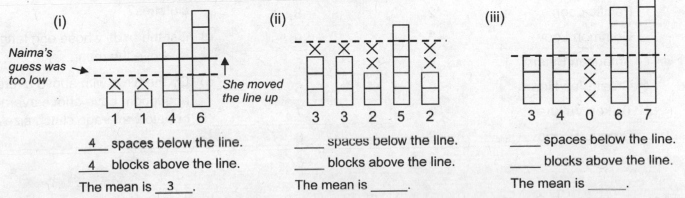

(i) Naima's guess was too low → She moved the line up

__4__ spaces below the line.

__4__ blocks above the line.

The mean is __3__.

(ii) ____ spaces below the line.

____ blocks above the line.

The mean is ____.

(iii) ____ spaces below the line.

____ blocks above the line.

The mean is ____.

 jump math
MULTIPLYING POTENTIAL

Probability & Data Management 2

PDM5-15: Mean (Advanced)

1. The number of spaces below the mean is the same as the number of blocks above the mean. Write a number sentence to show this.

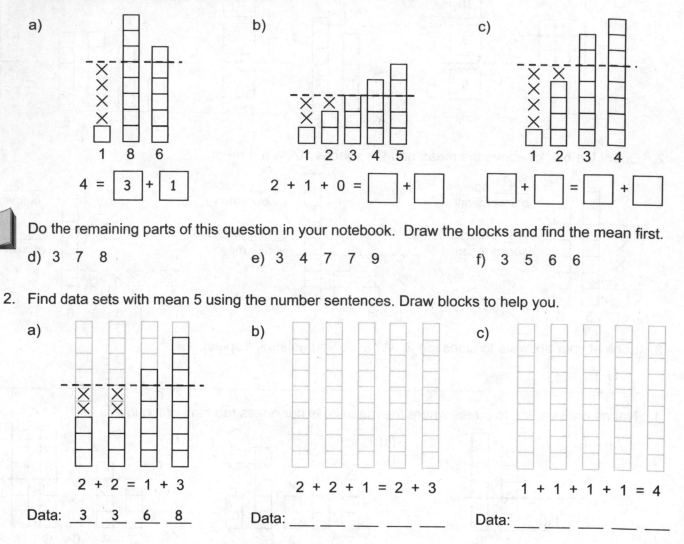

a)

1   8   6

4 = [3] + [1]

b)

1   2   3   4   5

2 + 1 + 0 = [ ] + [ ]

c)

1   2   3   4

[ ] + [ ] = [ ] + [ ]

Do the remaining parts of this question in your notebook. Draw the blocks and find the mean first.

d) 3 7 8   e) 3 4 7 7 9   f) 3 5 6 6

2. Find data sets with mean 5 using the number sentences. Draw blocks to help you.

a)

2 + 2 = 1 + 3

Data: _3_ _3_ _6_ _8_

b)

2 + 2 + 1 = 2 + 3

Data: ___ ___ ___ ___ ___

c)

1 + 1 + 1 + 1 = 4

Data: ___ ___ ___ ___ ___

3. Lily found some data about Canadian birds' eggs.

Bird	Clutch size (number of eggs in the nest)	Egg length (cm)
Pacific Loon	2	8
Common Loon	3	9
American Bittern	4	5
Great Blue Heron	6	6
Turkey Vulture	2	7
Greater Scaup	8	6
Snow Goose	3	8

a) What is the mean length of the eggs?

b) What is the mean size of the clutches?

c) List the birds whose egg length is above the mean.

d) Do the birds with above average egg length have above average or below average clutch size?

jump math
MULTIPLYING POTENTIAL.

PDM5-16: Stem and Leaf Plots

The **leaf** of a number is its right-most digit.

The **stem** is all its digits <u>except</u> the right-most digit.

NOTE: The stem of a one-digit number is 0 since there are no digits except the right-most one.

(48)<u>7</u>

↗ stem   ↖ leaf

----

1. Circle the stem and underline the leaf.

   a) <u>5</u> *no stem*　　b) (3)<u>7</u>　　　　c) 1 2 3　　　　d) 3 1　　　　e) 9 0 0 0

   f) 8 7 2　　　　g) 8 3　　　　h) 8 3 1　　　　i) 8 3 1 0　　　　j) 4 0 7 1

2. For each group of numbers, cross out the numbers that have the same stem.

   a) 78　74　94　　　　b) 89　90　91　　　　c) 291　287　28　29

3. In each group of numbers, circle the stems and write the stems from smallest to largest.

   a) (1)3　9　8　(2)4　(6)4　(1)8　(2)5　　b) 26　29　48　53　27　9　44　　c) 102　98　86　76　103　95

   <u> 0 </u>　<u> 1 </u>　<u> 2 </u>　<u> 6 </u>　　　　　　___ ___ ___ ___　　　　___ ___ ___ ___

4. Here is how you can make a stem and leaf plot for the data set 38 29 26 42 43 34:

Step 1:			Step 2:			Step 3:		
Write the stems in order, from smallest to largest.	stem	leaf	Then write each leaf in the same row as its stem:	stem	leaf	Finally put the leaves in each row in order, from smallest to largest.	stem	leaf
	2			2	96		2	69
	3			3	84		3	48
	4			4	23		4	23

For each plot, put the leaves in the correct order. Then list the data from smallest to largest.

a)

stem	leaf
2	41
3	856
5	32

→

stem	leaf
2	14
3	
5	

b)

stem	leaf
0	4
1	95
2	380

→

stem	leaf

<u> 21 </u>　<u> 24 </u>　___ ___ ___ ___　　　　___ ___ ___ ___ ___ ___

5. Use the following data to create stem and leaf plots.

   a) 9 7 12 19 10　　　　b) 99 98 102 99 101　　　　c) 88 91 104 98 110 111 96 87

6. Numbers with the same stem must have the same number of digits. True or false? Explain.

PDM5-17: The Mode, Median, and Range

1. To find the **median** of a data set, put the data in order. Count from either end until you reach the middle.

   2   3   ⑥   7   11   2   3   (7   9)   11   15
   The median is 6.   *The median is half way between 7 and 9.*
                               The median is 8.

   Circle the middle number or numbers. Then find the median.

   a) 2 4 6 7 8   b) 2 3 3 8   c) 7 9 13 14 26   d) 3 4 6 10 11 17

2. Stem and leaf plots make it easy to find the smallest and largest data values.

   (i)   Look for the <u>smallest</u> leaf in the <u>first</u> row to find the **smallest** data value.

   (ii) Look for the <u>largest</u> leaf in the <u>last</u> row to find the **largest** data value.

   (iii) Then find the **range (**the difference between the largest and the smallest value).

   a)
stem	leaf
8	244
9	89
10	014

   Smallest: __82__
   Largest: __104__
   Range: __22__

   b)
stem	leaf
0	569
1	247
2	13

   Smallest: ____
   Largest: ____
   Range: ____

   c)
stem	leaf
9	569
10	188
12	2

   Smallest: ____
   Largest: ____
   Range: ____

3. Is the data spread out more above or below the median?

   a) 3 4 4 (4) 5 9 11

   range *below* median: [4] – [3] = [1]

   range *above* median: [11] – [4] = [7]

   The data is spread out more ___above___ the median.
   above/below

   b) 13 17 20 25 26 27 30

   range *below* median: [ ] – [ ] = [ ]

   range *above* median: [ ] – [ ] = [ ]

   The data is spread out more _____ the median.
   above/below

4. Anna's marks on 10 tests were: 4   6   6   6   6   6   9   12   11   14

   a) Create a stem and leaf plot for the data.

   b) Which value is hardest to read from the stem and leaf plot?

      • range   • mean   • median   • mode (the value that occurs the most often)

      Explain.

   c) Find the mean and median. Describe the data. Is it spread out more …

      (i) above or below the mean?   (ii) above or below the median?

PDM5-18: Choices in Data Representation

1. In the first week of April, Mandy kept track of the number of robins she saw on her walk to school.

	Monday	Tuesday	Wednesday	Thursday	Friday
Number of Robins	2	3	5	9	11

a) Do you notice a trend through the week? If so, what is it? _____

_____

b) Draw a line graph to display her findings. Don't forget to include a title and clear labels!

2. Draw a bar graph to display the following data. Choose your scale carefully.

City	Edmonton (E)	Ottawa (O)	Montreal (M)	Washington (W)	Beijing (B)
Average annual snowfall (cm)	130	222	214	42	30

3. Sonia's math test scores (out of 100) for the year were …

Test #	1	2	3	4	5	6	7	8	9	10
Mark	68	75	82	78	75	78	78	86	93	91

a) Draw a stem and leaf plot and a broken line graph for the scores.

b) Answer the following questions and say which graph you used to find the answer.

(i) On how many tests did she score between 70 and 80?

(ii) What mark did she score most often?

(iii) Did her mark tend to increase or decrease throughout the year?

(iv) What was her highest score?

(v) Which graph makes it easier to …

A. find the number of data values between 70 and 80?

B. see a trend in the marks?

C. see the most frequent value?

The different ways an event can happen are called **outcomes** of the event.

When Alice plays a game of cards with a friend, there are 3 possible outcomes: Alice (1) wins, (2) loses or (3) the game ends without a winner or a loser (this is sometimes called a <u>tie</u> or a <u>draw</u>).

REMEMBER: A coin has 2 sides, heads and tails.   A die has six sides, numbered 1 to 6.

----

1. Fill in the chart.

		Possible Outcomes	Number of Outcomes
a)	1 2 / 3 4	You spin a 1, 2, 3 or 4	4
b)	1¢		
c)	The final game of the Stanley Cup.		
d)	(die)		
e)	6 • 9		
f)	• 6		

2. You draw a marble from a box. How many different outcomes are there in each of the following cases?

a)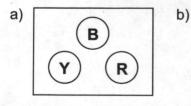

b)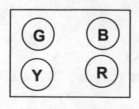

_____ outcomes   _____ outcomes

3. List all the outcomes that are …

a) even numbers

b) odd numbers

c) greater than 5

PDM5-20: Describing Probability

- If an event cannot happen it is **impossible**.
  For example: Rolling the number 8 on a die is <u>impossible</u> (since a die only has the numbers 1, 2, 3, 4, 5, and 6 on its faces).

- If an event <u>must</u> happen it is **certain**.
  For example: When you roll a die, it is <u>certain</u> that you will roll a number less than 7.

- It is **likely** that you would spin yellow on the spinner shown (since more than half the area of the spinner is yellow).

- It is **unlikely** that you would spin red on the spinner shown (since there is only a small section of the spinner that is red).

- When an event is expected to occur exactly half the time, we say that there is an **even** chance of the event occurring.
  For example: When you flip a coin, there is an <u>even</u> chance of flipping heads or tails.

----

1. Complete each statement by writing "more than half", "half" or "less than half".
   HINT: Start by finding half of the number.

   a) 2 is _____ of 6

   b) 5 is _____ of 9

   c) 7 is _____ of 10

   d) 4 is _____ of 8

   e) 5 is _____ of 11

   f) 6 is _____ of 15

   g) 5 is _____ of 12

   h) 9 is _____ of 16

2. What fraction of your spins would you expect to be red: "even," "more than half," or "less than half"?

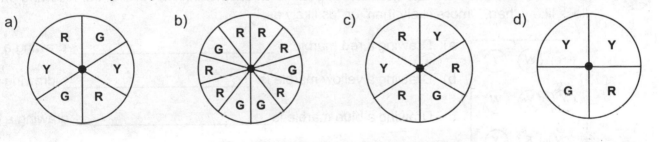

   _____   _____   _____   _____

3. Describe each event as "even," "likely" or "unlikely."

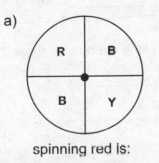

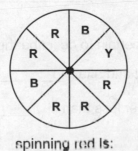

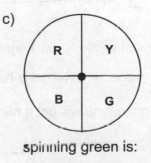

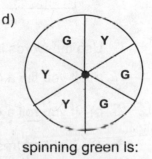

   spinning red is: spinning red is: spinning green is: spinning green is:

   _____   _____   _____   _____

4. Using the words "certain", "likely", "unlikely" or "impossible", describe the likelihood of...

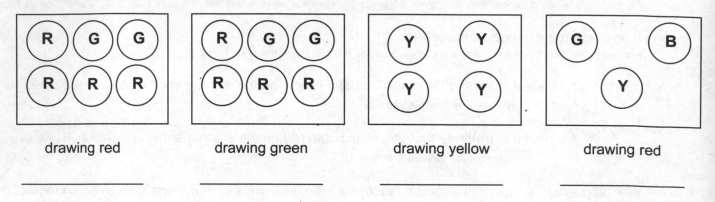

drawing red   drawing green   drawing yellow   drawing red

_____ _____ _____ _____

5. Describe each outcome as "impossible", "unlikely", "likely" or "certain."

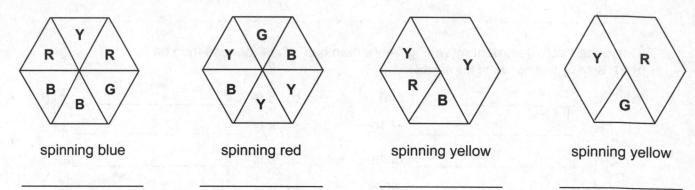

spinning blue   spinning red   spinning yellow   spinning yellow

_____ _____ _____ _____

6. Count the number of marbles of each colour. Fill in each blank with one of the following phrases: "less likely than," "more likely than" or "as likely as."

a) Drawing a red marble is _____ drawing a green.

b) Drawing a yellow marble is _____ drawing a red.

c) Drawing a blue marble is _____ drawing a green.

d) Drawing a white marble is _____ drawing a blue.

e) Drawing a red marble is _____ drawing a white.

7. Use the words impossible, likely, unlikely or certain to describe the following events.

a) If you flip a coin once, you will get a head and a tail. _____

b) If you roll a die once, you will get a number less than six. _____

c) Eight metres of snow will fall today. _____

NOTE: You can show the likelihood of events using a **probability line**.

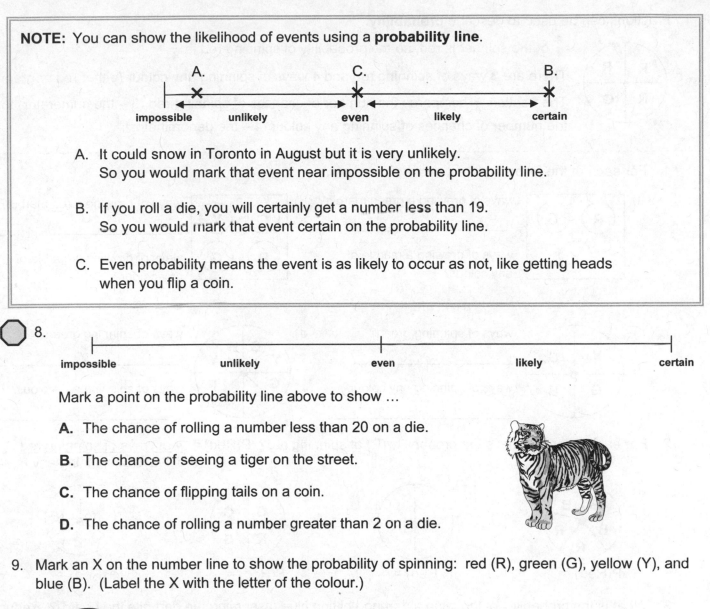

A. × — impossible   unlikely
C. × — even
B. × — likely   certain

A. It could snow in Toronto in August but it is very unlikely.
So you would mark that event near impossible on the probability line.

B. If you roll a die, you will certainly get a number less than 19.
So you would mark that event certain on the probability line.

C. Even probability means the event is as likely to occur as not, like getting heads when you flip a coin.

8.

| impossible | unlikely | even | likely | certain |

Mark a point on the probability line above to show …

A. The chance of rolling a number less than 20 on a die.

B. The chance of seeing a tiger on the street.

C. The chance of flipping tails on a coin.

D. The chance of rolling a number greater than 2 on a die.

9. Mark an X on the number line to show the probability of spinning: red (R), green (G), yellow (Y), and blue (B). (Label the X with the letter of the colour.)

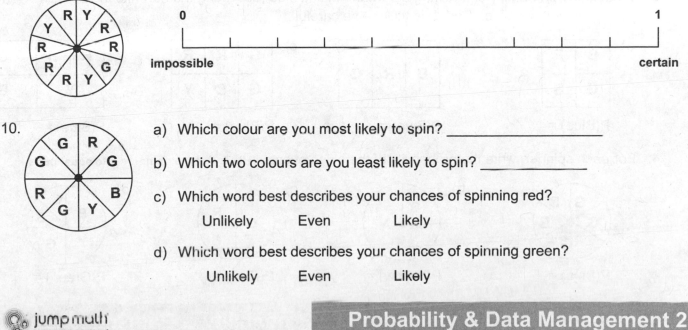

0   1

impossible   certain

10.

a) Which colour are you most likely to spin? _____

b) Which two colours are you least likely to spin? _____

c) Which word best describes your chances of spinning red?
    Unlikely   Even   Likely

d) Which word best describes your chances of spinning green?
    Unlikely   Even   Likely

PDM5-21: Probability

Fractions can be used to describe **probability**.

$\frac{3}{4}$ of the spinner is red, so the probability of spinning red is $\frac{3}{4}$.

There are 3 ways of spinning red and 4 ways of spinning any colour (either red or green).

The fraction $\frac{3}{4}$ compares the number of chances of spinning red (3 – the numerator) to the number of chances of spinning any colour (4 – the denominator).

---

1. For each of the following situations, how many …

   a) ways of drawing a green marble?
   _____

   ways of drawing a marble of any colour?
   _____

   b) ways of drawing a red marble?
   _____

   ways of drawing a marble of any colour?
   _____

   c) ways of spinning green?
   _____

   ways of spinning any colour?
   _____

   d) ways of spinning green?
   _____

   ways of spinning any colour?
   _____

2. For each spinner, what's the probability (P) of spinning red? P(Red) = $\frac{\text{\# of ways of spinning red}}{\text{\# of ways of spinning any colour}}$

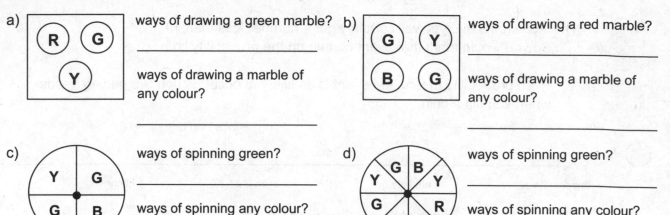

   a) P(Red) =   b) P(Red) =   c) P(Red) =   d) P(Red) =

3. What is the probability of throwing a dart and hitting blue (assuming the dart hits the board)? Reduce your answer if possible. Part d) is tricky – be careful.

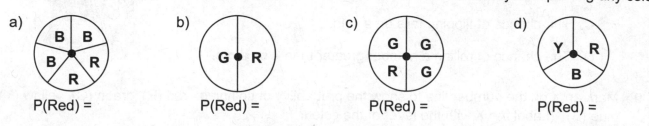

   a) P(Blue) =   b) P(Blue) =   c) P(Blue) =   d) P(Blue) =

4. For each spinner, write the probability of the given events. **HINT: Cut the spinners into equal parts.**

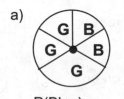

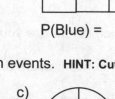
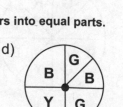

   a) P(Blue) =   b) P(Yellow) =   c) P(Red) =   d) P(Green) =

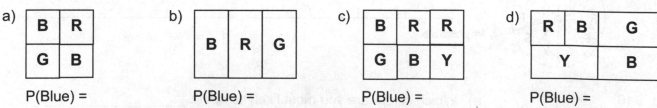

jump math
MULTIPLYING POTENTIAL

Probability & Data Management 2

PDM5-21: Probability (continued)

REMEMBER: A die has the numbers from 1 to 6 on its faces.

5. a) List the numbers on a die.

    b) How many outcomes are there when you roll a die?

6. a) List the numbers on a die that are even.

    b) How many ways can you roll an even number on a die?

    c) What is the probability of rolling an even number on a die?

7. a) List the numbers on a die that are greater than 4.

    b) How many ways can you roll a number greater than 4?

    c) What is the probability of rolling a number greater than 4 on a die?

8. a) List the numbers on a die that are less than 3.

    What is the probability of rolling a number less than 3 on a die?

    b) List the numbers on a die that are odd.

    What is the probability of rolling an odd number on a die?

    c) List the numbers on a die that are multiples of 3.

    What is the probability of rolling a multiple of 3 on a die?

9. Write a fraction that gives the probability of spinning …

    Spinner with numbers: 1, 3, 7, 1, 6, 5, 9, 4

    a) the number 1.
    b) the number 3.
    c) an even number.
    d) an odd number.
    e) a number less than 5.
    f) a number greater than 5.

10. Write a fraction that gives the probability of spinning …

    Spinner with letters: A, E, C, T, A

    a) the letter A.
    b) the letter C.
    c) the letter E.
    d) a vowel.
    e) a consonant.
    f) a letter that appears in the word "Canada,"

11. Design a spinner on which the probability of spinning red is $\frac{3}{8}$.

1. A game of chance is <u>fair</u> if both players have the same chance of winning. Which of the following games are fair? For the games that aren't fair, who has the better chance of winning?

a)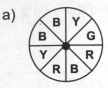

Player 1 must spin red to win.

Player 2 must spin blue to win.

Is it fair?   Y   N

b)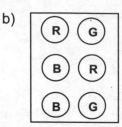

Player 1 must draw red to win.

Player 2 must draw blue to win.

Is it fair?   Y   N

2. Imogen throws a dart at the board. Write the probability of the dart landing on each colour.

P(R) = _____

P(G) = _____

P(Y) = _____

P(B) = _____

R		
G	Y	R
B		

3. Write letters A, B, and C on the spinner so that the probability of spinning …

A is .3.

B is .5.

C is .2.

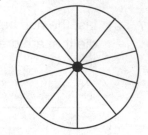

4. When two or more events have the same chance of occurring, the events are <u>equally</u> likely.

Are your chances of spinning red and yellow equally likely? Explain.

a)

b)

5. a) How many children are in the class?

   b) A child is picked to make the morning announcement.

      (i) What is the probability the child is a girl?

      (ii) What is the probability the child is a 9-year-old boy?

   c) Make up your own problem using the numbers in the chart.

Age	Number of Boys in a Class	Number of Girls in a Class
9	2	1
10	5	3
11	4	7

Kate plans to spin the spinner 15 times to see how many times it will land on yellow.

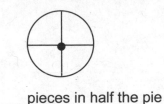

$\frac{1}{3}$ of the spinner is yellow. Kate **expects** to spin yellow $\frac{1}{3}$ of the time. Kate finds $\frac{1}{3}$ of 15 by dividing by 3: $15 \div 3 = 5$. She expects the spinner to land on yellow 5 times.

(The spinner may not actually land on yellow 5 times, but 5 is the <u>most likely</u> number of spins.)

----

1. Shade <u>half</u> of the pie. How many pieces are in the pie? How many pieces are in half the pie?

a)

b)

c)

_____ pieces in half the pie

_____ pieces in the pie

_____ pieces in half the pie

_____ pieces in the pie

_____ pieces in half the pie

_____ pieces in the pie

2.

	Number of pieces in a pie	How many pieces make half?
a)	4	
b)	8	
c)	12	

3. Write the number of pieces in the pie and the number of pieces shaded.
   Then circle the pies where <u>half</u> the pieces are shaded.

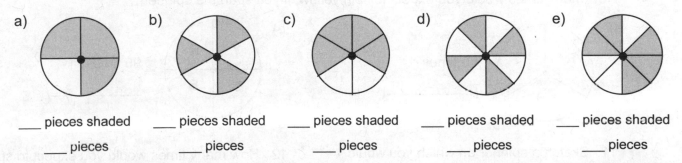

a)

b)

c)

d)

e)

___ pieces shaded

___ pieces

___ pieces shaded

___ pieces

___ pieces shaded

___ pieces

___ pieces shaded

___ pieces

___ pieces shaded

___ pieces

4. Circle the pies where half the pieces are shaded. Put a large 'X' through the pies where less than half the pieces are shaded.
   HINT: Count the shaded and unshaded pieces first.

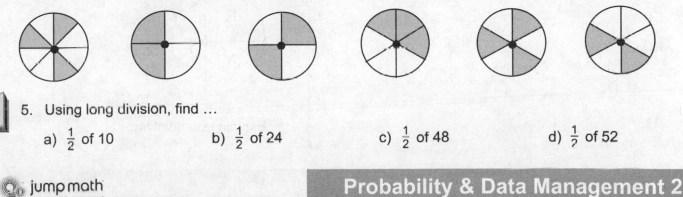

5. Using long division, find ...

   a) $\frac{1}{2}$ of 10

   b) $\frac{1}{2}$ of 24

   c) $\frac{1}{2}$ of 48

   d) $\frac{1}{2}$ of 52

Probability & Data Management 2

6. 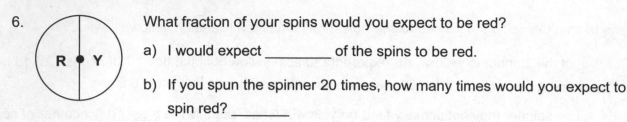 What fraction of your spins would you expect to be red?

     a) I would expect _____ of the spins to be red.

     b) If you spun the spinner 20 times, how many times would you expect to spin red? _____

7. If you flip a coin 40 times, how many times would you expect to flip heads? Explain.

8. Using long division, find …

     a) $\frac{1}{3}$ of 60 is _____   b) $\frac{1}{3}$ of 42 is _____   c) $\frac{1}{4}$ of 52 is _____   d) $\frac{1}{4}$ of 84 is _____

9. For each spinner below, what fraction of your spins would you expect to be red?

     a)   I would expect _____ of the spins to be red.

     b)

10. How many times would you expect to spin yellow, if you spun the spinner …

     a)   66 times? _____

     b)   96 times? _____

11. Sketch a spinner on which you would expect to spin red $\frac{3}{4}$ of the time.

12. How many times would you expect to spin yellow if you used the spinner 100 times?

Explain your thinking.

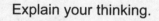

Answer the questions below in your notebook.

1.

Tanya and Daniel play a game of chance with the spinner shown.
If it lands on yellow, Tanya wins.
If it lands on red, Daniel wins.

Green	Red	Yellow
${\rlap{||||}{\text{卌}}}$	||||	卌 卌

a) Tanya and Daniel play the game 20 times. How many times would you <u>predict</u> that the spinner would land on red?

b) When Tanya and Daniel play the game they get the results shown in the chart. Daniel says the game isn't fair. Is he right? Explain.

2. Place the point of your pencil inside a paper clip in the middle of the circle.

Hold the pencil still so you can spin the clip around the pencil.

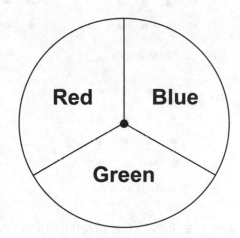

a) If you spin the spinner 30 times, how many times would you predict spinning red?
Show your work.
HINT: Think of dividing 30 spins into 3 equal parts.

b) Spin the spinner 30 times.
Make a tally of your results.
Did your results match your expectations?

3. Write numbers on the spinners to match the probabilities.

a)

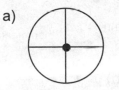

The probability of spinning a 3 is $\frac{1}{4}$.

b)

The probability of spinning an even number is $\frac{5}{6}$.

c)

The probability of spinning a multiple of 3 is $\frac{2}{5}$.

d)

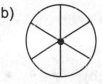

The probability of spinning a 2 is $\frac{1}{2}$.

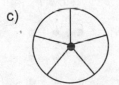

1. Join the dots in the given column OR row.

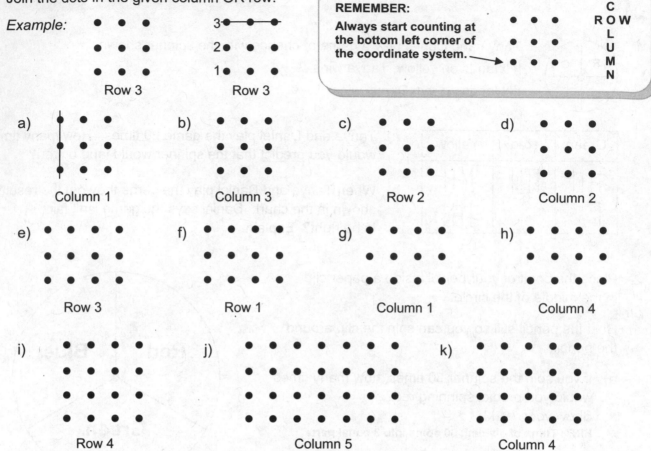

REMEMBER:
Always start counting at the bottom left corner of the coordinate system.

C
R O W
O
L
U
M
N

2. Join the dots in the given column AND row.

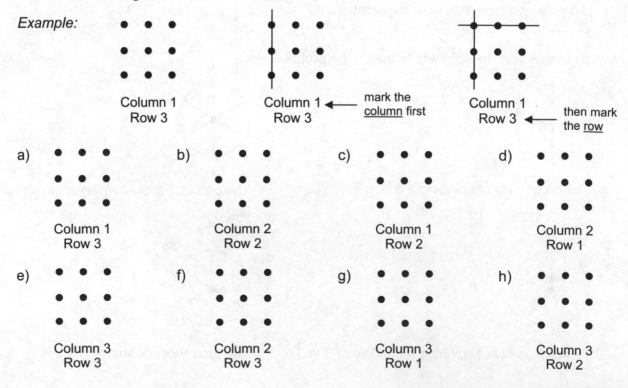

3. Join the dots to find a hidden letter. Write each letter beside the array.

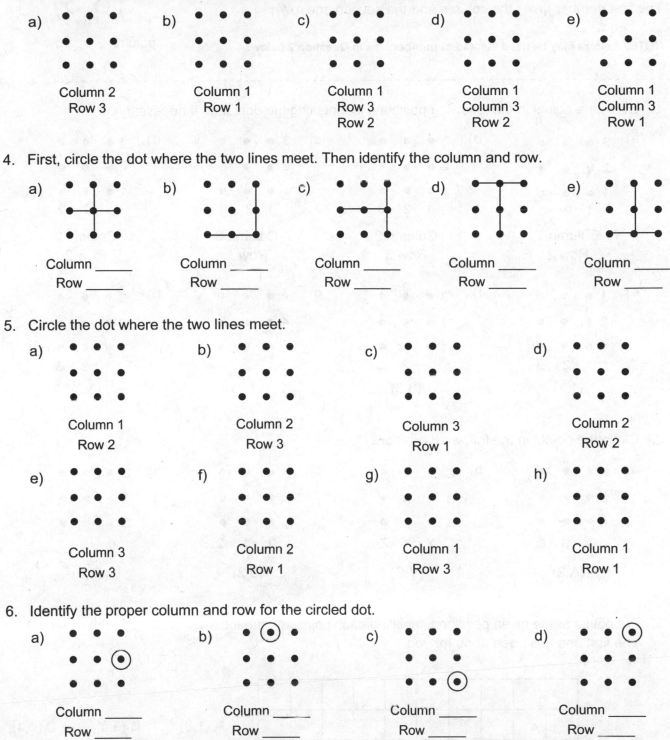

a) Column 2
    Row 3

b) Column 1
    Row 1

c) Column 1
    Row 3
    Row 2

d) Column 1
    Column 3
    Row 2

e) Column 1
    Column 3
    Row 1

4. First, circle the dot where the two lines meet. Then identify the column and row.

a) Column _____
    Row _____

b) Column _____
    Row _____

c) Column _____
    Row _____

d) Column _____
    Row _____

e) Column _____
    Row _____

5. Circle the dot where the two lines meet.

a) Column 1
    Row 2

b) Column 2
    Row 3

c) Column 3
    Row 1

d) Column 2
    Row 2

e) Column 3
    Row 3

f) Column 2
    Row 1

g) Column 1
    Row 3

h) Column 1
    Row 1

6. Identify the proper column and row for the circled dot.

a) Column _____
    Row _____

b) Column _____
    Row _____

c) Column _____
    Row _____

d) Column _____
    Row _____

7. Draw a 4-by-4 array on grid paper and circle a dot in the array. Ask a friend to name the column and the row of the dot.

8. Draw an array on grid paper and write a letter backwards or forwards (i.e. ⊦ or ⊣) on the array. Then write out the column and row numbers of the lines that make up the letter.

G5-19: Coordinate Systems

Rows and columns can be identified by a pair of numbers in a bracket.
The first number gives the column and the second, the row.

$(5,3)$

column   row

NOTE: Letters may be used instead of numbers, as in Question 2 below.

---

1. Circle the points in the following positions (connecting the dots first, if necessary).

a)
```
3 • • •
2 • • •
1 • • •
  1 2 3
```
Column 1
Row 2

b)
```
3 • • •
2 • • •
1 • • •
  1 2 3
```
Column 2
Row 3

c)
```
3 • • •
2 • • •
1 • • •
  1 2 3
```
Column 3
Row 1

d)
```
3 • • •
2 • • •
1 • • •
  1 2 3
```
Column 2
Row 2

e)
```
3 • • •
2 • • •
1 • • •
  1 2 3
```
(1,1)

f)
```
3 • • •
2 • • •
1 • • •
  1 2 3
```
(3,3)

g)
```
3 • • •
2 • • •
1 • • •
  1 2 3
```
(1,3)

h)
```
3 • • •
2 • • •
1 • • •
  1 2 3
```
(3,2)

2. Circle the points in the following positions.

a)
```
3 • • •
2 • • •
1 • • •
  A B C
```
(A,2)

b)
```
C • • •
B • • •
A • • •
  X Y Z
```
(Y,C)

c)
```
2 • • •
1 • • •
0 • • •
  0 1 2
```
(0,2)

d)
```
2 • • •
1 • • •
0 • • •
  0 1 2
```
(2,0)

3. Put points at the given positions, labelling each point with the letter written beside the ordered pair.
The first one has been done for you.

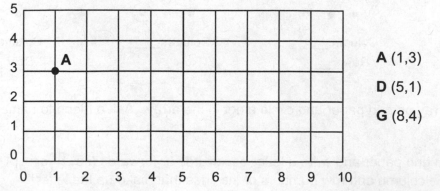

A (1,3)	**B** (9,5)	**C** (4,4)
D (5,1)	**E** (0,0)	**F** (10,3)
G (8,4)	**H** (2,3)	**I** (6,2)

G5-19: Coordinate Systems (continued)

4. Circle the points in the following positions.

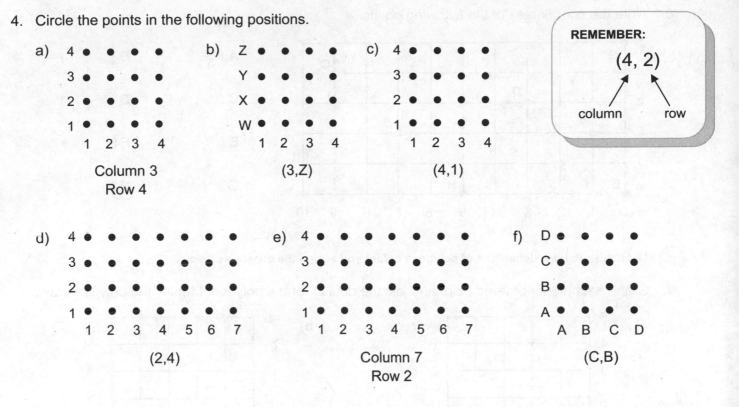

a) Column 3 Row 4

b) (3,Z)

c) (4,1)

d) (2,4)

e) Column 7 Row 2

f) (C,B)

REMEMBER:

(4, 2)

column   row

5. Put points at the given positions, labelling each point with the letter written beside the ordered pair.

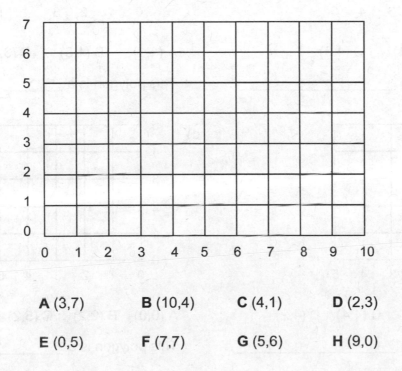

A (3,7)   B (10,4)   C (4,1)   D (2,3)

E (0,5)   F (7,7)   G (5,6)   H (9,0)

6. Write the coordinates of the following points.

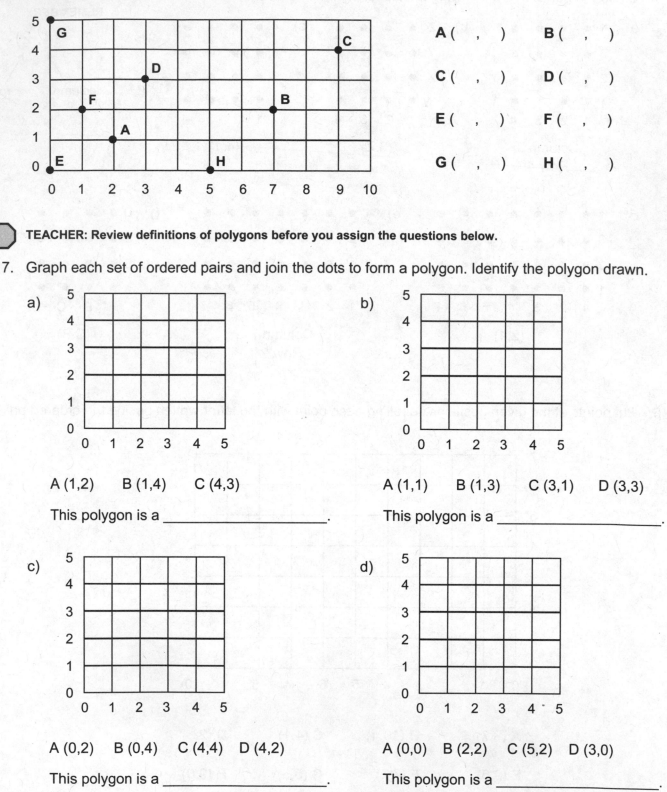

A (,)   B (,)

C (,)   D (,)

E (,)   F (,)

G (,)   H (,)

⬡ **TEACHER: Review definitions of polygons before you assign the questions below.**

7. Graph each set of ordered pairs and join the dots to form a polygon. Identify the polygon drawn.

a)

A (1,2)   B (1,4)   C (4,3)

This polygon is a _____.

b)

A (1,1)   B (1,3)   C (3,1)   D (3,3)

This polygon is a _____.

c)

A (0,2)   B (0,4)   C (4,4)   D (4,2)

This polygon is a _____.

d)

A (0,0)   B (2,2)   C (5,2)   D (3,0)

This polygon is a _____.

BONUS

8. Draw a polygon on grid paper. Tell a friend the coordinates of the vertices of your polygon and see if they can name the polygon.

Josh **slides** a dot from one position to another. Slides may be described using the words right, left, up and down.

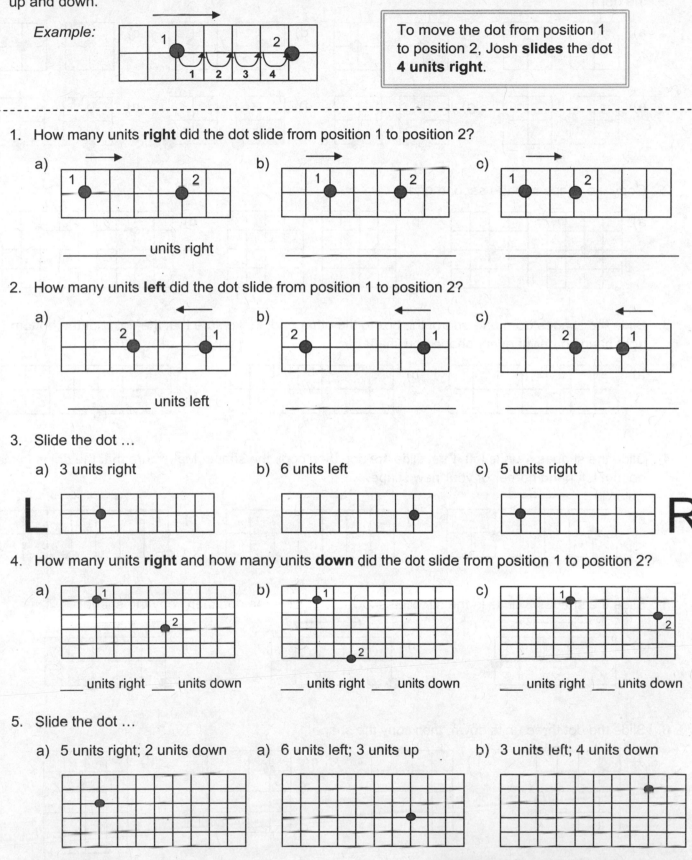

Example:

To move the dot from position 1 to position 2, Josh **slides** the dot **4 units right**.

1. How many units **right** did the dot slide from position 1 to position 2?

a)

_____ units right

b)

_____

c)

_____

2. How many units **left** did the dot slide from position 1 to position 2?

a)

_____ units left

b)

_____

c)

_____

3. Slide the dot …

a) 3 units right

b) 6 units left

c) 5 units right

L   R

4. How many units **right** and how many units **down** did the dot slide from position 1 to position 2?

a)

___ units right ___ units down

b)

___ units right ___ units down

c)

___ units right ___ units down

5. Slide the dot …

a) 5 units right; 2 units down

a) 6 units left; 3 units up

b) 3 units left; 4 units down

1. Copy the shape into the second grid. (Make sure your shape is in the same position relative to the dot.)

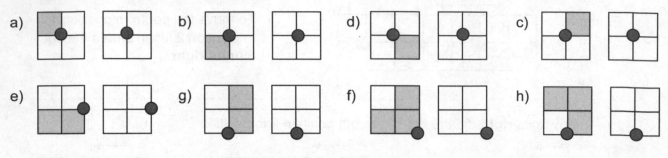

2. Copy the shape into the second grid.

a) 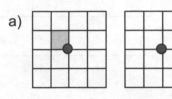   b) 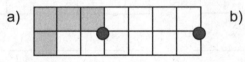   c)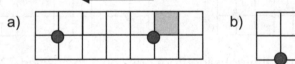

3. Slide the shapes from one end of the box to the other end. Make sure that the dot is at the bottom right hand corner of every shape you shade.

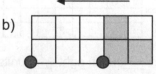
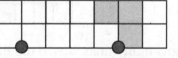
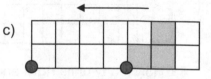

4. Slide the shapes 4 units left. First slide the dot, then copy the shape. Make sure that the dot is in the bottom left hand corner of your new shape.

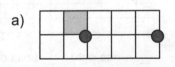
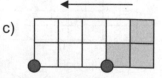

5. Slide the shapes 3 units in the direction shown. First slide the dot, then copy the shape.

a)   b)   c)

6. Slide the dot three units down, then copy the shape.

a) 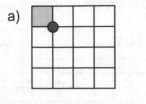   b) 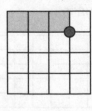   c) 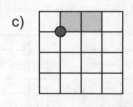   d)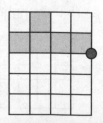

G5-22: Slides (Advanced)

In a **slide** (or **translation**), the figure moves in a straight line without turning. The image of a slide is congruent to the original figure.

Helen slides (or translates) a shape to a new position by following these steps.

1. Draw a dot in a corner of the figure.
2. Slide the dot (in this case, 4 right and 1 down).
3. Draw the *image* of the figure.

Join the two dots with a translation arrow to show the direction of the slide.

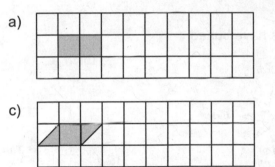

Slide the box 4 right and 1 down.

---

4. Slide each shape 4 boxes to the right. (Start by putting a dot on one of the corners of the figure. Slide the dot four boxes right, then draw the new figure.)

a)

b)

c)

d)

4. Slide each figure 5 boxes to the right and 2 boxes down.

a)

b)

3. Describe how figure A moved to position B. Use the word "translation" in your answer.

4. Amy says she used a slide to move figure A to position B. Is she correct? Explain.

1. This is the star map of a constellation. The names of the stars are given in Arabic.

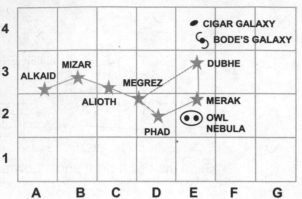

a) The star named "Bear" is in the square E3.
What is its name in Arabic? _____.

b) The "Goat" lives in C3.
What is its Arabic Name? _____.

c) Alkaid star is in the square _____.

d) The Owl Nebula is in square _____.

e) How many squares up from the Owl Nebula is Bode's Galaxy? ____

f) Which star is 2 squares left and 1 square up from Phad? _____

2. The map shows part of Treasure Island, where pirates have buried gold and silver.

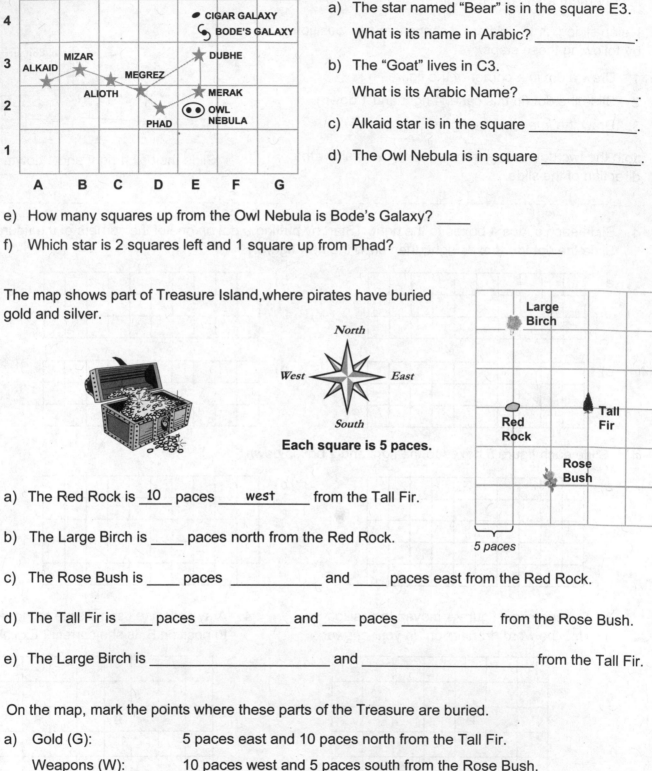

Each square is 5 paces.

5 paces

a) The Red Rock is __10__ paces ____west____ from the Tall Fir.

b) The Large Birch is ____ paces north from the Red Rock.

c) The Rose Bush is ____ paces _____ and ____ paces east from the Red Rock.

d) The Tall Fir is ____ paces _____ and ____ paces _____ from the Rose Bush.

e) The Large Birch is _____ and _____ from the Tall Fir.

3. On the map, mark the points where these parts of the Treasure are buried.

a) Gold (G):   5 paces east and 10 paces north from the Tall Fir.

   Weapons (W):   10 paces west and 5 paces south from the Rose Bush.

   Silver in Bars (S): 10 paces south and 5 paces east from the Large Birch.

b) What two landmarks is the silver buried between? _____

This map shows all of the Treasure Island.

Each edge on the map represents 1 kilometre.

The Round Lake is at point (2.5, 4).

4. What is at point …

   a) (3, 2)? _____

   b) (5, 5)? _____

   c) (3, 5)? _____

   d) (6.5, 3.5)? _____

5. What are the coordinates of …

   a) the Old Lighthouse? _____

   b) Lookout Hill? _____

   c) the Clear Spring? _____

6. What is …

   a) 1 km west of Bear Cave? _____

   b) 1.5 km south of the Fort? _____

   c) 1 km north and 1.5 km west of the Treasure?

   _____

7. Fill in the blanks.

   a) The Old Lighthouse is __4.5__ km ___east___ of Round Lake.

   b) The Treasure is _____ km _____ of the Fort.

   c) The Bear Cave is _____ km _____ of the Treasure.

   d) Lookout Hill is _____ km _____ and _____ km south of the Bear Cave.

   e) The Clear Spring is _____ km _____ and _____ km _____ of the Old Lighthouse.

   f) The Bear Cave is _____ of the Fort.

   g) The Treasure is _____ of Lookout Hill.

8. Make your own question using the map and ask your partner to answer it.

G5-24: Reflections

O'Shane **reflects** the shape by flipping it over the mirror line. Each point on the figure flips to the opposite side of the mirror line, but stays the same distance from the line. O'Shane checks to see that his reflection is drawn correctly by using a mirror.

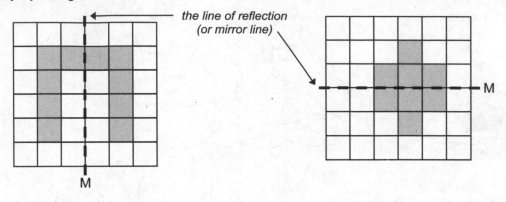

the line of reflection (or mirror line)

1. Draw the reflection of the shapes below.

a)

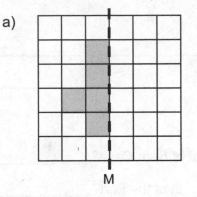

b)

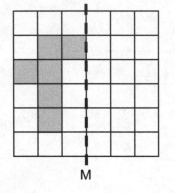

c)

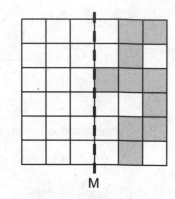

2. Draw the reflection, or flip, of the shapes.

a)

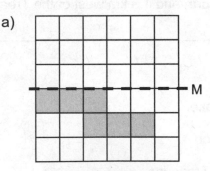

b)

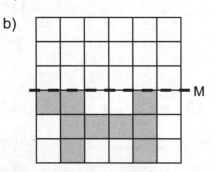

c)

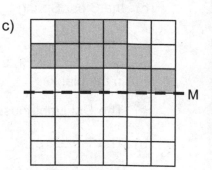

3. Draw your own shape in the box below. Now draw the flip of the shape on the other side of the mirror line.

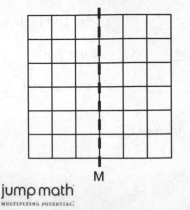

BONUS: Are the shapes on either side of the mirror congruent? Explain your answer.

_____

_____

_____

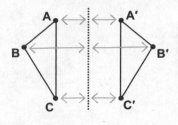

When a point is reflected in a mirror line, the point and the image of the point are the same distance from the mirror line.

A figure and its image are congruent but face in opposite directions.

---

4. Reflect the point P through the mirror line M. Label the image point P′.

a)   b)   c)   d)

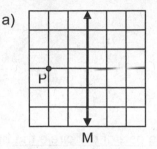   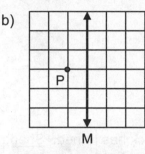   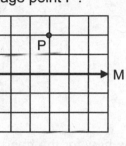   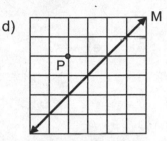

5. Reflect the set of points P, Q and R through the mirror line. Label the image points P′, Q′ and R′.

a)   b)   c)   d)

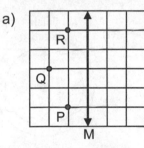   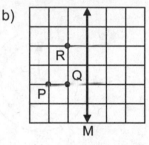   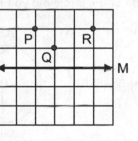   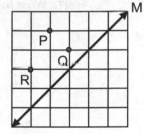

6. Reflect the figure by first reflecting the vertices of the figure.

a)   b)   c)

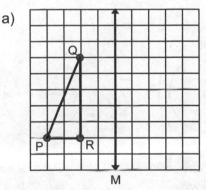   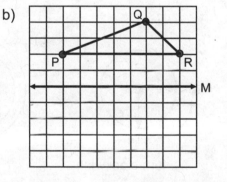   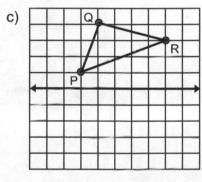

7. Circle the pictures that <u>do not</u> show reflections. Explain how you know the figures you circled aren't reflections. **REMEMBER: The image must be congruent to the figure and face the opposite direction.**

a)   b)   c)

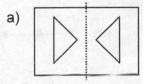   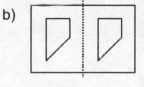   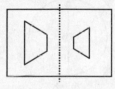

8. Draw a mirror line on grid paper. Draw a polygon with 3 or 4 sides and draw a dot at each vertex. Reflect the polygon through the mirror line by first reflecting each of the vertices.

TEACHER:
Review the meaning of the terms "clockwise" and "counter clockwise" for this lesson.

1. Name the fractions shown in the pictures.

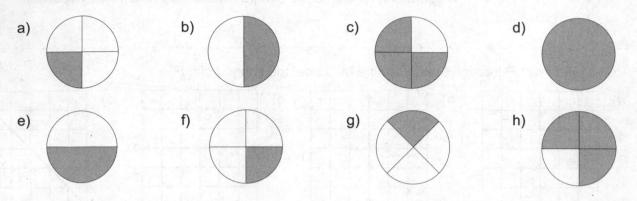

a)   b)   c)   d)

e)   f)   g)   h)

2. The picture shows how far the hand of the clock has turned. <u>Shade the part of the circle the hand has moved across</u>. Then, in the box, write what fraction of a turn the hand has turned.
   HINT: What fraction of the circle did you shade?

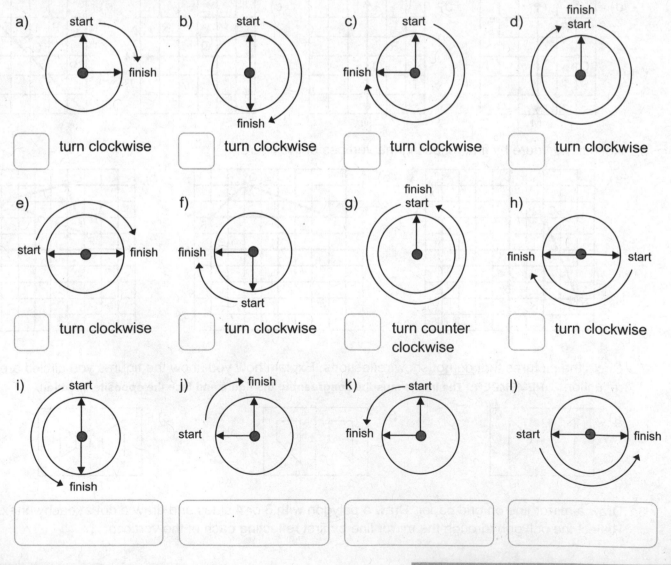

a) start / finish   b) start / finish   c) start / finish   d) finish start

☐ turn clockwise   ☐ turn clockwise   ☐ turn clockwise   ☐ turn clockwise

e) start / finish   f) finish / start   g) finish start   h) finish / start

☐ turn clockwise   ☐ turn clockwise   ☐ turn counter clockwise   ☐ turn clockwise

i) start / finish   j) finish / start   k) start / finish   l) start / finish

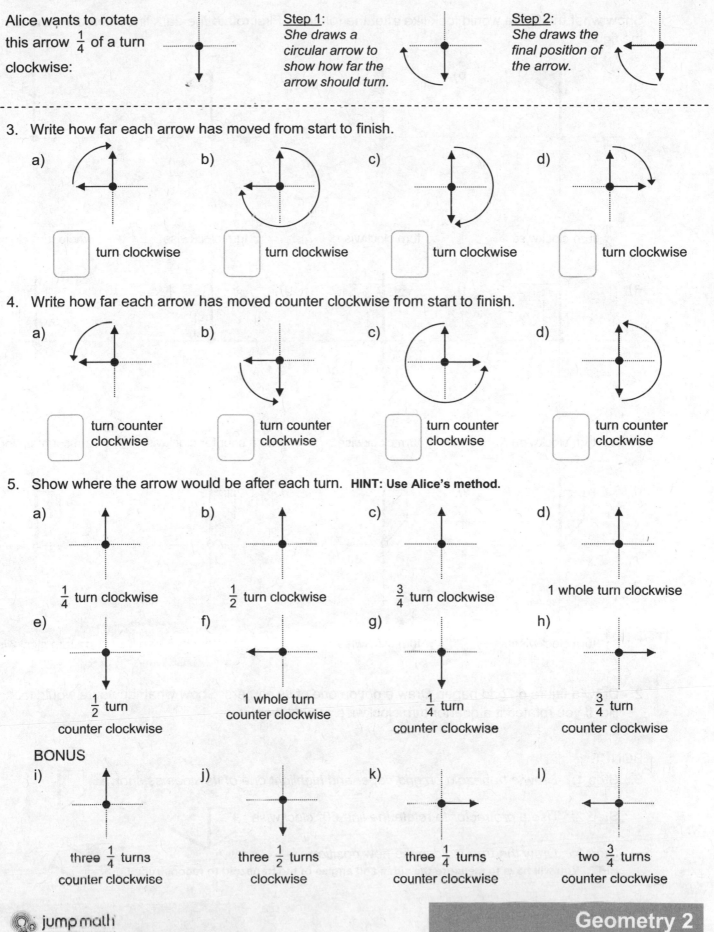

Alice wants to rotate this arrow $\frac{1}{4}$ of a turn clockwise:

Step 1:
She draws a circular arrow to show how far the arrow should turn.

Step 2:
She draws the final position of the arrow.

3. Write how far each arrow has moved from start to finish.

a) ☐ turn clockwise

b) ☐ turn clockwise

c) ☐ turn clockwise

d) ☐ turn clockwise

4. Write how far each arrow has moved counter clockwise from start to finish.

a) ☐ turn counter clockwise

b) ☐ turn counter clockwise

c) ☐ turn counter clockwise

d) ☐ turn counter clockwise

5. Show where the arrow would be after each turn. **HINT: Use Alice's method.**

a) $\frac{1}{4}$ turn clockwise

b) $\frac{1}{2}$ turn clockwise

c) $\frac{3}{4}$ turn clockwise

d) 1 whole turn clockwise

e) $\frac{1}{2}$ turn counter clockwise

f) 1 whole turn counter clockwise

g) $\frac{1}{4}$ turn counter clockwise

h) $\frac{3}{4}$ turn counter clockwise

BONUS

i) three $\frac{1}{4}$ turns counter clockwise

j) three $\frac{1}{2}$ turns clockwise

k) three $\frac{1}{4}$ turns counter clockwise

l) two $\frac{3}{4}$ turns counter clockwise

jump math
MULTIPLYING POTENTIAL

Geometry 2

G5-26: Rotations (Advanced)

1. Show what the figure would look like after the rotation. First rotate the dark line, then draw the rest of the figure.

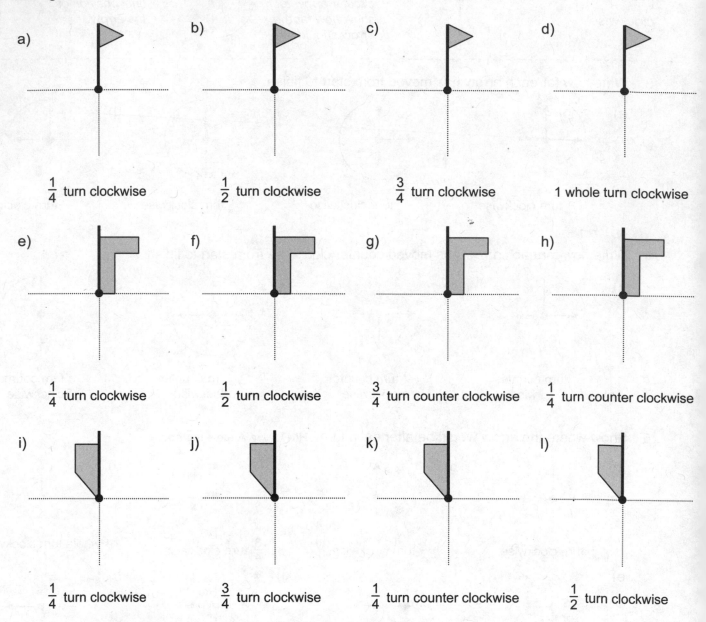

a)
$\frac{1}{4}$ turn clockwise

b)
$\frac{1}{2}$ turn clockwise

c)
$\frac{3}{4}$ turn clockwise

d)
1 whole turn clockwise

e)
$\frac{1}{4}$ turn clockwise

f)
$\frac{1}{2}$ turn clockwise

g)
$\frac{3}{4}$ turn counter clockwise

h)
$\frac{1}{4}$ turn counter clockwise

i)
$\frac{1}{4}$ turn clockwise

j)
$\frac{3}{4}$ turn clockwise

k)
$\frac{1}{4}$ turn counter clockwise

l)
$\frac{1}{2}$ turn clockwise

2. Draw a figure on grid paper. Draw a dot on one of its corners. Show what the figure would look like if you rotated it a quarter turn clockwise around the dot.

BONUS

3. Step 1: *Draw a trapezoid on grid paper and highlight one of its sides as shown.*

   Step 2: *Use a protractor to rotate the line 60° clockwise.*

   Step 3: *Draw the trapezoid in the new position.*
   HINT: You will have to measure the sides and angles of the trapezoid to reconstruct it.

jump math
MULTIPLYING POTENTIAL

G5-27: Rotations and Reflections

1. Rotate each shape 180° around centre P by showing the final position of the figure.

   Use the line to help you.

2. Rotate each shape 180° around centre P.

   HINT: First highlight an edge of the figure and rotate the edge (as in Question 1).

3. Rotate each shape 90° around point P in the direction shown:

4. Rotate each shape 90° around the point in the direction shown:

   HINT: First highlight a line on the figure and rotate the line 90°.

   a)

   b)

5. Reflect each shape in the mirror line.

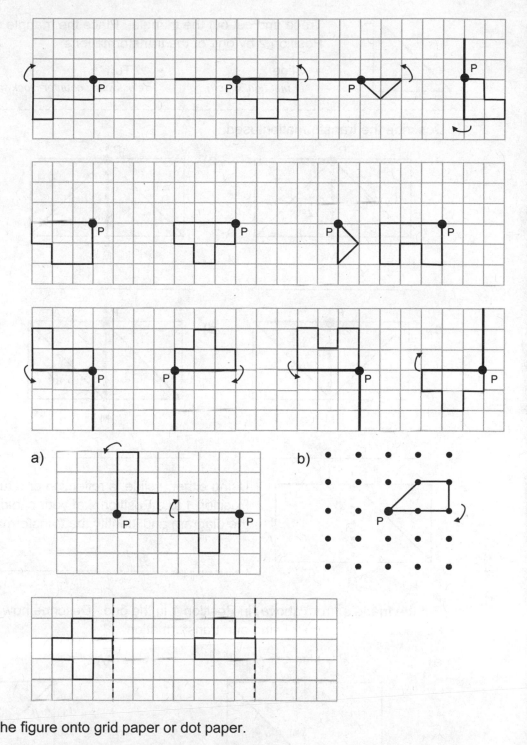

6.

   a) Copy the figure onto grid paper or dot paper.

   b) Pick any point on the figure as a centre of rotation.

      Turn the figure $\frac{1}{4}$ or $\frac{1}{2}$ turn around the point.

      Then slide the figure in any direction.

      Describe the transformations you used.

   c) Rotate the figure around any point, then reflect it in a mirror line of your choice. Describe your transformation.

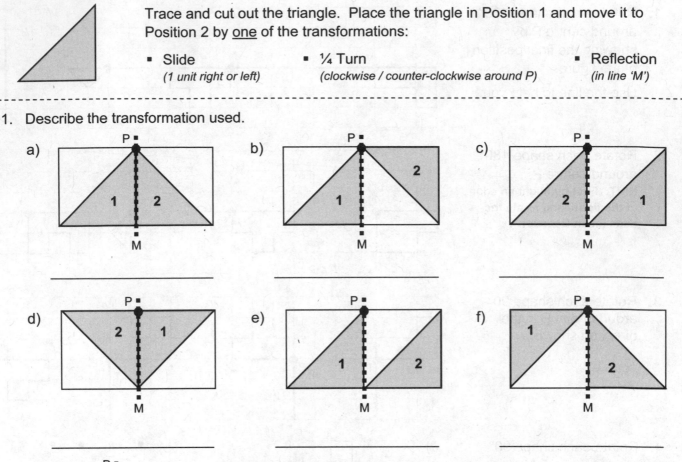

Trace and cut out the triangle. Place the triangle in Position 1 and move it to Position 2 by <u>one</u> of the transformations:

- **Slide**
  (1 unit right or left)
- **¼ Turn**
  (clockwise / counter-clockwise around P)
- **Reflection**
  (in line 'M')

---

1. Describe the transformation used.

a) b) c)

d) e) f)

2.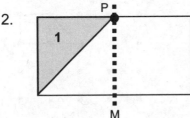

Using either a slide, a reflection or a turn, move the triangle from Position 1 to a Position 2 of your choice. Add the second triangle to the diagram and identify the transformation you used below.

3. Put the triangle (from above) in Position 1 in the grid. Describe how you can move the figure from Position 1 to Position 2 using <u>one</u> transformation.

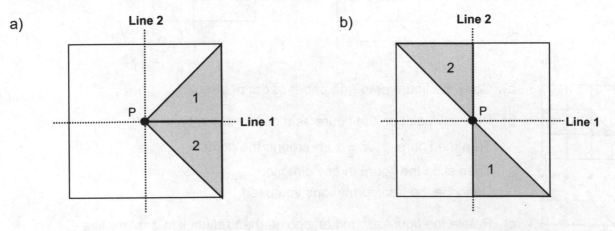

a) b)

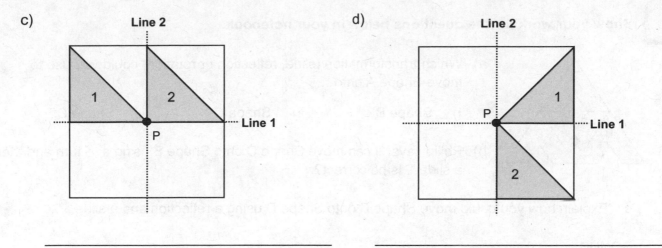

c) _____

d) _____

4. Describe how the figure moved from Position 1 to Position 2 by using <u>two</u> transformations.
(Some questions have more than one answer – try to find them.)

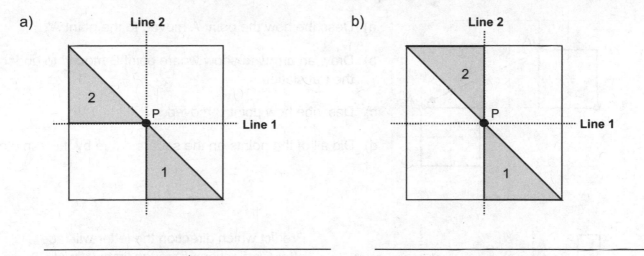

a) _____

b) _____

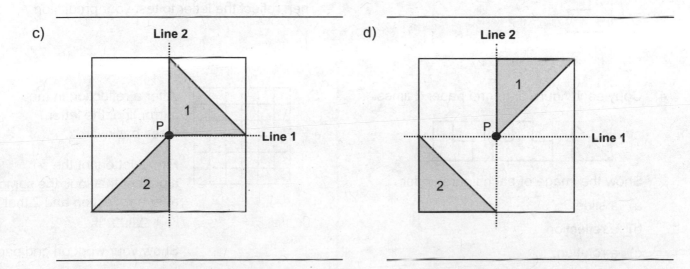

c) _____

d) _____

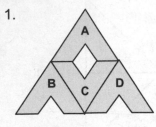 Show your work for the questions below in your notebook.

1.

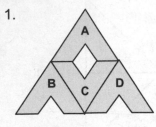

a) Which transformation (slide, reflection or rotation) could you use to move Shape A onto …

   i)   Shape B?   ii)   Shape C?   iii)   Shape D?

b) Philip says: "I can move Shape C onto Shape B using a ½ turn and then a slide." Is he correct?

c) Explain how you could move Shape C onto Shape D using a reflection and a slide.

BONUS

d) You could move Shape C onto Shape D using only a turn. Mark the centre of the rotation.

2. The picture shows a translation of a square.

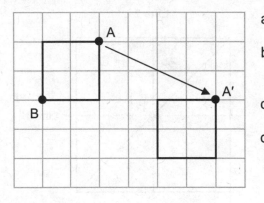

a) Describe how the point A moved to the point A'.

b) Draw an arrow to show where point B moved to under the translation.

c) Describe how point B moved.

d) Did all of the points on the square move by the same amount?

3.

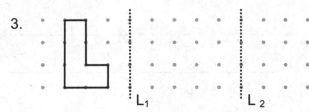

L₁   L₂

Predict which direction the letter will face after 2 reflections (through lines L_1 and L_2).

Then reflect the letter to test your prediction.

4. Copy each figure onto grid paper 3 times.

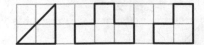

Show the image of each figure under …

a) a slide.

b) a reflection.

c) a rotation.

5.

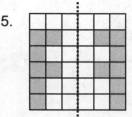

After a reflection in the mirror line, the letter F faces backwards.

Find 2 letters of the alphabet that look <u>the same</u> after a reflection and 2 that look <u>different</u>.

Show your work on grid paper.

G5-30: Building Pyramids

** For the exercises on this page you will need modeling clay (or plasticine) and toothpicks (or straws).

To make a skeleton for a **pyramid**, start by making a base.
Your base might be a triangle or a square.

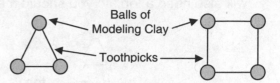

Now add an edge to each vertex on your base and join the edges at a point.

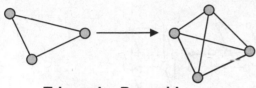

Triangular Pyramid

Square Pyramid

After you have made a triangular pyramid and a square pyramid, try to make one with a five-sided base (a pentagonal pyramid). Then fill in the first three rows of the chart below.

- -

1.

	Draw Shape of Base	Number of Sides of Base	Number of Edges of Pyramid	Number of Vertices of Pyramid
Triangular Pyramid				
Square Pyramid				
Pentagonal Pyramid				
Hexagonal Pyramid				

2. Describe the pattern on each column of your chart.
   Use the pattern to fill in the row for the hexagonal pyramid.

3. Describe any relationships you see in the columns of the chart.
   EXAMPLE: What is the relationship between the number of sides in the base of the pyramid and the number of vertices or the number of edges in the pyramid?

4. How many edges and vertices would an octagonal pyramid have?

Geometry 2

G5-31: Building Prisms

To make a skeleton for a **prism**, start by making a base (as you did for a pyramid). However, your prism will also need a top, so you should make a copy of the base.

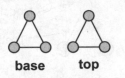
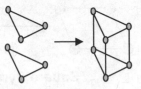
base   **top**

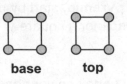
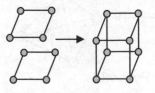
base   **top**

Now join each vertex in the base to a vertex in the top.

After you have made a triangular prism and a cube, try to make a prism with two five-sided bases (a pentagonal prism). Then fill in the first three rows of the chart below.

1.

	Draw Shape of Base	Number of Sides of Base	Number of Edges of Prism	Number of Vertices of Prism
Triangular Prism				
Cube				
Pentagonal Prism				
Hexagonal Prism				

2. Describe the pattern in each column of your chart.
   Use the pattern to fill in the row for the hexagonal prism.

3. Describe any relationships you see in the columns of the chart.

4. How many edges and vertices would an octagonal prism have?

jump math
MULTIPLYING POTENTIAL

Geometry 2

G5-32: Edges, Faces, and Vertices

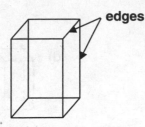

edges

The **faces** are the flat surfaces.

Faces meet at **edges**.

Candice builds a skeleton of a rectangular prism using wire.

She covers the skeleton with paper.

The dotted lines show the *hidden* edges.

1. Draw dotted lines to show the hidden edges.

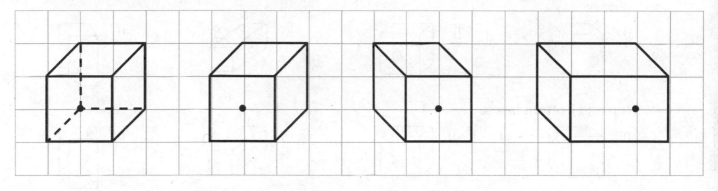

2. Shade all of the edges (the first one is started).
   Count the edges as you shade them.

a) __ edges b) __ edges c) __ edges d) __ edges

e) __ edges f) __ edges g) __ edges h) __ edges

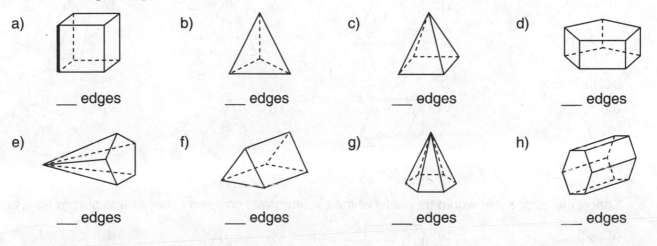

3. Vertices are the points where the edges of a shape meet.
   Put a dot on each vertex. Count the vertices.

a) __ vertices b) __ vertices c) __ vertices d) __ vertices

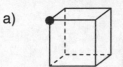

Geometry 2

G5-32: Edges, Faces, and Vertices *(continued)*

4. Shade the...

    front face:

    a) 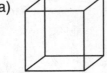   b)   c)   d)

    back face:

    e)   f)   g)   h)

    side faces:

    i)   j)   k)   l)

    top and **bottom** faces:

    m)   n)   o)   p)

    back face:

    q)   r)   s)   t)

    bottom face:

    u)   v)   w)   x)

5. Shade the edges that would be hidden if the skeleton was covered in paper and placed on a table.

    a)   b)   c)   d)

BONUS

6. Shade the edges that would be hidden if the skeleton was covered with paper and was hung above you in the position shown.

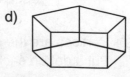

G5-33: Prisms and Pyramids

The solid shapes in the figure are called **3-D shapes**.

Faces are the flat surfaces of a shape, **edges** are where two faces meet, and **vertices** are the points where 3 or more faces meet.

faces
edges
vertices

Pyramids have a **point** opposite the base. The base of the shape is a polygon; for instance, a triangle, a quadrilateral or a square (like the pyramids in Egypt), a pentagon, etc.

Prisms do not have a point. Their bases are the same at both ends of the shape.

---

1. Count the faces of each shape.

a)

___ faces

b)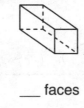

___ faces

c)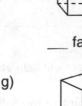

___ faces

d)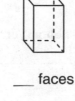

___ faces

e)

___ faces

f)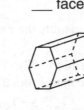

___ faces

g)

___ faces

h)

___ faces

2. Using a set of 3-D shapes and the chart below as reference, answer the following questions.

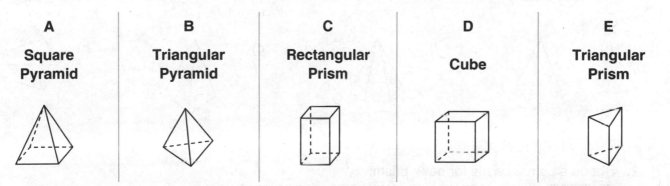

A	B	C	D	E
Square Pyramid	Triangular Pyramid	Rectangular Prism	Cube	Triangular Prism

a) Describe each shape in terms of its faces, vertices and edges. The first one has been done.

	A	B	C	D	E
Number of Faces	5				
Number of Vertices	5				
Number of Edges	8				

b) Did any shapes have the same number of faces / vertices / edges? If so, which shapes share which properties?

Melissa is exploring differences between pyramids and prisms. She discovers that …

- A **pyramid** has **one base**.
  (There is one exception – in a triangular pyramid, any face is a base.)

  Example:

- A **prism** has **two bases**.
  (There is one exception – in a rectangular prism any pair of opposite faces are bases.)

  Example:

IMPORTANT NOTE:
The base(s) are not always on the "bottom" or "top" of the shape.

TEACHER:
The activity that goes with this worksheet will help your students identify the base of a 3-D figure.

1. Shade a base <u>and</u> circle the point of the following pyramids. The first one is done for you.
   NOTE: The base will not necessarily be on the "bottom" of the shape (but it is *always* at the end opposite the point).

   a)   b)   c)   d)

   e)   f)   g)   h)

2. Shade a pair of bases for each prism.
   REMEMBER: Unless all its faces are rectangles, a <u>prism</u> has <u>two bases</u>.

   a)   b)   c)   d)

   e)   f)   g)   h)

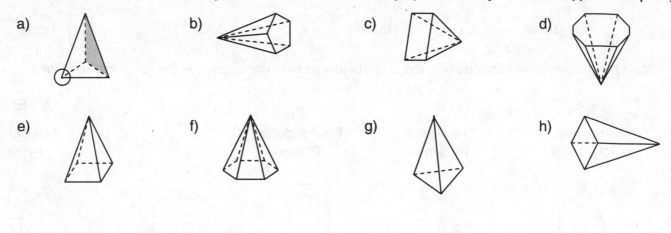

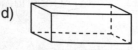
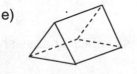
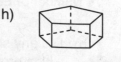

3. Kira has many prisms and pyramids. Can you circle the ones that have **all congruent faces**?

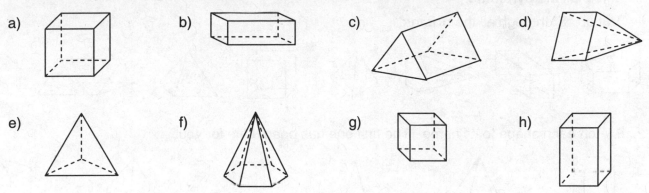

a)   b)   c)   d)

e)   f)   g)   h)

4. Shade a pair of opposite bases for each prism. Shade the base of each pyramid.

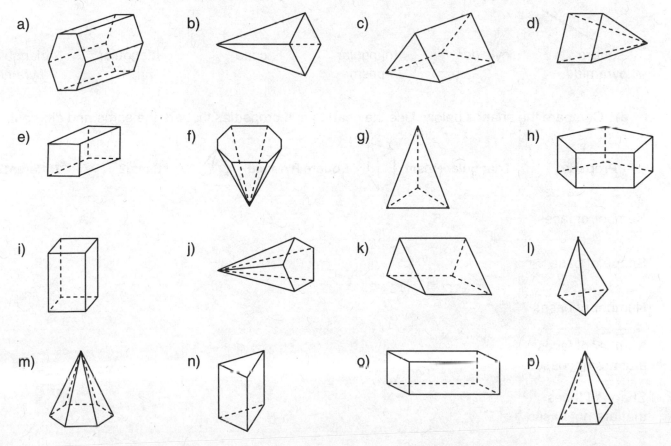

a)   b)   c)   d)

e)   f)   g)   h)

i)   j)   k)   l)

m)   n)   o)   p)

5. "I have a hexagonal base." Name two 3-D shapes this could describe.

G5-35: Properties of Pyramids and Prisms

1. Circle all the **pyramids**.
   Put an "X" through all the **prisms**.

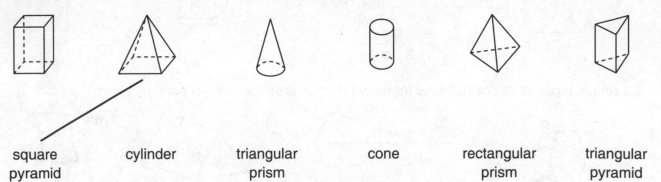

2. Match each shape to its name. The first one has been done for you.

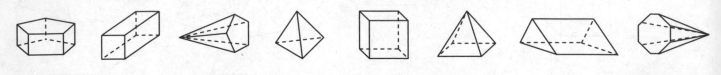

| square | cylinder | triangular | cone | rectangular | triangular |
| pyramid | | prism | | prism | pyramid |

3. a) Compare the shapes below. Use the chart to find properties that are the <u>same</u> and <u>different</u>.

Property	Triangular Prism	Square Pyramid	Same?	Different?
Number of faces	5	5	✓	
Shape of base				
Number of bases				
Number of faces that are <u>not</u> bases				
Shape of faces that are <u>not</u> bases				
Number of edges				
Number of vertices				

   b) Copy and finish writing the following sentences:

   "A triangular prism and a square pyramid are the <u>same</u> in these ways …"

   "A triangular prism and a square pyramid are <u>different</u> in these ways …"

4. a) Complete the chart. Use the actual 3-D shapes to help you. Colour the number of sides in each base to help you name your shape.

| Shape | Name | Number of ... | | | Pictures of Faces |
		edges	vertices	faces	* In each case, circle the base(s)

b) Count the number of sides in the base of each pyramid.
Compare this number with the number of vertices in each pyramid.
What do you notice?

c) Count the number of sides in the base of each prism.
Compare this number with the number of vertices in each prism.
What do you notice?

5. Write a paragraph outlining how the shapes are the <u>same</u> and how they are <u>different</u>.

a)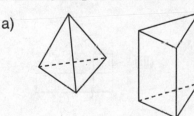

b)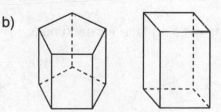

BONUS

6. In your notebook, draw rough sketches of as many everyday objects you can think of that are (or have parts that are) pyramids or prisms.

jump math
MULTIPLYING POTENTIAL

Geometry 2

G5-36: Nets and Faces

TEACHER:
Give your students copies of the nets for the following 3-D shapes (from the Teacher's Guide) and have them cut, fold and glue the nets into the proper shapes.

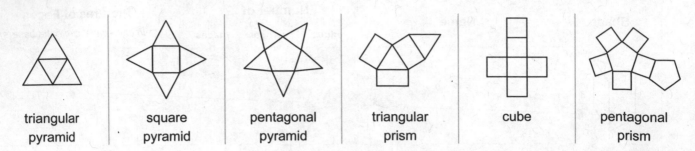

triangular pyramid   square pyramid   pentagonal pyramid   triangular prism   cube   pentagonal prism

1.

Name of Figure	Shape of Base	Number of Faces	Number of Edges

2. Draw the missing face for each net.

(i) 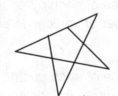 (ii) (iii)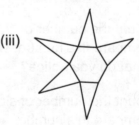

a) What is the shape of each missing face?

b) Are these nets of pyramids or of prisms?

_____

3. Draw the missing face for each net.

(i) 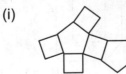 (ii) 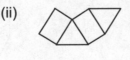 (iii)

a) What is the shape of each missing face?

b) Are these nets of pyramids or of prisms?

_____

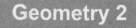Geometry 2

4. Shade the base of each shape below, then fill in the chart.

a)   **A:**   **B:**   **C:**

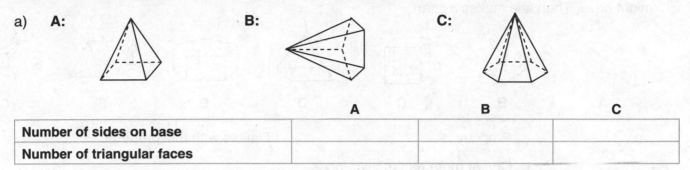

	A	B	C
Number of sides on base			
Number of triangular faces			

What relationship do you see between the numbers in the two rows of your chart?

b)   **D:**   **E:**   **F:**

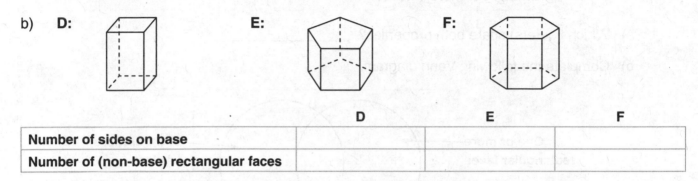

	D	E	F
Number of sides on base			
Number of (non-base) rectangular faces			

What relationship do you see between the numbers in the two rows of your chart?

4. How many of each type of face would you need to make the desired 3-D shape?

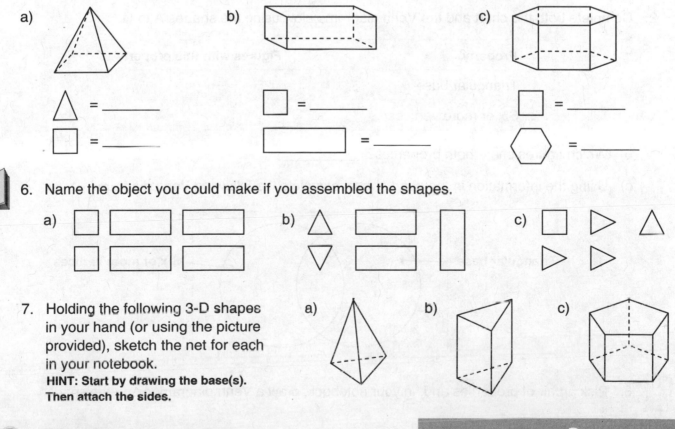

a)

△ = _____

▢ = _____

b)

▢ = _____

▭ = _____

c)

▢ = _____

⬡ = _____

6. Name the object you could make if you assembled the shapes.

a)

b)

c)

7. Holding the following 3-D shapes in your hand (or using the picture provided), sketch the net for each in your notebook.

    HINT: Start by drawing the base(s).
    Then attach the sides.

a)   b)   c)

G5-37: Sorting 3-D Shapes

Eve sorts the following figures using a Venn diagram. She first decides on two properties that a figure might have. Then she makes a chart.

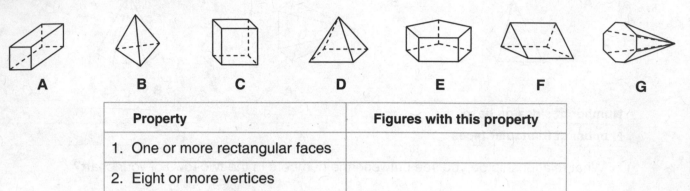

Property	Figures with this property
1. One or more rectangular faces	
2. Eight or more vertices	

1. a) Which figure(s) share both properties? _____

    b) Complete the following Venn diagram.

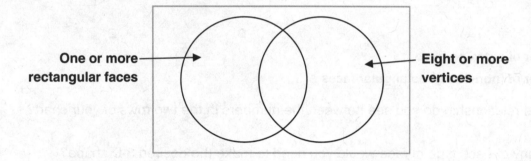

One or more rectangular faces   Eight or more vertices

2. Complete both the chart and the Venn diagram below using the shapes A to G.

    a)

Property	Figures with this property
1. Triangular base	
2. Six or more vertices	

    b) Which figures share both properties? _____

    c) Using the information in the chart above, complete the following Venn diagram.

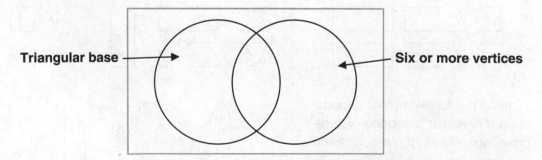

Triangular base   Six or more vertices

3. Pick a pair of properties and, in your notebook, draw a Venn diagram to sort the shapes.

G5-38: Tessellations

A **tessellation** is a pattern made up of one or more shapes that completely covers a surface (without any gaps or overlaps).

Some shapes that can be used to tessellate are:

A square

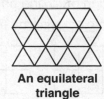

An equilateral triangle

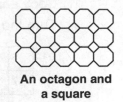

An octagon and a square

---

1. Show how you can tessellate a region of space by using …

   a) hexagons

   b) equilateral triangles

   c) hexagons and triangles

   d) trapezoids

2. The picture shows how you can tessellate a grid using an 'L' shape.

   a) Add at least 6 more 'L' shapes to the tessellation.

   b) On grid paper, show how you could use the shapes below to tessellate the grid.

      (i)

      (ii)

BONUS

3. Create a shape that will tessellate.

   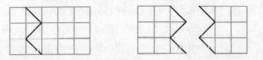

   Cut out a grid paper rectangle and cut the shape into 2 pieces (any way you like).

   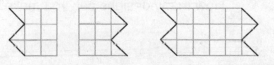

   Tape the two opposite ends together.

4. Find a letter of the alphabet that tessellates.

jump math
MULTIPLYING POTENTIAL

Geometry 2

1. Copy each design onto grid paper and cut the figure out.
   Turn the design <u>clockwise</u> by the given amount, then sketch what it looks like in the grid provided.

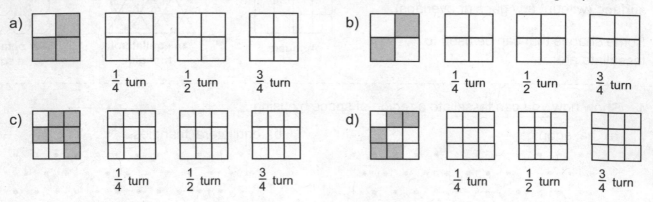

2. Show what each design would look like after a reflection in the mirror line.

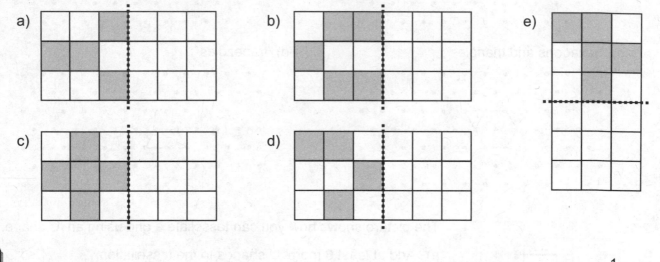

3. Design a 3 by 3 grid pattern that looks the same after ...   a) a half turn.   b) a $\frac{1}{4}$ turn.

4.

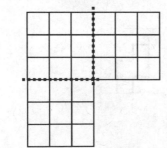

   Make a design that looks the same after a reflection in either mirror line. How many designs can you make?

5. Show what the design would look like after each <u>clockwise</u> turn.

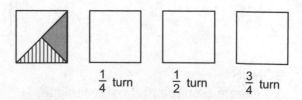

6. Make your own design on grid paper and show what the design would look like after a rotation, a reflection and a combination of rotations and reflections.

1. Show what each design would look like after ...

   ▪ a reflection in the mirror line:

   ▪ a ¼ turn counter clockwise around point P:

   a) 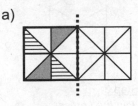   b) 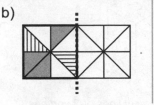   c) 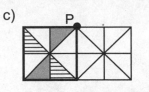   d)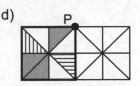

2. a) Colour the sections of the left-hand square using at least 3 colours.

      Then create a border design by <u>rotating</u> the square a $\frac{1}{4}$ turn repeatedly.

   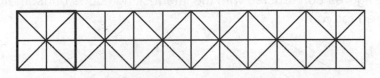

   b) Choose a different set of 3 colours and again colour in the left-hand square.
      Then create a border design by <u>reflecting</u> the square.

   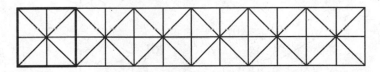

3. Show what each shape would look like after ...

   a) 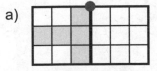   b) 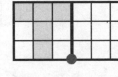   c) 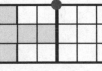   d)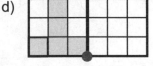

   $\frac{1}{4}$ turn counter clockwise $\frac{1}{4}$ turn clockwise $\frac{1}{4}$ turn counter clockwise $\frac{1}{4}$ turn clockwise

4. Trace and cut out the shape below. Make a pattern by ...

   a) Sliding the shape repeatedly one unit right:

   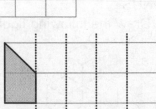

   b) Reflecting the shape repeatedly in the mirror lines:

   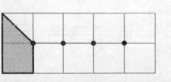

   c) Rotating the shape repeatedly 180° around the dots:

   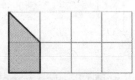

G5-41: Isoparametric Drawings

Steps to drawing a **cube** on isometric dots:

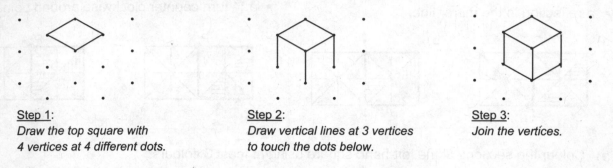

Step 1:
Draw the top square with
4 vertices at 4 different dots.

Step 2:
Draw vertical lines at 3 vertices
to touch the dots below.

Step 3:
Join the vertices.

---

1. Draw the following figures constructed with the interlocking cubes on isometric dot paper. The first one has been started for you.

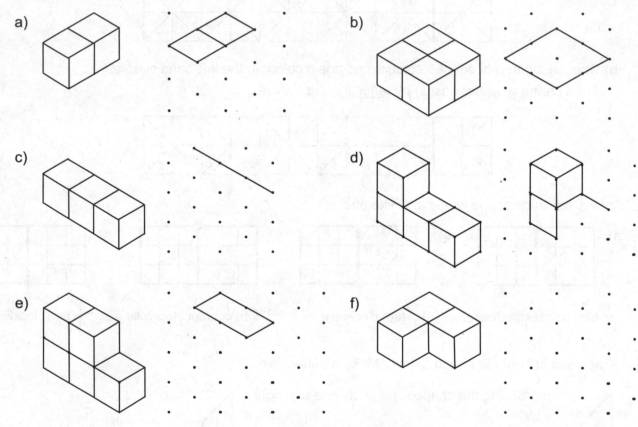

a)

b)

c)

d)

e)

f)

BONUS
2. Draw the following figures constructed with interlocking cubes on isometric dot paper.

a)

b)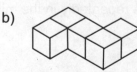

c)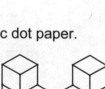

d)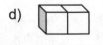

e)

f)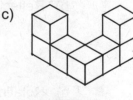

G5-42: Building and Drawing Figures

1. Build with blocks or interlocking cubes.

    a)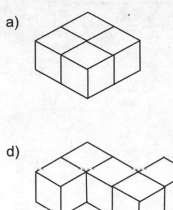

    b)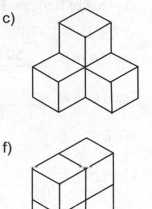

    c)

    d)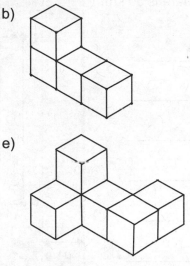

    e)

    f)

2. Fill in the numbers in the "mat plan", then build the figure. The first one was done for you.

    a)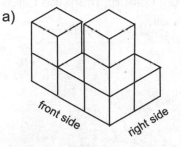

    front side   right side

    mat plan →
    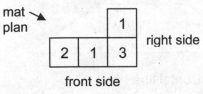

		1
2	1	3

    right side

    front side

    b)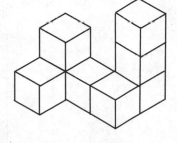

    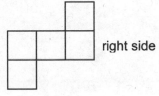

    right side

    front side

    c)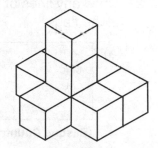

    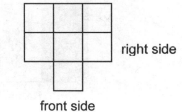

    right side

    front side

3. Draw a "mat plan" (as in Question 2), then build the figure.
    HINT: Shade the squares facing the front side.

    a)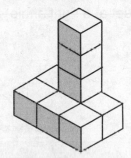

    b)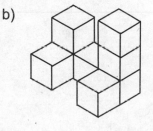

    c)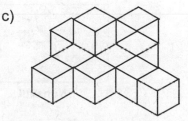

4. Build three figures with 10 cubes. Draw a mat plan for each.

Geometry 2

G5-43: Geometry in the World

1. A ship is sailing from Navy Board Inlet to the Gulf of Boothia. Each square is 50 km. Describe its path.

   From A to B: _____50 km north_____ .

   From B to C: _____ .

   From C to D: _____ .

   From D to E: _____ .

   From E to F: _____ .

   From F to G: _____ .

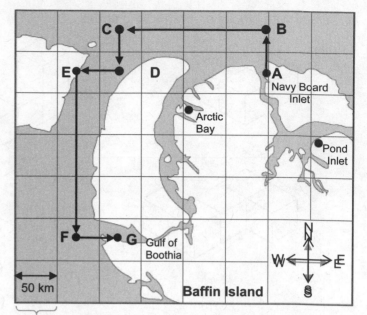

2. Draw any lines of symmetry you see in the flags.

   a)

   (Basque Country) Spain

   b)

   Barbados

   c) What polygons are suggested by the flag of Nunavut? Explain.

   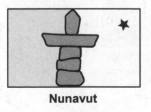

   Nunavut

3. Using different colours, mark the following lines in the quilt.

   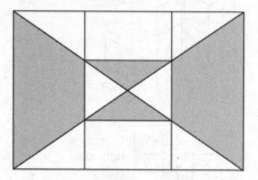

   a) a horizontal line

   b) a vertical line

   c) a pair of intersected lines

   d) a pair of perpendicular lines (lines that meet at a right angle)

4. Say which transformation could be used to move Shape A to each of the labelled positions in this ancient Roman Mosaic:

   - rotation CW   - rotation CCW   - reflection   - translation

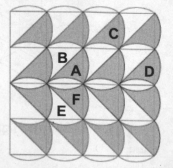